A PASSION FOR TRUTH

A PASSION
FOR TRUTH

Hans Küng and His Theology

ROBERT NOWELL

CROSSROAD · NEW YORK

1981
The Crossroad Publishing Company
18 East 41st Street, New York, NY 10017

Printed in the United States of America

Library of Congress Cataloging in Publication Data

Nowell, Robert, 1931-
A passion for truth.

Bibliography: p.
Includes index.
1. Küng, Hans, 1928-   I. Title.
BX4705.K76N68   230   80-26760
ISBN 0-8245-0039-3

Contents

Acknowledgements

My thanks are due above all to Hans Küng and his colleagues at the Institut für Ökumenische Forschung in Tübingen for their help and hospitality, and especially to Dr Margret Gentner for keeping me supplied with essential documents; to Michael Walsh and Stephen Poole of Heythrop College Library and to the friars and staff of the Catholic Central Library; to Fr. Yves Congar, O.P., for throwing light on a dark passage in the Church's recent history; to all the various friends with whom I have discussed various aspects of this book; to Charles and Mary Muller for their hospitality at a crucial stage in writing it; and to my wife for her help, encouragement, forbearance, and common sense.

I am grateful to the following for permission to quote from the works named: Search Press/Burns and Oates Ltd (Hans Küng, *Justification, Structures of the Church*, and *The Church*; Peter Harris and others, *On Human Life*; Walter Kasper, *Jesus the Christ*).
Sheed and Ward Ltd (Hans Küng, *The Council and Reunion* and *Truthfulness*; Nicholas Lash, *His Presence in the World*).
Gill and Macmillan Ltd (James Mackey, *Tradition and Change in the Church*).
T. and T. Clark Ltd (Karl Barth, *Church Dogmatics*).
Darton, Longman and Todd (Michael Novak, *The Open Church*; Karl Rahner, *Theological Investigations*).
Oxford University Press (A. V. Miller's translation of Hegel's *Phenomenology of Spirit*).
Cambridge University Press (E. M. Butler, *The Tyranny of*

Greece over Germany; James T. Burtchaell, *Catholic Theories of Biblical Inspiration since 1810*).

The Rev Kenneth Baker, S.J., editor of *Homiletic and Pastoral Review* (Karl Rahner's critique of *Infallible?* and his response to Küng's response).

ROBERT NOWELL

Abbreviations

To avoid spattering the text with too many footnotes, the most frequently cited books by Küng and some other works are referred to by abbreviated titles:

Challenge: The Christian Challenge, Collins, London, 1979.

Christian: On being a Christian, Collins, London, 1977.

Church: The Church, Burns and Oates, London, 1967.

Church Dogmatics: Karl Barth, *Church Dogmatics*, T. and T. Clark, Edinburgh, 1936–1962.

Diskussion: Hermann Häring and Josef Nolte (eds.), *Diskussion um Hans Küng 'Die Kirche'*, Herder, Freiburg/Basle/Vienna, 1971.

The Documents of Vatican II, Walter M. Abbott, SJ (ed.), Geoffrey Chapman, London/Dublin, 1966.

Fall: Norbert Greinacher and Herbert Haag (eds.), *Der Fall Küng: Eiene Dokumentation*, Piper, Munich, 1980.

Fehlbar?: Fehlbar? Eine Bilanz, Benziger, Einsiedeln/Zürich/Cologne, 1973.

God: Does God Exist?, Collins, London, 1980.

Gott: Existiert Gott?, Piper, Munich, 1978.

Hasler: August Bernhard Hasler, *Wie der Papst unfehlbar wurde. Macht und Ohnmacht eines Dogmas*, Piper, Munich, 1979.

Infallible?: Infallible? An Enquiry, Collins, London, 1971.

Justification: Justification: The Doctrine of Karl Barth and a Catholic Reflection, Burns and Oates, London, 1965.

Leid: Gott und das Leid, Benziger, Einsiedeln/Zürich/Cologne, 1967.

The Living Church, Sheed and Ward, 1963.

Menschwerdung: Menschwerdung Gottes. Eine Einführung in Hegels theologisches Denken als Prolegomena zu einer künftigen Christologie, Herder, Freiburg/Basle/Vienna, 1970.

Reden: 500 Jahr Eberhard-Karls-Universität Tübingen 1477–1977. Reden zum Jubiläum, Attempto Verlag, Tübingen, 1977.

Reunion: The Council and Reunion, Sheed and Ward, London, 1961.

Signposts: Signposts for the Future, Doubleday, New York, 1978.

Structures: Structures of the Church, Burns and Oates, London, 1965.

Theologian: The Theologian and the Church, Sheed and Ward, London/Melbourne/New York, 1965.

Truthfulness: Truthfulness: The Future of the Church, Sheed and Ward, London/Sydney, 1968.

Wahrheit: Walter Jens (ed.), *Um nichts als die Wahrheit. Deutsche Bischofskonferenz contra Hans Küng,* Piper, Munich, 1978.

Way: Hermann Häring and Karl-Josef Kuschel (eds.) with Margaret Gentner, *Hans Küng: His Work and His Way,* Collins (Fount), London, 1979.

Why Priests?: Collins (Fontana), London, 1972.

AAS: *Acta Apostolicae Sedis.*

CIC: *Codex Iuris Canonici.*

DS: Denziger-Schönmetzer, *Enchiridion Symbolorum, Definitionum et Declarationum de Rebus Fidei et Morum,* 33rd edition, Herder, Barcelona/Freiburg/Rome/New York, 1965.

HPR: *Homiletic and Pastoral Review.*

The English translation of *Does God Exist?* appeared too late for me to be able to make use of it while writing the book, but page references to it have been inserted where appropriate.

Letters and documents for which no source is given have been quoted from the documentation issued by the German bishops' conference on 18 December 1979.

I

Loyalty Disavowed

For many Christians – perhaps especially for those not in communion with Rome – there was always something too good to be true about Hans Küng. He combined the very qualities that many of the Catholic Church's detractors have regarded as totally incompatible: a passion for truth and loyalty to Rome, an open-minded willingness to accept the fruits of critical enquiry and adherence to what from the outside was seen as a closed dogmatic system. For such people the Doctrinal Congregation's statement of 18 December 1979 denying Küng the label 'Catholic theologian' confirmed what they had long feared or suspected, that a commitment to truth could not for long be combined with a commitment to Rome. Either one was ready to follow the search for truth wherever it might lead, or one accepted that the Church was somehow in possession of the truth, in which case searching for it might even be a dangerous distraction.

For others there had always been a disturbing and unsettling element in Küng's work. He asked awkward questions, raked up old issues which surely had long since been settled. He encouraged a different and unwelcome pattern of Christian belief and practice from the passive obedience so often held up as the model of true Catholicism. For such people, many of whom had already dismissed Küng as somehow on the fringes of orthodoxy if not actually heretical, the Doctrinal Congregation's sudden verdict came as a relief. It confirmed what they had long believed, that the challenges Küng offered could safely be ignored.

11

Yet both views surely take too narrow and pessimistic a view of Catholicism. They run the risk of reducing the Church to a sect. If the Church does not have room for loyal dissent, if it can only embrace those of one particular cast of mind, then it is failing in its mission of bringing the good news of salvation to all mankind. What is at issue in the case of Hans Küng is twofold: whether the Church is committed to the truth, or primarily to its past; and whether it is truly catholic, truly universal in its appeal, or simply confined to those of a particular temperament and cultural background.

But even many who are willing to allow Hans Küng some place on their map of orthodoxy often push him out into the border areas. They are apt to see him as some kind of Catholic maverick: as the safety-valve any institution needs if it is to be able to cope with the pressures that inevitably build up within it, or as representing merely the under-standable reaction to the excesses of the past, to the intellectual totalitarianism that marked the Church over the greater part of the last century and before. Yet this again, surely, is to miss the point. Hans Küng's criticism has its origins in the way he takes the Church extremely seriously indeed as the means for bringing mankind the good news of salvation. What he is concerned about is that it should be free to preach and live the gospel, no longer smothered by the irrelevancies and stupidities that so often prevent its message being heard.

In this way his work is not solely or even primarily a matter of criticism. His fundamental aim is to enable men and women today to accept this gospel and to accept the Church to which they owe the gospel. What he is endeavouring to do is thus to make sense of Christianity in a way that does justice both to the original message and to the two-thousand-year history of how that message has been received and transmitted in human society.

In all this there are certain basic assumptions and presuppositions that need to be brought out. Küng assumes that Christian faith is fundamentally reasonable, that what we are called on to believe in response to God's gracious revelation of himself does not contradict our reason however much it may transcend it. In other words, belief for the Christian is not something irrational, even if its complete rational justification may be impossible to attain within the limits of this life and must await the next. In this way Küng is all the time trying to overcome the tension between our limited understanding and what our faith demands of us, in contrast to those who if anything glory in the irrational element in faith and in the way in which the demands of faith can so often seem to cut clean across our reasonable human categories.

A second basic assumption concerns the way in which we arrive at and recognize the truth. For Küng the truth clearly is something that imposes itself, not something that can be imposed. Nor is truth something that is simply given, in the way that a quiz-master supplies the answers. Rather is it something that men and women have to struggle to reach through the normal human process of argument and reflection. Truth is not won without effort: as with geometry, there is no royal road. In this way the truth is something that emerges from the debate and discussion within the Church — and a key question at once becomes how it is recognized. The point here, however, is that it is not something that is simply produced like a rabbit out of a hat.

Above all what throughout his work Küng endeavours to be concerned about is the truth, no matter what the price that has to be paid for it. What matters is that his arguments should hold water, not that this position or that should be shored up. He is very fond of quoting Pope Gregory the Great: 'If scandal is taken at the truth, then it is better to allow scandal to arise than to abandon the truth' (*Reunion*, p. 62).

His theology is of course no more than one man's interpretation within the plurality of possible interpretations of the Christian message that he and others see as both legitimate and essential in the Church. He may naturally experience the same difficulty that anyone else experiences over admitting the validity of an interpretation other than the one they have struggled to attain, but its right to exist he would not question. But he would argue convincingly that his own interpretation falls within the mainstream of orthodox tradition; and certainly it is an interpretation that has found a remarkable echo among his contemporaries. Hans Küng is an example of what in our apparently irreligious age may seem a paradoxical but is perhaps not that rare a phenomenon, the best-selling theologian. Whatever other criticism may be made of it, his way of seeing the gospel and the Church does not set up the obstacles to acceptance that too often surround many a more 'official' proclamation of Christian belief. His work has moreover encouraged many Catholics not to lose patience with the institutional Church, not to break loose. The fact that he has now been officially disavowed will encourage the very contempt for the Church's authority and structures that over the years his work as a theologian did so very much to diminish.

Nor is his appeal simply to those within or on the fringes of the Catholic Church. The way he is more concerned with the truth than with saving institutional appearances has given his work an immense appeal to Anglicans and Protestants, who are apt to see the Reformation quarrel from which they are descended as a struggle between the claims of truth and the claims of the institution, with the Protestants on the side of the truth. In this way the official Church's disavowal of him as a Catholic theologian can only have damaging repercussions in the ecumenical field, however much Anglicans and Protestants may have realized that on particularly neuralgic issues Küng represented one possible interpretation of the Catholic tradition and not some kind of contemporary Catholic consensus. The manner of the disavowal also awakens all the intense suspicion of Rome and Roman ways that lies buried just beneath the surface, especially in England where 'no popery' has been described as the residual religion of the English. A Church which attempts to silence theologians without a fair trial is not the kind of Church most other Christians would want to contemplate uniting with.

In establishing himself as a theologian Hans Küng was immensely helped by being the right man at the right time. He emerged just at the time when Pope John XXIII was freeing the Church from the constricting pressures that had warped its intellectual development over the past century or so: the crushing of modernism had meant not just that the answers the modernists had suggested were condemned but that even the questions they had tried to answer were greeted with suspicion. Theologians of an earlier generation whose labours provided the groundwork for the Second Vatican Council – men like Rahner, Congar, de Lubac, von Balthasar – had had to work against a background of hostility and harassment by the Church's central authorities in Rome. Küng on the other hand was able to benefit from the new climate of intellectual freedom that their efforts had helped to establish. For a large part of his career he may have been involved in a running battle with the Doctrinal Congregation and latterly with the German bishops' conference acting on the Roman authorities' behalf, but the battle was conducted for the most part in public and had apparently ended in a draw, with Küng's orthodoxy unimpugned, until the sudden crackdown of 18 December 1979.

Vatican II was in fact the pivotal point in Küng's career. It is noteworthy that his ecclesiastical hero remains Pope John XXIII, who by summoning that council made it realistic for Catholics to hope for better things and took the first decisive step towards bringing them about – just as in the political field his hero remains John F. Kennedy, whose brief presidency gave a similar emobodiment to secular hope. And it was against the background of Vatican II that Hans Küng both consolidated his reputation in the German-speaking world and first became known to readers of English.

To English-speaking Catholics more than most the announcement of Vatican II came as a shock. A tradition of strong loyalty to Rome combined with a suspicion of theology encouraged the view that major change in the Church was not just unlikely but impossible, and when major change started happening few people can have been more bewildered – though they adapted with remarkable ease. In these circumstances Hans Küng came forward as an interpreter able to explain clearly the logic and sense of the radical upheavals that were taking place in people's understanding of the Church and of what was involved in being a Christian. At the same time by being committed so strongly to the cause of reform he emerged not just as a spokesman but as a symbol of what was taking place. He became identified with the radically new understanding of the Church legitimized by Vatican II in a way that his older contemporaries, men like Rahner and Congar, did not.

Beyond this, the circumstances of his first publication in English enabled those who were upset by what he was saying and by the clarity with which he was saying it (especially when translated by Cecily Hastings) to dismiss him as a paperback theologian – though why it should be held to detract from a theologian's work that he reaches a wide audience is a mystery, especially when one considers that theologians like Origen and Augustine, were they working in today's conditions, would undoubtedly qualify for this derogatory label.

During the Council and even more afterwards developments within the Church and Küng's reactions to them combined to emphasize his symbolic role as the theologian who articulates what many ordinary Catholics feel but are unable to express in terms that will make headway against the official theology they are reacting against. He has an outstanding gift for homing in on just the problems and difficulties that are causing most anxiety, and his full-length discussion of infallibility – the central issue in the disciplinary measures eventually taken by Rome – was sparked off by his need to take seriously both Pope Paul VI's encyclical *Humanae vitae*, with its reaffirmation of previous popes' condemnation of artificial birth control, and the widespread rejection of this stand by ordinary Catholics. At the same time he was bitterly disappointed by the conservative backlash that even before *Humanae vitae* (and even during the Council) had set in under Paul VI, and did not hestitate to say so – above all in the foreword to *Infallible? An Enquiry*.

The dispute occasioned by that book and the further dispute generated by Küng's approach to Christology in *On Being a Christian* enhanced his role as the leader of His Holiness's loyal opposition. (Küng has in fact compared *Infallible?* to a parliamentary question from Her Majesty's loyal opposition.[1]) But it is a role that does not fit him easily. He is not a natural rebel. If he finds himself in opposition, it is because he is forced there by inner conviction. His rebellion, if one should call it that, is the expression of his loyalty to the Church. That loyalty is so deep-rooted that he cannot conceive of its coming into conflict with the passionate commitment to the truth that is the other pole of his nature. Where other Catholics may be tempted to sacrifice truth to loyalty (and before Vatican II sometimes felt they had to if they wished to stay in the Church) Küng sees no essential conflict between his commitment to the truth and his commitment to the Church. For it is precisely because it is at the service of the truth, and precisely because despite all its scandalous shortcomings it has indeed been able to proclaim the truth, that the Church can lay claim to his or to anyone else's loyalty.

Indeed, the *Leitmotiv* of Küng's work is his passionate anxiety to preach this gospel which it is the Church's mission to proclaim. What he is concerned about is making Christian belief accessible once more in an age when too many people outside the Church are put off Christianity because they think it involves doing violence to the accepted 'scientific' way of understanding the world, and when too many people inside the Church cling to Christianity precisely because they see it as offering a bulwark against the contemporary world. In opposition to both these tendencies, Küng is concerned for Christian faith to be something alive and vital: not a valued fossil survival from the past, the institutional equivalent of the coelacanth, not an optional extra like a taste for Elizabethan miniatures or Haydn quartets, but the irreplaceable foundation of life as a whole. For Küng being a Christian is ultimately the only finally satisfactory way of being human.

Behind the theologian there thus stands a preacher. Originally Hans Küng saw his vocation in terms of working as a priest in some Swiss town or village, and it was only by accident that he was diverted into becoming a professional academic theologian. But in many ways it is the original vocation that has remained primary. It was in order to be able to preach the gospel that Hans Küng undertook the study of theology in the first place, and it is in order to be able to go on preaching the gospel that he continues to explore and expound what those strange and unsettling events of nearly two thousand years ago mean for us today.

Preaching the gospel is of course something not to be undertaken lightly, and the preacher has to be sure that what he is proclaiming is the message of God and not of men. That from the standpoint of the Catholic Church's central authorities in Rome is now a matter of dispute as far as Hans Küng is concerned. Whether this is actually so the reader of the pages that follow will, I hope, be better able to judge.

1 In his foreword to the book by August Bernhard Hasler, *Wie der Papst unfehlbar wurde*, Piper, Munich, 1979, p. xiii. It was the publication of this foreword to a book the Roman authorities found exceptionally provocative and embarrassing that seems to have played the chief part in bring about the disciplinary measures taken later that year.

2

The Making of a Theologian

It took some time for the English-speaking world to realize
that Hans Küng was not German but Swiss. He was a professor at a German university, operating within the
German academic and intellectual world, and journalists
knowing little more of him than that he held a chair at
Tübingen would automatically pin the label 'German' on
him. Yet the fact that he is Swiss provides a key to understanding many facets of the positions he has adopted,
particularly in his relations with the Church authorities.

One striking thing about the Swiss, apart from the tiny
Romansch-speaking minority, is that culturally they are
identified with much larger and more powerful nations on
their doorstep while having remained and remaining politi-
cally distinct. In Europe they provide (along with the not
very happy example of Belgium) the exception to the
tendency that ever since the French Revolution and the
Napoleonic wars has increasingly aligned national with
linguistic frontiers. Thus, while culturally the German-
speaking Swiss belong to the German-speaking world, a
world which throughout the nineteenth century was
moving steadily towards political unification, their
membership of it is automatically somewhat askance and
critical. In a sense they were all along pioneers of the
political pluralism that, since the collapse of Hitler's
enlarged *Reich*, has become established as the pattern, with
Germany itself divided into two and Austria developing its
own identity without hankering after either past imperial
glories or absorption in a greater Germany.

Moreover, the Swiss were able to enjoy a political development healthier and less disastrous than their fellow-German-speakers in these two other countries. They trace their democratic tradition back to the alliance that linked the original three cantons of Uri, Schwyz and Unterwalden in 1291: historians may question the precise date and even more the legend of the solemn oath sworn on the Rütli, the meadow above the lake of Lucerne, but are agreed that the confederation has its origins at least in the early fourteenth century. Swiss democracy is thus a native growth. In tragic contrast, Germany has suffered from the fact that all the major political and social changes it has undergone have resulted from outside pressure. It has never enjoyed a successful domestic revolution or programme of reform. The sixteenth-century Peasants' Revolt was brutally suppressed, with Luther's encouragement. In the next century Germany became the battlefield of Europe in the Thirty Years' War, from which it emerged an exhausted and devastated patchwork of petty despotisms. The French Revolution and the Napoleonic invasion that followed brought about a half-hearted rationalization of the country's political geography, but liberal and democratic ideals could hardly withstand the pressure of the autocratic tradition. The Weimar Republic was the outcome of defeat in the First World War rather than of popular uprising; and however firmly rooted the democratic institutions of the Federal Republic may have become, they too are basically something imposed from outside following the collapse of the Nazi régime. Nor in the religious field was the toleration of nonconformity at all encouraged by the policy of *cuius regio eius religio*, which established local homogeneity as the norm.

One effect of this is that ideas first mooted in England during our seventeenth-century civil war, and long since taken for granted, still retain a certain novelty in Germany and still have to justify their existence. There is a tendency always to reach back to the eighteenth-century *Aufklärung* or enlightenment to lay bare the roots of contemporary thought. Beyond this, the diffused autocracy that marked the eighteenth century, with some two hundred odd petty absolutist states, and that still in a more concentrated form persisted in the nineteenth, encouraged the habit of deference to authority. Initiatives needed official approval to succeed. Throughout, the painful lesson of history for the Germans has been that nonconformity and dissidence do not pay: major radical changes have resulted not from the efforts of their advocates within society but from the intervention of some external power, some *deus ex machina*. This helps to explain why to this day German society retains an authoritarian stamp that can bewilder even those who recognize the country's many virtues and achievements. Along with the inflexibility that is built into the syntax of the very language they speak, it also helps to explain why many Germans seem to find it singularly hard to tolerate dissent and to bring dissent and disagreement into constructive dialogue with the rest of the community. The idea of loyal opposition can be rather a difficult one for the German mind to grasp. All this has a distinct bearing on the disputes in which Hans Küng has been embroiled, particularly on that between him and the German bishops' conference over *On being a Christian* and the absence of friendly relations between him and the majority of German bishops. Relevant here is Küng's reaction when I told him about the reactions of Monsignor Alan Clark, now Bishop of East Anglia, to an article I wrote on his appointment as auxiliary of Northampton in 1969, pointing out that he was neither the choice of the clergy of the diocese nor (because of his role as chairman of an association of 'conservative-minded' priests at a time of dissension following *Humanae vitae*) really that suitable a candidate for episcopal office.[1] Bishop Clark's response was to invite me to lunch, and we have been on good terms ever since. Hans Küng looked both surprised and sad. 'That could never happen here,' he said.

It is not only in their political traditions and presup-positions that the Swiss are marked off from their German neighbours. There is also a distinction in the field of Church order that makes Swiss Catholicism unique. It is only in the Swiss dioceses of Basle, Chur and St Gall – and strictly speaking also in the Czech archdiocese of Olomouc, though under present political conditions this latter case is of academic interest only – that there has survived the tradition of the free election of the bishop of the diocese by the cathedral chapter. This is in any case an attenuation of the earlier tradition – amply documented by Antonio Rosmini in the fourth chapter of his pioneering work *The Five Wounds of the Church*, published in 1848 and placed on the Index in 1849 – of the election of the bishop by the clergy and people of the diocese. Elsewhere, apart from a limited right of election enjoyed by dioceses in the rest of the German-speaking world, this tradition survives only in two legal fictions: that whereby the Pope is elected by the college of cardinals, representing the parish clergy of Rome; and that whereby bishops of the Church of England are 'elected' by the cathedral chapter after nomination by the sovereign, even if since 1977 that nomination has been in the hands of the Church rather than of the Prime Minister. Furthermore, in the traditionally Catholic parts of Switzerland the practice has also persisted of parish priests being elected by the community they are called to serve – and having to stand for re-election at four-year intervals. Long before the Council Swiss Catholics thus took for granted a degree of internal Church autonomy and democracy that even half a generation after Vatican II many Catholics elsewhere would regard as impossibly and irres-ponsibly radical. It is a tradition Hans Küng has been swift to defend when he has seen it threatened, as in 1967 when the Holy See started taking an unhealthy interest in the

election of the new Bishop of Basle, or in 1969 when a
fellow-priest criticized the popular election of parish
priests.[2]

All this helped to form Hans Küng's cultural heritage.
He was born in a solidly Catholic part of Switzerland, in
the small town of Sursee at the northern end of the
Sempacher See. His grandfather had established himself in
the shoe trade and was successful enough to have three
shops in different towns. His father took over the one in
Sursee itself. (Today it is run by one of Hans Küng's sisters
and her husband.) Here, in a former inn with at its corner a
madonna marking where in the seventeenth century a fire
ravaging the town had stopped, Hans Küng was born on 19
March 1928, the eldest of a family of two boys and five
girls. It seems to have been a happy and contented child-
hood. Certain the Küngs form a friendly and united family,
hospitable to outsiders and in no way closed in on themselves. Also his native town has remained a, probably the,
focal point in Hans Küng's life, a centre to which he is
continually coming back and where his roots are. When
land prices were by today's standards ridiculously cheap
the Küng children persuaded their father to buy a plot of
land down by the lakeside, and here they have built and
share three holiday homes: one owned by Hans Küng and
his uncle, another by three of his sisters and their husbands,
the third by the remaining two sisters and brothers-in-law.
(As we shall learn, his brother died in his early twenties.)

Sursee is thus where Hans Küng is normally to be found
when he is not at Tübingen or engaged on the lecture tours
that have taken him right round the globe and even as far as
Peking. Here he can relax with swimming and sailing, or in
the winter go off skiing in the nearby mountains. But as
often as not relaxation is not allowed to get in the way of a
steady flow of work. Not only does he enjoy good health
but he also has remarkable energy and stamina, blessings he
attributes to his upbringing. Five hours' sleep a night he

regards as plenty: the eight hours' sleep some people need he is apt to dismiss as fit only for babies. Thus he is the kind of person who will get up at five in the morning and have a swim in a neighbour's pool before setting off to drive a hundred and fifty miles to preside over a colloquium of his doctoral students.

As a German-speaking Swiss growing up in the 1930s and 1940s, Hans Küng could hardly avoid being aware of what was happening in Germany, just the other side of a frontier less than thirty miles to the north of Sursee. His earliest memory of reading a newspaper for its political news dates from when he was six: the Nazi assassination of the Austrian Chancellor Engelbert Dollfuss in 1934, a grim precursor of the absorption of Austria by Nazi Germany in the Anschluss four years later. What was going on in Europe as the Nazis consolidated their hold on Germany and then swallowed Austria, dismembered Czechoslovakia and attacked and overran Poland made a deep impression on him and was stored away in a capacious memory. When in 1940 his class at school was set an essay on the causes of the war, the twelve-year-old Hans Küng had so much of the detailed political history of the past seven years at his fingertips that his contribution was of remarkable length. In all this he was sharing the anxiety felt by the vast majority of Swiss, who watched what was happening in full awareness that their turn might come next. 1940 was the year General Guisan, the Swiss commander-in-chief, made a famous speech to his senior officers on the hallowed soil of the Rütli, advocating a policy of defending a central Alpine redoubt if Switzerland were attacked, rather than trying to keep its frontiers intact: it was a speech that helped to stiffen Swiss resistance generally at a time when the very idea of resistance could have appeared quixotic and impractical.

School at that time was still in Sursee. When he was fourteen the time came for him to move on to the

Gymnasium or grammar school, and for this his parents sent him as a dayboy to the cantonal capital of Lucerne, thirteen miles to the south-east, where the *Gymnasium* was not only inter-denominational, with Protestants and Jews as well as Catholics among Hans Küng's fellow pupils, but co-educational too: many Catholic families preferred to send their sons to boarding schools in central Switzerland where they would be safely segregated both from the world and from girls. Hans Küng was thus brought up in a mature and resilient Catholicism that was fully capable of coming to terms with the world in which it lived.

A sharp contrast was provided by the seven years that followed leaving school. These were spent at the German College in Rome, an institution founded by Pope Julius III in 1552 at the instigation of Ignatius of Loyola, united in 1580 with the Hungarian College to form the Pontifical German-Hungarian College, and run by the Jesuits (except for the years from the society's suppression by Clement XIV in 1773 until the college's re-opening in 1818 after its closure in 1798 under the revolutionary republic). The choice was deliberate. Hans Küng's vocation to the priesthood had crystallized during his last years at school, and if he was going to be a priest there would be no half-measures about it. To prepare himself for pastoral work in his native Switzerland he wanted both the strict discipline of what for the German-speaking world was the very model of a Tridentine seminary and at the same time the solid theological education he would obtain at the Gregorian University, also Jesuit-run, where students from the Germanicum, along with students from most of the other national colleges, went for their lectures. So it was to Rome that Hans Küng went at the age of twenty in 1948, after taking his *Matura* or school-leaving examination, and donned the red cassock that distinguishes students of the Germanicum from their fellows at other colleges.

Like every other Swiss lad who was fit, Hans Küng was

liable for military service. He would have been allotted to a signals regiment providing communications for aircraft and for anti-aircraft artillery, since he had done two courses for radio operators. But he never actually started his military service, since immediately after his *Matura* he visited England for the first time for a holiday before starting life as a student in Rome, and from then on until ordination he was always out of the country.

Like most Catholics at that time, the twenty-year-old Hans Küng took the officially approved theology and officially approved Catholic attitudes very seriously indeed. In those days Catholics tended to keep to themselves any doubts they might have about the wisdom or expediency of a particular aspect of Vatican policy or about the coherence, plausbility or even truth of a particular teaching; and if any doubts were expressed they were expressed in very respectful and deferential terms. By and large it was only in the climate of free speech created and fostered by Vatican II that ordinary Catholics began to compare notes and to make the painful discovery that some of what they had striven so loyally to accept, understand, preach and defend was something they had to discard out of very loyalty to the Catholic faith they professed.

The clearest example of this process is the rethinking of the Church's attitude to birth control which took place during the 1960s. A generation of young, idealistic, well-educated and articulate Catholics took seriously the traditional condemnation of artificial birth control proclaimed by Pius XI in his 1930 encyclical *Casti connubii* in opposition to the cautious approval expressed by the Anglican episcopate at the Lambeth Conference earlier that year. They tried valiantly to live up to this teaching and to put into practice the principles of the safe period sanctioned by Pius XII. But increasingly they found that this teaching could only be lived in practice at the cost of considerable strain and artificiality; and the closer they examined it the more difficult it became to justify it in theory. As a result, when in 1968 Paul VI reaffirmed the traditional condemnation in his encyclical *Humanae vitae* there was an outburst of protest. Since then there has been tacit acceptance by most bishops and priests of a right of dissent on this issue. It has been recognized, implicitly if not explicitly, that one can remain a loyal Catholic while refusing to accept the papal condemnation of artificial contraception. The question raised by some of John Paul II's statements on this subject is not just whether his own attitude is not more intransigent than that of his predecessors but whether he is trying to establish such an attitude as the norm throughout the Church and thus bring to an end a decade of relative toleration.

Hans Küng's theological education and development followed a course similar to the evolution of his contemporaries' thinking on birth control. His rejection of what may be termed the official Roman school of theology does not spring from ignorance or from an inadequate appreciation of what it is trying to do and why it is doing it. Rather it comes from having taken this theology seriously and having put it to the test only to find that it just does not work.

Two aspects of this official Roman theology should be noted. One is the nineteenth century development summed up in Pius IX's alleged remark: *'La tradizione, son' io!'* ('Tradition? *I* am tradition'). Instead of scripture providing the criterion for assessing and evaluating what the Church was doing, or rather scripture as consistently read and interpreted in the Church, what came to matter was the Church's teaching authority, particularly as focused — and during the nineteenth century it increasingly came to be focused — in the person of the pope. Tradition thus came to mean what Rome saw it as meaning. The Irish theologian James Mackey has traced this development through the work of the Roman theologians Perrone (1794–1876) and Franzelin (1816–1886):

> But he [Perrone], like many later theologians, became so interested in establishing the teaching authority of the Catholic hierarchy, that he finally adopted as his definition of tradition 'the living, authoritative preaching of the word of God by the hierarchy', and he regarded this preaching as the proximate rule of faith. This tendency continued after him, it was crystallized in the work of Franzelin at the time of the First Vatican Council, and it lasted into the first half of the present century. The definition of tradition came to be restricted to the official teaching of the Roman Catholic hierarchy. The broader perspectives of Möhler's work were ignored, as was Newman's essay on development of dogma.
>
> What was wrong with this restrictive tendency is very simply stated and very easily seen. All the emphasis was placed on the authority of office, which the hierarchy alone possesses. The result was that the very prerogatives which the hierarchy possesses in order to fulfil its task, the helps it was promised by Christ – its infallibility, in short – tended to be seen as an almost automatic concomitant of official pronouncements, guaranteed by law. The hierarchy defined a certain dogmatic development. The hierarchy was infallible by divine law. Therefore the defined dogma was really part of the faith. And despite all the denials, the impression was really conveyed that the so-called proximate rule of faith was a supreme rule of faith, supreme even over the word of God itself.[3]

The danger thus grew of any objective sense of tradition becoming buried by the subjective need continually to re-interpret that tradition in keeping with the demands of the moment. It meant starting at the wrong end, with what was felt to be required by the contemporary situation, almost as it were with an instinctive reaction, and then seeking to justify that by recourse to the tradition – which in this way was continually being challenged and reinterpreted by the present instead of being allowed to offer the present its own sometimes unwelcome challenge. For theology the starting-point tended to become the pronouncement recorded in Denzinger, that invaluable compendium of the doctrinal statements of popes and councils which was first published in 1854 by the German theologian Heinrich Denzinger and which in its successive editions has established itself as an essential theological tool. The temptation grew for the task of theology to be seen as somehow justifying these pronouncements on the basis of scripture and tradition rather than as allowing scripture and tradition to amplify and provide the context for what were usually statements made in the course of a doctrinal dispute – and where necessary to correct and criticize them.

The other aspect of this Roman theology that needs to be mentioned here is its treatment of grace and the supernatural. These were seen as forming another and distinct slice of life superimposed on the natural world. This two-tier theory, as Hans Küng has termed it, could at worst lead to a kind of pious schizophrenia, with natural and supernatural assigned to separate compartments and hardly if ever coming into contact with each other. It also encouraged the attitude that saw only somebody's strictly religious behaviour as important and, except where sexual matters were concerned, largely discounted how he or she behaved in the world as a whole.

But what disfigured the official Roman theology was not just that it harboured ideas that were increasingly shown to be inadequate and misleading. What disfigured it was rather the totalitarian manner in which it was all too often imposed and its ruthless intolerance of competing theologies. It may be the task of the Church's authorities to defend essential doctrines when these come under attack or are in danger of being eroded. But all too often this century what they have seemed concerned to defend has been not so much doctrine itself as a particular interpretation of it. What before Vatican II was the final outburst of this authoritarian obscurantism took place while Hans Küng was a student in Rome. In his 1950 encyclical *Humani generis* Pius XII condemned some of the recent developments that had been taking place in theology, particularly in French theology. In 1953 came his ending of the worker-priest experiment, with as a side-effect a purge of many prominent French Dominicans who had temporarily to seek refuge elsewhere. The final flicker of this particular wave of suppression came in 1961 when the Holy Office was able to bring about the suspension of two teachers at the Pontifical Biblical Institute, the Jesuits Stanislas Lyonnet and Maximilian Zerwick. They were only reinstated in 1964 or thereabouts.

Among the targets of this rearguard action by Pius XII against the 'new wave' of French theology was the French Jesuit Henri de Lubac's attempt to overcome the gulf between natural and supernatural in his book *Le surnaturel*, published in 1946, as Hans Küng explained in his summary of this episode in *Does God Exist?* (*Gott*, pp. 572 – 3; cf. *God*, pp. 519 – 520):

> Pius XII, however, reacted to this *théologie nouvelle* nearly as sharply as Pius X, whom he was later to canonize, had done to 'modernism'. There was no question at all of allowing any genuine discussion. Just four years after the publication of de Lubac's *Le surnaturel* there appeared, on 12 August 1950, what could be seen as a new Syllabus of Errors, the encyclical *Humani generis* 'concerning certain false opinions which threaten to sap the foundation of Catholic teaching'. This encyclical condemned the methods and many of the results of this 'new' theology (and philosophy) that deviated from neo-scholasticism. De Lubac's view of the supernatural was explicitly rejected and at the same time the

doctrine of the possibility of a natural knowledge of God was reasserted with a renewed intensity . . .

Pius XII's words were followed by deeds. Without legal proceedings of any kind Henri de Lubac and other French Jesuit theologians were removed from their teaching posts and often also banned from the places where they had been working. They were banned from writing on the subject in dispute and were not able to defend themselves in any way; Teilhard de Chardin . . . had earlier been silenced. It was only the highly adaptable Jean Daniélou, who at that time was remarkably progressive, who was able to go on teaching in Paris and subsequently even to do very well for himself in the Church (he was made a cardinal by Paul VI). Fear pervaded the Church's promising institutions of learning throughout France: their staff did not enjoy legal protection. On 1 November of that same Holy Year 1950, Pius XII, despite the theological considerations that could be brought against such a step both from inside and from outside the Catholic Church, defined Mary's bodily assumption into heaven as a dogma. And a few years later the theological purge of the Jesuits was followed, in the wake of the ban on worker-priests in 1953, by a purge of Dominicans, among whom were such out- standing theologians as M.-D. Chenu and Yves Congar who had, with great commitment, advocated the Catholic Church adopting a new relationship towards the world, towards the working class, and towards other Churches, and had also proposed a thorough-going reform of the Church's structures. Here too there was no question of any legal proceed- ings: books were banned, people were banned from writing, people were removed from their posts or moved from one post to another, and some even exiled for a time.

What in the latter case seems to have been under threat was not so much the freedom of expression of French Dominican theologians (though that was very much involved) as the democratic constitution of the Order of

Preachers. The Master General, Father Emanuel Suarez, had been ordered by Rome to bring the French Dominicans back into line. What Rome wanted, so the French were given to understand, was for the provincials to be nominated by the central authorities instead of being freely elected by the friars of each province. To avoid this, the provincials of the Paris, Lyons and Toulouse provinces resigned, and four prominent theologians – Boisselot, Chenu, Congar and Féret – moved out of Paris, though three of them did not go very far: Boisselot went to Dijon, Chenu to Le Havre, Féret to Nancy. Congar went the furthest afield, to Jerusalem, but he was only there from February 1954 to the end of April that year, followed by a spell in Rome itself from November 1954 to February 1955, while in 1956 the Master General (then Father Michael Browne, who was made a cardinal in 1962 – Father Suarez had been killed in a car crash in June 1954) sent him to stay with his English brethren at Cambridge.

Congar had earlier fallen foul of the Holy Office through his pioneering work *Vraie et fausse réforme dans l'Eglise*, a book which was to have a considerable impact on Hans Küng when he caught up with it as a doctoral student in Paris. *Vraie et fausse réforme* was actually published in 1950 a couple of months after *Humani generis* had appeared with its onslaught against what French theologians were up to. But it was only in February 1952 that the Holy Office acted by banning a second edition as well as translations of the work. The ban was issued at a time when the work of setting a second edition up in type had reached page 350. The printers had been asked to keep the type of the first edition instead of distributing it, but unfortunately they had failed to do so. A second *impression* would not have been forbidden by the Holy Office's decree, according to the advice available from canon lawyers; and apparently this loophole also extended to a second impression made by photographic means, though Congar refused to get round the ban this way. A second edition only became possible after the Council, when it was authorized (by word of mouth) by Cardinal Ottaviani himself, the secretary of the Holy Office and at Vatican II one of the staunchest defenders of the old Roman ways.

Three points in all this are worth underlining in slightly greater detail. One is the part played by the fact that French theologians, unlike their German counterparts, do not normally enjoy the protection afforded by being employed by a state institution. By an accident of history, Catholic theological education in the German-speaking world takes place to a substantial extent in faculties of Catholic theology that form part of state universities. This means that most German theologians enjoy something like the Church of England parson's freehold, as became clear in consequence of the disciplinary measures taken against Hans Küng himself in December 1979. The local bishop's approval is needed before an appointment can be made to a theological chair, as everyone was sharply reminded in October 1979 when Cardinal Joseph Ratzinger, Archbishop of Munich and formerly himself a professor of theology at Tübingen, did not actually refuse to sanction the appointment of Johannes Baptist Metz to a chair at Munich but persuaded the Bavarian government minister responsible to appoint the runner-up to the post instead.[4] The local bishop can also withdraw this official approval or *missio canonica* and ask the state authorities to provide an acceptable substitute, as Bishop Georg Moser of Rottenburg-Stuttgart eventually had to do in Küng's case after the failure of an appeal to Rome. But withdrawal of *missio canonica* does not mean loss of professorial chair. In this way a German academic theologian's livelihood has not depended on the continued approval of the Church authorities, as it has done for his French or Italian colleagues. Furthermore, many German professors of theology have been secular priests, whereas membership of a religious order can provide a means for exerting pressure on a theologian who is a member – even though the superiors general of orders such as the Dominicans and the Jesuits have a fairly honourable record when it comes to shielding their members from the depradations of the Holy Office. This fact that German professors of theology are virtually unsackable, along with such things as the tangled impenetrability of Karl Rahner's prose style, helped to keep German theology relatively immune from the intellectual reign of terror that persisted almost until the Second Vatican Council assembled – though Rahner himself was regarded with the deepest suspicion by the Holy Office and at one stage was forbidden to write another word about concelebration.[5]

The second point is that, certainly in France and quite probably elsewhere too, the attack on the worker-priest movement was if anything more damaging to the Church than the attack on theologians. From the worker's point of view it looked as if after all the Church were on 'their' side and not on 'ours'. And within the French context the damage was all the greater because of the long struggle the French Church has had to free itself of the suspicion of hankering after the bad old days of the *ancien régime*: the mainspring of Archbishop Marcel Lefebvre's rebellion has been not so much love of the Latin Mass as an inability to accept and come to terms with the French Revolution. Beyond this, the ban on the worker-priest movement tended to cut theology off from its roots: the movement had helped to provide the practical raw material that any living theology needs and had thus given French post-war theology a particular cutting edge and relevance that on their own the study and the library could not offer.

The third point is that the suppression of the worker-priest movement illustrates the essentially arbitrary way in which the Church operated – and still, to far too great an extent, operates. To a substantial degree the worker-priest movement survived for as long as it did because it had a powerful advocate in Cardinal Emmanuel-Célestin Suhard, Archbishop of Paris. Not only is he said to have insisted on discussing this question only with the Pope himself, with whom he had been a fellow-student at the Gregorian, and not with subordinate prelates in the Roman Curia, but he is said to have replied to the Pope on one occasion: 'It is not the Bishop of Rome but the Bishop of Paris who will one day have to account to God for the souls of the workers of Paris.'[6] It may be significant that it was only after his death (on 30 May 1949) that the Holy Office issued its decree against Communism (1 July 1949). Certainly his successor, Cardinal Maurice Feltin, though equally committed a defender of the worker-priest movement, did not carry the same clout in Rome. And the actual clampdown had to wait until Monsignor Paolo Marella had succeeded Monsignor Angelo Roncalli, the future Pope John XXIII, as nuncio in 1953.[7]

The banning of the worker-priest movement illustrates the extent to which before Vatican II whether the Church operated justly or unjustly depended not so much on the existence of legal structures and systems as on the personalities and attitudes of its office-holders and on the amount of power each was able to exert – as well as on the shifting balance of power among them. In this way it was an arbitrary despotism, however well-intentioned all the despots may have been and however fairly many of them in practice behaved. Nor is it correct to speak of all this purely in the past tense. To a considerable extent the system is still in being.[8]

If over the past decade and a half it has no longer operated in quite the same repressive way, that is largely because there has been a dramatic shift in public opinion within the Church. This found both its cause and expression in the Second Vatican Council: those taking part and those observing it from outside St Peter's came to realize not only that the Church could survive heated debate on doctrinal issues but that such disagreement was essential to it, since it was only by public discussion of this kind that the Church could best fulfil Paul's injunction to 'test everything' and 'Hold fast what is good' (1 Thess. 5:21). As a result Catholics have no longer been prepared to accept the authoritarian suppression of free speech or of efforts to make the Church's mission more effective, while those in authority have been readier to react with argument than with suppression when policies or attitudes are called into question. One of the most disturbing implications of the disciplinary measures taken against Hans Küng, as well as of the Doctrinal Congregation's renewed vigour in pursuing what it sees as doctrinal deviation on the part of other theologians, is that these may indicate a reversion to a more repressive exercise of authority in the Church.

But even at the Council the whole issue of proper intellectual and academic freedom within the Church tended to remain a little obscured. It was only brought fully out into the open in one of the last speeches to be made, by the newly appointed Archbishop (later Cardinal) Michele Pellegrino of Turin:

> It is without a doubt the right and duty of authority to keep a closer watch on the clergy, since their mistakes are more damaging. But this ought always to be done with due respect for human dignity, to which also belongs the freedom of speech that is acknowledged to everyone.
>
> Nor should we think there is no danger lurking in this matter. We are all of course grateful to the supreme authority of the Church for having at the time overcome the extremely serious threat of modernism. But who would dare assert that in that necessary repression the rights and personal dignity of the clergy were always scrupulously maintained, whether it was a question of priests aflame with youthful zeal, or bishops, or cardinals of Holy Roman Church?

And lest anyone should think all this and similar matters belong to the past, I think it is enough if I mention having a few years ago found a member of a religious order who was living in involuntary 'exile' on account of doctrinal opinions which he had put forward but which today we are happy to read in papal and conciliar documents. Everybody knows this kind of case is not unique.

It is hardly necessary to point out that in theology too there are very many things which, even though they are maintained undisturbed for a long time, are nevertheless, with the progress of research, recognized as being in need of revision; and that the range of subjects on which people are free to reach their own conclusions is perhaps much larger than is thought by those without experience of the hard and often dangerous work of this kind of research.

It is only on condition that freedom in seeking the truth is acknowledged to all Catholics that there can take place that dialogue within the Church which Pope Paul VI wanted to be 'of frequent occurrence and on an intimate level' and 'ready to listen to the variety of views which are expressed in the world today' (*Ecclesiam suam* § 113, AAS 1964 p. 657).

I would add that, if everyone knows he or she is able to express his or her opinion with due and healthy freedom, he or she will act with that truthfulness and sincerity that ought always to shine forth in the Church. Acting in any other way means it is hardly possible to avoid the abominable plague of falsehood and hypocrisy.[9]

Thanks to this intervention, the Council's constitution on the Church in the world of today adds the clause 'whether clerical or lay' to its mention of the lawful freedom of enquiry, thought and speech that belongs to all the faithful just to emphasize that the clergy, who are usually the only members of the Church against whom the ecclesiastical authorities can bring sanctions to bear, are not to be deprived of the freedom that in the past was too often denied them.[10]

All this may seem to add up to a rather negative picture of the intellectual climate during the last years of Pius XII's pontificate, the time when Hans Küng was a student in Rome. But the change brought about by John XXIII and his Council has been so radical and has gone so deep that it is easy for Catholics to forget and for non-Catholics to be unaware just how bad things were. In Bishop Christopher Butler's admitted exaggeration, 'it was the best of all possible religions, and everything in it an intellectual scandal'.[11] Nor was this something that affected merely theologians or even merely the clergy. The caution that theologians and clergy needed to exercise to make sure that their enquiries and pronouncements did not come into conflict with what the Curia regarded as orthodoxy trickled down to influence the man and woman in the pew. Ordinary Catholics became wary of saying what they thought, or even of expressing their beliefs in terms other than those repeated from the catechism. There was always the lurking danger of unwittingly uttering heresy and talking oneself out of the Church. The Catholic's job was to believe what was propounded for his or her belief by those placed in spiritual authority above him or her, no matter whether it made sense or not:

> In our day, an impersonal, notional system has replaced personal belief as the primary fact in the consciousness of Catholics. Ask a Catholic what his faith is, and he replies with the words of the catechism. Ask him what he *believes*, and he won't tell you unless he trusts you. He may even be afraid to admit his beliefs to himself, lest they reveal him as a 'heretic'. Many Catholics repress their doubts and questions.[12]

And in theology itself this kind of attitude did if possible even more damage by seeing theology in excessively objective terms, as if it were the study of data as impersonal and abstract as those of physics or geography. In these circum-

stances, Nicholas Lash has pointed out, the test of orthodoxy is no longer what a man believes, but what he says:

> To put the point slightly differently, theology, as
> divorced from belief, becomes talking about some-
> body else's idea of God. Teaching theology means
> getting one person to accept another person's under-
> standing of God. Since very often it is not, for either
> teacher or pupil, their own understanding of God that
> is involved, theology ceases to be discourse about God,
> the living God, at all.[13]

Too abstract and impersonal an approach to theology can
in this way mask a terrfying absence of belief.

The change in Catholic attitudes brought about by the
Council should not, however, be seen as some kind of
abrupt break. Rather, it was the rediscovery of older and
more robust viewpoints, the bringing to the surface of what
had long lain hidden and unacknowledged. It was a continuous development, even if one speeded up and com-
pressed into a few years. In this sense it was a revolution.

The uncanny thing about Hans Küng's coming to
maturity as a theologian is the way it mirrored this
development within the Church. He started from almost
unquestioning acceptance of the Church as it then was and
obedience to the claims it made on him. By his own account
he even sounds a little priggish. Asked if as a student he had
accepted without any reservations at all the encyclical
Humani generis (which had been drafted largely by his
professors at the Gregorian) along with the definition of the
Assumption and the rest of the triumphalist fabric of the
Catholicism of that Holy Year 1950, he answered (*Way*,
p. 130):

> Yes, I did to start with. The definition of the Assump-
> tion, for example, struck me as a suitable expression
> of the Catholic understanding of the faith on the basis
> of the organic theory of the development of dogma
> being served up to us at that time. And in talking to

students from German universities I used to criticize the 'arrogance' and the 'mania for criticism' shown by the German professors of theology who had their doubts on this question and who were described as rationalistic. For the rest I used to be pretty slavish in keeping to the uncommonly strict rules of the German College, rules that in some respects weren't even sensible, and I didn't understand at all the freer attitude of my older fellow-students who had come into the German College straight off the Italian campaign and just could not come to terms with this Tridentine regulation of their entire life.

What he was looking for was some clue that would justify the imposing edifice with which he was presented. It was when no such clue was forthcoming that he began to question what he was being offered.

Much of the strength and appeal of Küng's work lies in the way his development was thus in advance of and parallel to that of many ordinary Catholics, though consciously worked out at the proper scholarly level. He was far enough ahead to be able to point out how the path was going, but never so far ahead as to lose touch. All he was doing was to take seriously what he was being offered and expecting it to make sense. Those who complain about the course his development has taken should recall that among its roots are the deficiencies of preconciliar Catholicism in its last flowering of triumphalist glory.

[1] 'How Not to Appoint a Bishop – II', *Herder Correspondence*, vol. 6 no. 6, June 1969, pp. 186–7.

[2] See items 92 and 93, p. 214, and item 114, p. 217, in Dr Margret Gentner's invaluable bibliography in *Hans Küng: His Work and His Way*.

[3] J. P. Mackey, *Tradition and Change in the Church*, Gill and Son, Dublin and Sydney, 1968, pp. 139–140.

[4] See Karl Rahner's outspoken denunciation of these goings on, 'Ich protestiere', *Publik-Forum*, 16 November 1979, pp. 15–19.

[5] Karl Rahner, art. cit., pp. 18 and 19.

[6] Gregor Siefer, *The Church and Industrial Society*, Darton, Longman and Todd, London, 1964, p. 119.

[7] Siefer, op. cit., p. 71.

[8] See Clifford Longley's analysis of the methods of work of the former Holy Office, now the Congregation for the Doctrine of the Faith, *The Times*, 25 September 1978.

[9] *Acta Synodalia Concilii Vaticani II*, Vatican Polyglot Press, Rome, 1970–77, vol. 4 fasc. 3, pp. 136–7; cf. Xavier Rynne, *The Fourth Session*, Faber and Faber, London, 1966, pp. 92–5, and *The Tablet*, 9 October 1965, pp. 1112–3.

[10] Cf. the commentary on this passage (*Gaudium et Spes* § 62) by Roberto Tucci, S.J., in Herbert Vorgrimler (ed.), *Commentary on the Documents of Vatican II*, Burns and Oates, London, 1967–69, vol. v, pp. 285–287. The commentary also quotes a slightly fuller extract from Archbishop Pellegrino's speech quoted above.

[11] B. C. Butler, 'Joy in Believing', *The Tablet*, 5 February 1966, p. 153; reprinted in Valentine Rice (ed.), *Searchings: Essays and Studies by B. C. Butler*, Geoffrey Chapman, London, 1974, p. 268.

[12] Michael Novak, *The Open Church: Vatican II, Act II*, Darton, Longman and Todd, London, 1964, p. 358.

[13] Nicholas Lash, *His Presence in the World: A Study of Eucharistic Worship and Theology*, Sheed and Ward, London and Sydney, 1968, p. 10. The whole of this first chapter – 'What on earth is theology?' – is very much to the point.

3

Rome and Paris

Nevertheless, a surprising amount was stirring under the apparently calm surface of preconciliar Catholicism. As long as the structure of doctrinal orthodoxy remained intact, there was toleration and even encouragement of a wide range of initiatives. The changes in the pattern of worship that, particularly for outsiders, were the most obvious effect of Vatican II had their origins in a liturgical movement that flourished with papal approval. In principle, too, successive popes were in favour of biblical studies, though ready to clamp down on some of their more disturbing findings and implications. There was movement and activity alongside the serene assurance of being in the right and the caution with which anything new was greeted.

There was even a first recognition of the place of public opinion within the Church. In a speech in 1950 – which, signficantly enough, did not find its way into the *Acta Apostolicae Sedis*, the official record of the Pope's and the Holy See's activities, though it is listed in the index to the relevant volume – Pius XII told the international congress of the Catholic press that it was only those who knew little or nothing about the Catholic Church who would be surprised to hear him talking about public opinion within the Church – 'about things that can be left open to discussion, of course'. There would, he said, be something missing from the Church's life if it had no public opinion – 'a defect for which pastors as well as the faithful would be responsible'.[1] In 1953, the same year that saw the suppression of the worker-priest movement, Karl Rahner built on this foundation a courageous essay that established 'the individual's, and above all the layman's, right to free speech within the Church'.[2] The older theologian pointed to the role Hans Küng was later to fill when he stated that people in the Church 'must learn that even in the Church there can be something like Her Majesty's Opposition'. This he saw as representing 'a genuine, divinely-willed opposition to all that is merely human in the Church and her official representatives'.[3]

At the same time things were stirring in the world at large. The generation that grew up during and after the war had more reason than most to question their elders' wisdom and authority. Not only had the war been the second in a quarter of a century to bring destruction to Europe, but it had ended with the disclosure that in the atomic bomb mankind now had at its disposal the means for collective suicide. Authority had forfeited the almost automatic trust earlier generations had been encouraged to place in it, the presumption that those in power knew what they were doing and had the competence to do it.

There were thus a number of influences at work to discourage in a clerical student too close a dependence on the received wisdom of the Roman schools. Hans Küng himself lists four factors that slowly weaned him from his original uncritical acceptance of official ways and modes of thought (*Way*, pp. 130–131). First was the crisis of Church leadership in the final years of Pius XII's pontificate. He saw the Curia, the Pope's administrative machinery, becoming more and more ossified and the Pope himself becoming more and more isolated. He was shocked by the abruptness with which the worker-priest movement in France was suppressed. He became disillusioned with the continuous inflation of statements by the Church's teaching authority, something which in practice ended up with the Pope reciting or putting his name to addresses and encyclicals written by people he knew personally because they were among his teachers. Being able to look behind the scenes led to the demythologization of a Pope whom he and his contemporaries had begun by idealizing.

Second was his growing dissatisfaction with the neoscholastic system of theology. It didn't, he found, deliver what it promised. His dissatisfaction centred particularly on the two-tier theory of natural and supernatural – one of the issues behind *Humani generis*. For him and his contemporaries, nature and grace, reason and faith, the natural and the supernatural could not be neatly separated off into different bundles in the way neoscholasticism wanted to do: reality was untidier and more demanding than that.

Third was the growing problem presented by the strict discipline imposed by the German College. The first time ecclesiastical obedience created difficulties for him was over the obligation to attend lectures (often no more than the reading out of textbook material) when it would have been simpler and quicker and made much better pedagogical sense to have read the material up on one's own.

Fourth was the conflict he was brought into with the college authorities through his taking seriously the post of chaplain to the German College's Italian employees. He saw it as part of his job to intervene on their behalf over such things as improving their accommodation and their pay and the possibility of getting married. No doubt the college authorities saw it as the chaplain's job to keep the domestic staff quiet and contented, not to start acting as their shop steward. One suspects that it took the young Hans Küng some time to learn that Christian behaviour does not always endear one to one's fellow Christians. One suspects, too, that he was not only taken aback but also hurt by the college authorities' lack of sympathy for his efforts on behalf of their staff.

At the same time his formal seminary education had an adventurous quality which comes as a forcible reminder that even in the heyday of neoscholasticism 'Rome' (or at least some parts of that complex entity) was far from closed to new ideas coming in from outside. His dissertation for his licentiate of philosophy was on Jean-Paul Sartre's atheistic humanism – a daring enough subject considering that all Sartre's works had been put on the Index of forbidden books in 1948, the very year Hans Küng began his studies – and that for his licentiate of theology on Karl Barth's doctrine of justification. Already themes were being sounded that would recur in his later work. There is no doubt an element of luck in it too, but throughout Hans Küng has had a happy knack of spotting the important issues and concentrating on them. This has enabled him to avoid false starts or wasted efforts spent exploring what turn out to be blind alleys. The study he has devoted to subjects in the past provides a springboard for current research.

Both his dissertation topics thus crop up in his later work – Sartre admittedly for the most part only in *Does God Exist?*, though throughout his career Hans Küng has been keenly aware of the general intellectual climate in which he is operating as a Catholic theologian and of the alternative visions of the world on offer. But Barth has coloured his entire work. Formally, of course, Küng cannot be described as Barth's pupil. But he early came under the older man's influence, and from 1955 onwards treasured a personal friendship that lasted until Barth's death in 1968 at the age of eighty-two.

What attracted Küng to Barth was the latter's very Protestantism: 'In him I saw the strictest possible development of the Protestant thing and at the same time a striving after a Catholic breadth' (*Way*, p. 135). But there was more to Barth for Küng than simply opening up the way into Protestant theology (*Way*, pp. 142–3):

> Beyond that Barth aroused my enthusiasm for theology as such. Before, theology was for me an essential

and obligatory exercise and a preparatory phase for
the pastoral work that was to come later. To begin
with it had comparatively little fascination for me,
certainly less than philosophy, art, music, psychology
. . . It was only now, brought up against Barth's theological system, which is enormously spacious and at
the same time organized down to the smallest detail,
that I could see clearly what theology as a field of
study was capable of. Barth's critical and constructive
grappling with the entire Christian tradition of the
past two thousand years and thus with the Catholic
tradition too, his grappling with the great thinkers of
the past and with the spirit of the age, his involvement
in practical questions not only in connection with the
Church's resistance to Hitler and the Nazis but also in
other Church disputes, all this established for me
lasting standards of theological thought and activity.
And in this you mustn't forget that for seven years it
was only in Latin that I had been listening to lectures,
only in Latin that I had been doing examinations, and
hence it was Latin books in particular that I had been
studying. It was Barth who reintroduced me to decent
German in theology with his powerful theological
language that may indeed often be a bit long-winded
but is nevertheless honed down to a fine polish.

Küng thus owed Barth a fourfold debt. First, because Barth
was the Protestant theologian who had come to dominate
theology in the German-speaking world (and outside it)
since the publication in 1918 of the first edition of his
commentary on Romans, Küng's own theology inevitably
took on the nature of a dialogue with Christians on the
other side of the Reformation divide. Barth brought Küng
into the centre of the Protestant theological world and
ensured that he would all the time be aware of its fundamental concerns. Barth was indeed himself a pioneer of the
ecumenical dialogue at this basic theological level. In the
winter term of 1928–29 he devoted a seminar to the first
part of Thomas Aquinas' *Summa Theologiae* and invited the

Jesuit Erich Przywara to Münster to debate with him at one session of this seminar in February 1929. In 1941 he welcomed a pupil of Przywara's, Hans Urs von Balthasar, then newly arrived in Basle as Catholic student chaplain, to his seminar on the Council of Trent with the words: 'The enemy is listening in.' This particular 'enemy' went on to write one of the first Catholic studies of Karl Barth ten years later.[4]

Second, Barth introduced Küng to a theological language that was based not on the philosophical tradition of Aristotle as mediated through Thomas Aquinas and his commentators but on the native German philosophical tradition running from Kant through to Hegel (*Justification*, p. 7):

> Catholic theologians have no small difficulty in trying to grasp the theology of Karl Barth, and this precisely because, quite apart from all matters of content, Barth thinks and speaks otherwise than they do. The vocabulary and the whole system of categories, the choice of words and the pattern of thinking are strange. Whereas the Catholic theologian generally thinks and speaks along Aristotelian and scholastic lines, Barth's thought and language take their shape from German Idealism. Barth has assimilated, especially through the theology of Schleiermacher, the whole development from Kant through Fichte and Schelling to Hegel. He has also drawn upon later Protestant theology, particularly that of Overbeck, Feuerbach, Strauss, and especially the theological existentialism of his own teacher, Herrmann.

Involved here is language in two senses: the strict sense of Latin, German or English; and the broader sense of a particular way of looking at the world and a particular set of categories for coming to terms with it. In both senses neo-scholasticism provided a straitjacket which made it difficult to escape from what was fundamentally the mental and intellectual world of the late Middle Ages, a world undisturbed by the Copernican revolution Kant claimed to have brought about in philosophy. There was indeed an ideological aspect to the use of Latin: it suggested that Christian faith was a system of timeless truths somehow abstracted from any actual incarnation in the changing world we live in and was therefore more fittingly expressed in a language that had ceased developing because it was dead. In both respects Barth was a liberating influence. Not only did he reintroduce Küng to 'decent German' in theology, but he also offered him a philosophical language capable of speaking more directly to his contemporaries.

Third comes Barth's insistence on the sheer otherness of God, on the fact that man may propose but it is definitely and always God who disposes. This insistence provides a useful corrective to the temptation Catholics seem to be exposed to of regarding God as somehow under the control of his Church instead of seeing the Church as continually subject to God's judgement. It may be because of what God has done for us in the past that we are called upon to place our trust in him – 'I am the Lord your God, who brought you out of the land of Egypt, out of the house of bondage' (Exod. 20:2) – but he is the God not of our past but of our present and still more of our future: 'And I will walk among you, and will be your God, and you shall be my people' (Lev. 26:12); and the future is something that, try as we may, we cannot control and pin down. The besetting temptation for the Church is to regard the salvation Christ has achieved for us as something past and safe and predictable and controllable and, in a way, 'dead'. There comes about a shutting off from any willingness to accept, let alone welcome, the challenge which God continually offers to our complacency. In this way God can too easily become reduced to purely human terms and categories. Barth's insistence on God's essential otherness and on God's transcendence of all purely human categories, on man's total dependence on God and his inability to do anything for himself beyond plunge himself yet deeper into the mire of sin, thus acts as a powerful antidote to the distortion of Catholicism that lets the Church elbow God aside as the focus of human aspirations. Küng's continual insistence on the provisional nature of the Church as something that points to rather than embodies the kingdom can thus be seen to have its roots in Barth, as well as being a re-discovery of orthodox balance after the exaggerated triumphalism of the recent Catholic past. So too can his unwillingness to transfer to the Church the infallibility that properly belongs to God alone.

Fourth, for Barth theology was no ivory-tower occupa-tion. Far from providing an escape from human anxieties and human difficulties, it involved him in the human struggle. Right from the start of his pastorate at Safenwil Barth took the workers' side: he joined the Social Democratic Party in 1915, and in 1919 celebrated May Day by marching with the Safenwil workers behind the red flag to nearby Zofingen. As a professor at Bonn Barth was at the heart of resistance to Nazi efforts to take over Church as well as State: he played a central role in the formation of the Confessing Church, and the declaration it adopted at its first synod held at Barmen in 1934 was largely his work. During the early stages of the war Barth, now a professor at Basle after having been sacked by the Nazis in 1935, made himself unpopular in his native Switzerland by his efforts to stiffen Swiss resistance to Hitler, and some of his lectures were banned by the censors.[5] Barth thus offered a model for the political commitment required of a theologian. Küng's career may lack the same note of overt political commit-ment, but the reason for that is the different circumstances in which it has unfolded. Both theologians stand for the freedom of the Church, both reject the idea of the Church making a practice of dictating to the state how it should go about its business, both insist on the Church's duty to bear witness when some aspect of what is involved in being a Christian comes under attack.

The discovery of Barth meant that new intellectual horizons were all the time opening up before the young Hans Küng. Indeed, the older theologian's monumental *Church Dogmatics*, never in fact to be completed, was still in course of publication, with volumes IV/1 and IV/2 only appearing in 1953 and 1955, and the last full volume, IV/3, being published (in two parts) in 1959 and 1960, by which time Küng had passed from being a student through pastoral work as an assistant priest in Lucerne to being a research assistant at Münster.

At the same time his awareness of life was being expanded in other and less pleasant ways. For his ordination and first Mass, both celebrated in St Peter's on 10 and 11 October 1954, his whole family came to Rome; and that was when they discovered his brother Georges, then aged twenty-three, was suffering from what turned out to be a brain tumour. At first the family thought all would be well when Georges went on from Rome to stay with friends in Italy for a holiday, but on his return to Switzerland he had to be taken into hospital at Zürich at once, and a year later he was dead.

This was a shattering blow for the whole Küng family. In the twentieth century parents no longer expect to bury any of their children, as they so frequently did right up to a century ago. For Hans Küng it meant that right at the start of his life as a priest he was brought sharply up against the central, ugly but inescapable fact of death, the mocking question to which Christian faith claims to be the only answer that is in any way satisfactory; and he was brought up against it in a particularly agonzing and personal way. No one, he was to write twelve years later (*Leid*, p. 8), could suppress the questions that suffering provoked: 'Is not all this misery crying to heaven? Indeed, is it not crying

against heaven and its God? Is it not an accusation against
the creator of this world that is more than full of suffering?'
Only the cross could provide an answer to these unavoidable questions, and that by offering the Christian not a way
past but a way through suffering; and it was an answer
anchored in hope in the future promised by God and
already breaking in on our present, the future when God
'will wipe away every tear from their eyes and death shall
be no more, neither shall there be mourning nor crying nor
pain any more, for the former things have passed away'
(Rev. 21:4, quoted by Küng at the conclusion of *Gott und
das Leid*, p. 69).

His brother's death coincided more or less with the conclusion of Hans Küng's studies in Rome and his move to
Paris in 1955 to start work on his doctorate. To go on to a
doctorate after ordination may at first sight seem a little
strange for someone whose intention was to work in the
pastoral ministry. But as far as Hans Küng was concerned a
doctorate was simply the final stage of making sure he was
properly trained to embark on the pastoral ministry he felt
himself called to undertake. Nor in fact are priests with
doctorates that uncommon in ordinary parish work: in
England and Wales, where doctorates are not prized as
highly as in the German-speaking world, nor so common a
conclusion of university studies, there are nearly seventy
out of about 4700 priests engaged in pastoral work, and
only about a quarter of these seventy are canon lawyers.

Hans Küng's bishop, Monsignor Franz von Streng of
Basle, had given him leave to spend a further two years
studying for his doctorate. In the event he needed only a
year, and was able to spend the rest of his time in Paris
starting what turned out to be twelve to thirteen years'
work on Hegel, culminating in *Menschwerdung Gottes*
published in 1970, while he was also able to make study-
trips to Amsterdam, Berlin, Madrid and London. This was
because the subject of his thesis – Karl Barth's doctrine of

justification – was the same as for his licentiate in Rome, and his professors in Paris found that he had already covered much of the ground.

The subject was one of three suggested by Hans Urs von Balthasar, the Swiss Catholic theologian whom we have already met as a participant in Barth's seminar on the Council of Trent and as the author of one of the first Catholic studies of Barth. Küng first visited Balthasar at his home in Basle in 1953, and the older theologian clearly gave him every help and encouragement. Küng speaks of him correcting him when he went wrong in his work on Barth, and despite the sundering row that blew up a quarter of a century later over *On being a Christian* he can never forget Balthasar's friendly gesture of solidarity in coming all the way to Paris when he had to defend his thesis for his doctorate (*Way*, p. 136). It was Balthasar, too, who saw to it that his thesis was published at the Johannes Verlag in Einsiedeln simultaneously with his gaining his doctorate.

Paris meant not only new and broader opportunities for study but also freedom after seven years of the restricted life of a Roman seminarian in the reign of Pius XII (*Way*, p. 147):

> First of all, Paris meant an immense liberation after all the business of being isolated and segregated in a Roman college, after all the compulsion and regulation of a life regimented from morning till night. At last one was free to plan one's life oneself again. It may sound rather odd even for seminarists today, but once again, as earlier during my days at the *Gymnasium* [in Lucerne], I could freely go to the theatre, to the cinema, to talks and lectures, when I had the time to do so. This contact with French cultural life and above all with the French university, with the Sorbonne and of course particularly with the Institut Catholique and with French theology, meant an undreamed-of enrichment for me.

Quite what a relief it must have been we can also deduce from the fact that it was during a visit to the opera – Verdi's *Rigoletto* – that he had decided to go to the Germanicum in Rome for his studies for the priesthood. The schoolboy in his late teens in Lucerne had been free to do what was forbidden to the seminarian in his early twenties in Rome. The freedom Paris represented also brought with it in a particularly strong form a temptation to which Hans Küng was susceptible in his student days – that of spending too much money buying too many books.

Theologically Paris was particularly important in two respects. One was in making Küng aware of the significance for the renewal of theology of the Fathers of the Church, above all the Greek Fathers whose importance has tended to be overlooked in a Church with an intellectual tradition largely shaped by that towering but uneven genius Augustine of Hippo. The French interest in patristics was exemplified by the series *Sources chrétiennes* which the Jesuits Henri de Lubac and Jean Daniélou started during the war in 1941 and which (with a few exceptions) provided bilingual texts (Greek and French or Latin and French) of a wide range of patristic literature: this helped to bring the Fathers out of the library into the individual scholar's or pastor's study. Moreover, one effect of *Humani generis* was to make patristics even more attractive, since it was clearly a less dangerous field of study than dogmatic theology.

The other was the interest it prompted in ecclesiology, and the key work here was Congar's *Vraie et fausse réforme dans l'Eglise*. It was only in Paris that Küng was able to catch up with this seminal work and absorb its message, a message that was to bear fruit particularly in *The Council and Reunion* five years later. Congar himself Küng had first met while in Rome, where, as we have seen, the French Dominican was stationed from November 1954 to February 1955.

The two years in Paris also saw the first slow beginnings

of what by the end of the 1950s had become a steady flow of articles from Hans Küng's pen. One of the earliest concerned the pastoral work he had been doing, at the Swiss bishops' behest, among Swiss au pair girls who had come to the French capital to learn the language.

Paris, and the visits to Amsterdam, Madrid and London as well as Berlin that concluded his student years, finally helped him polish his enviable mastery of foreign languages. Besides his native German – which for a Swiss is some way towards a foreign language anyway, since the Swiss speak their own markedly distinct variety of German at home and among themselves, and the first year of primary school is spent making the transition to standard high German – Hans Küng is fluent in French, Italian, Spanish and English, with Dutch as a language he can read and understand but does not normally have to speak. If this array of linguistic ability should seem a little out of the ordinary, it is worth reflecting that, along with the command of Latin and Greek and the working knowledge of Hebrew that Küng also possesses, it represents something like the requisite minimum for a contemporary theologian if he is to be able to master his subject and to keep up with the ebb and flow of theological discourse around the world. In this as in other respects Küng is nothing if not professional.

[1] Quoted by Karl Rahner, *Free Speech in the Church*, Sheed and Ward, New York, 1959, pp. 14–15, and by Küng himself in *The Council and Reunion*, p. 66.
[2] Rahner, *Free Speech*, p. 26. It took six years for this work to appear in English.
[3] Rahner, *Free Speech*, pp. 36–37.
[4] Eberhard Busch, *Karl Barth: his life from letters and autobiographical texts*, SCM Press, London, 1976, pp. 182–3, 302, 362. Hans Urs von Balthasar's study is *Karl Barth: Darstellung und Deutung seiner Theologie*, Verlag Jakob Hegner, Cologne, 1951.
[5] Busch, *Karl Barth*, pp. 68–70, 82, 106; 222–248; and 303–311.

4

Justification

It is surely a little startling for a theologian to begin his career by calmly showing that on the one issue which has traditionally been accepted as the major dividing line between Protestant and Catholic the two sides were in fact in essential agreement. Yet in effect this is what Küng did in his doctoral thesis. If today this achievement is not what most people immediately call to mind in connection with Hans Küng, there are a number of reasons for this state of affairs. One is all the other startling things he has gone on to do, notably his critique of infallibility. Another is that the discovery of common ground where it was always assumed there was unbridgeable disagreement has become almost a commonplace of the ecumenical dialogue at the theological level, as is shown by the substantial agreement recorded by the Anglican/Roman Catholic International Commission on such traditionally divisive issues as the eucharist (1971) and the ministry and ordination (1973).

A third, and more important, reason concerns the subject matter of Küng's thesis. Not only is justification no longer felt to be a live issue by probably the majority of Christians today − whereas questions of eucharistic doctrine and worship and of the recognition of other Churches' ministries are very much live issues − but it is one to which many feel almost a positive aversion. 'It has rightly been observed that the question most disputed at the time of the Reformation now leaves people in the Protestant Churches just as cold as those in the Catholic Church', Küng was to observe seventeen years later in *On being a Christian* (p. 581).

There are, of course, still quite a number of Christians who are very much concerned about the question. Anglicans of a conservative evangelical outlook, for example, feel strongly that it has not been done justice to in official dialogue between the Anglican Communion and the Church of Rome, whether at the national or international level. But both their fellow-Anglicans of different brands of Churchmanship and their Catholic partners in dialogue are apt to find their eyes glazing over in boredom when justification comes up for discussion. It has become extraordinarily difficult for twentieth-century Christians, let alone their post-Christian agnostic contemporaries, to think themselves back into the minds of their sixteenth-century ancestors and understand how this question could be so divisive, to the point of bloodshed. No doubt this is because what is at issue is not *how* salvation works – which from one point of view is what the question of justification is about – but whether it works at all and what if anything salvation means. The questions now, as Küng has pointed out, basing himself on the work of his Tübingen colleague Norbert Greinacher, concern the meaning of life, man's freedom and responsibility, and the social dimension of salvation (*Christian*, p. 582).

Yet, as Küng goes on to point out in his later book, justification remains as vitally important a doctrine as ever – or indeed perhaps even more so – in a society where increasingly people are judged by what they have achieved. Thinking in terms of efficiency finally becomes a serious threat to the humanity of man, and liberation from this pressure and from this threat comes about from realizing that achievements are not what ultimately matters and that, in Pauline language, man is justified by faith alone, not by what he has done (which in any case is to say the least ambiguous) but by his trust in God (*Christian*, pp. 583–590).

In our day it is thus more a question of making someone's

worth and standing in the community and his or her self-respect depend on what he or she has or has not done. For the Reformers, what they were protesting against was the tendency they saw in the Church of their time to make salvation dependent on human achievement rather than on the mysterious and unpredictable workings of God's grace. Instead of religion representing man's attempt to respond honestly, humbly and openly to the challenge God presented him with and the demands he made on him, a challenge and demands that could not be defined or limited in advance, it was seen by the Reformers as having become deformed into a matter of man trying to bring God under his control and manipulate him for his own ends. Very much involved here was the way in which, in the popular mind at least, the eucharist and the priesthood took on more than a tinge of magic. The priest was seen as the man who had power over God and could bring God down on to the altar: the old pagan Roman religion, whose rites were meant to bind the gods to serve human purposes, had had its revenge. In this context the Reformers' insistence that man's salvation depended on God alone and that of himself man could do nothing rapidly because the central theological issue of the dispute that grew out of a German Augustinian friar's anxiety over whether he was saved while living in a Church recognized on all sides to be in desperate need of reform and forming part of a society undergoing the stresses and strains of readjusting to new horizons, new knowledge, new and upsetting ways of doing old things. Paradoxically the rightness of the Protestant emphasis on man's dependence on God alone for his salvation and the worthlessness of human achievements is underlined by the way in which the Protestant work ethic has fostered a society dominated by the idea of achievement. The problem, as we have seen, remains, even if the Protestant answer may merely have encouraged it to recur in a sharper and more intractable form.

Strictly speaking, of course, in his book Hans Küng is not specifically concerned with the doctrine of justification as enunciated by Luther or Calvin or any of their contemporaries among the Reformers. The scope of the book is clearly indicated by its sub-title: 'The Doctrine of Karl Barth and a Catholic Reflection.' But it would be futile to try to interpose a distinction on this point between the man who was the greatest living exponent of the Reformed tradition and the Reformers themselves. Barth may have aligned himself with the best Catholic tradition as against Luther in seeing the central dogma of Christianity as not justification but the mystery of Christ (*Justification*, p. 118). But what is at issue is not the extent to which Barth joins with Luther and his immediate followers in seeing justification as the one *articus stantis aut cadentis ecclesiae*, the one article of faith by which the Church stands or falls. What is at issue is whether Barth is true to the insights that made the Reformers see justification as the crucial and divisive issue in their challenge to what they came to regard as a Church corrupt not merely in its discipline but in its doctrine too.

Barth certain saw no compromise possible between the Reformers' view of justification and that put forward by the Council of Trent (*Church Dogmatics*, IV/1 p. 626):

> It is difficult to see in the Tridentine doctrine of justification anything better than what Paul [in Gal. 1:8–9] meant by another gospel. It has no light from above. It is admirably adapted to serve as a touchstone to show where we all stand in the matter. There are Protestant doctrines of justification – we will not enter into them now – which do not pass this test because they themselves are far too Tridentine. The aim of that Council was to be a reforming Council, and in many of its practical decisions this is what it actually was. But with its doctrine of justification the Roman Church closed the door to self-reformation and deprived itself of all possibility of seizing the

initiative in uniting the divided Church. It was impossible for the Evangelical Churches to return to fellowship with Rome when the decisive point of dispute was handled in this way. They could not surrender truth to unity. This reaction of the Roman Church was convincing proof that the Reformation application of the Pauline (and not only the Pauline) texts to the contemporary situation was both meaningful and necessary here at the very heart of the tragic controversy, and that it will remain so – seeing that the Roman Church cannot very well go back on that decree. A Church which maintains that its official decisions are infallible can commit errors which are irreformable. It has more than once done so.

That would seem to leave no room at all for rapprochement.

Küng's way of tackling the question was to devote the first part of his thesis to expounding what Barth had to say about the theology of justification and the second part to an attempted Catholic response. Barth is not the easiest of writers to summarize: he tends to think in page-long paragraphs where others think in sentences, and he depends on the effect of wave after wave of passionate argument washing over the reader and bearing him away. For this reason the first part of *Justification* can seem much heavier going than any other of Küng's writings – including the as yet untranslated study of Hegel, *Menschwerdung Gottes*.

This first part culminates in the question (*Justification*, p. 89): 'Does the Catholic theology of justification take justification seriously as the sovereign act of God's grace?' A long and painstaking analysis of the Catholic theology of justification, based on scripture and bolstered by lengthy and frequent quotations from the Fathers and from more recent theologians, as well as from formal doctrinal definitions, particularly the decree of the Council of Trent, reveals the answer to be that it does; and moreover that Barth for his part also takes justification seriously as the justification of *man* (*Justification*, pp. 263–264). Küng's finding is thus that 'on the whole there is fundamental agreement between the theology of Barth and that of the Catholic Church' and that on this question of justification 'Barth has no valid reason for a separation from the ancient Church' (p. 268). He concludes (p. 271):

It is without any doubt, then, significant that today there is a fundamental agreement between Catholic and Protestant theology, precisely in the theology of justification – the point at which Reformation theology took its departure. Despite all the difficulties, have we not, after these 400 years, come decidedly closer to one another also on the theological level?

Moreover, he suggests that a large part of the divergences in other fields, such as ecclesiology and sacramental theology, could likewise disappear if similar efforts were made to achieve a properly balanced and theologically sound presentation of the Catholic position instead of adopting a one-sided polemical approach (p. 267).

To all this Barth's response was generous. He had already seen Küng's Rome dissertation for his licentiate. According to Küng this had filled him with amazement and had made him wonder whether he was dealing with an old or a young man (*Way*, p. 143). Barth had just celebrated his seventieth birthday, *Festschrift* and all, the grand old man of Protestant theology with a reputation stretching back for very nearly forty years and with one more double volume of *Church Dogmatics* still to come; and here was a twenty-nine-year-old Catholic priest who had summed up his critique of Trent by saying he had 'treated the matter superficially' (*Justification*, p. 221).

Barth responded by giving Küng's book his blessing and approval. In a letter to Küng which acted as a foreword Barth testified that the younger theologian had 'fully and accurately reproduced my views as I myself understand them'. He could not hide his 'considerable amazement' at such a conclusion, and all he could say was: 'If what you have presented in Part Two of this book is actually the teaching of the Roman Catholic Church, then I must certainly admit that my view of justification agrees with the Roman Catholic view; if only for the reason that the Roman Catholic teaching would then be most strikingly in accord with mine' (*Justification*, pp.xvii–xviii). But he went on to argue that he should be allowed to plead mitigating circumstances for having been 'guilty of a persistent misunderstanding and, consequently, of a persistent injustice regarding the teaching of your Church, especially that of the Fathers of Trent' – even though he never went for a third time to the church of Santa Maria Maggiore in that city at the foot of the Alps to utter the contrite words *Patres, peccavi.*

Justification raises one fundamental question which so far Küng seems not to have tackled directly either in the book itself or in his subsequent writings. He demonstrated that to a considerable extent Catholics and Protestants had been arguing past each other, and that when one took the language of both sides to pieces they could be seen to be saying the same things but in terms which they took to denote a fundamental difference. The reader is thus left with the impression that the controversy has throughout been more semantic than real (*Justification*, p. 211):

> Protestants speak of a declaration of justice and Catholics of a making just. But Protestants speak of a declaring just which includes a making just; and Catholics of a making just which supposes a declaring just. Is it not time to stop arguing about imaginary differences?

Again, pointing out that applying too narrow a concept of justification as a yardstick could block any access to Barth's teaching, Küng writes (*Justification*, p. 217):

It would not even be noticed that what Barth and with him many Protestants call 'justification' largely coincides with what we Catholics call 'redemption' and that many expressions that sound heretical ought to be understood as completely orthodox: e.g. '*all* men are justified in Christ,' although it agrees with Scripture, may seem to Catholic ears to imply apokatastasis [Origen's idea that eventually all men and even the devil himself would be saved, an idea repeatedly condemned as unorthodox despite its obvious congruence with the infinite nature of God's mercy] which Barth, however, categorically rejects [because it would involve limiting God's gracious freedom and his justice: cf. *Church Dogmatics* II/2, pp. 295, 422]. In ordinary Catholic usage – and in agreement with Scripture – this would mean nothing other than the totally orthodox statement that '*All* men are *"redeemed"* in or by Jesus Christ'.

If the disagreement thus turns out to be a matter of verbal misunderstanding rather than of real difference, the question immediately arises why we have had to wait four hundred and fifty years to solve what is apparently more a semantic than a genuine difficulty. It would be intolerably patronizing to assume that our Reformation forebears were less skilled than we are at disentangling shadow and substance, and quite clearly they felt that momentous issues were at stake. It is difficult to avoid the conclusion that the theological issues carried such a heavy charge then, and now no longer do so, because they were then acting as the vehicle for other non-theological issues, the outcome of the intense social and cultural pressures European society was then experiencing, which at that time could only find expression by acting as a kind of explosive propellant for the purely theological questions.

It is thus tempting to argue that the decisive factors in schism and in the maintenance of schism are not primarily theological but social, cultural and economic, and this without either trivializing the theological disputes involved or indulging in the kind of reductionism that starts from the premise that theology is anyway merely a disguise for other concerns. The point would be not that the theological issues are unimportant but that the theological line of cleavage at a critical moment coincides with and is reinforced by other lines of cleavage, and that without this coincidence the purely theological dispute would be something that the Church would be able to contain and overcome without being split in two. On this hypothesis it could, for example, be argued that the Monophysite heresy reflected the tensions in the relations between on the one hand Syria and Egypt and on the other the imperial capital of Constantinople, and that what today would take the form of an independence movement or war of liberation then took on the form of heresy and schism. Indeed, in *A Study of History* Arnold Toynbee argued that Islam represented the final and successful Syriac protest against Hellenization, earlier and unsuccessful protests having been represented by the Nestorian and Monophysite 'heresies' which he saw as 'attempts to retain a religion which was Syriac in origin as an heirloom in the Syriac heritage'.[1] Similarly the American theologian Peter Chirico has suggested that 'many a heresy and a schism took its origin from the failure to distinguish a universal Christian meaning from a Christian meaning rooted solely in a particular time and place'[2] – in other words, that it proved impossible to disentangle the universal from the particular, the timeless from the time-bound, the essential from the accidental, in trying to translate Christianity out of one culture into another.

Looking at it from the other point of view, major obstacles to Christian unity tend these days to come from differences not so much of doctrine as of ecclesial life styles. What worries non-Catholics about the prospect of reunion with Rome is not so much infallibility (especially when this is subjected to so much interpretation as to become virtually innocuous for most practical purposes) as the inquisition: it is the way the Catholic Church sets about things that upsets them rather than what it says. Similarly a major stumbling block in the way of greater Church unity in England is not so much the Church of England's doctrinal position − which may be somewhat blurred by its twin traditions of comprehensiveness and tolerance but which is not totally impossible to pin down − as its cherished status as Church of the nation and the established Church of the realm: it is far too easy to see the Church of England as a religious endorsement of the English class system, no longer perhaps the Tory party but certainly the upper classes at prayer.

To test this hypothesis what would be needed would be a thorough and honest appraisal of all the major schisms and heresies that have littered the Church's history in an attempt to disentangle the theological from the non-theological factors involved, in as far as this is possible, and then seeing to what extent the purely theological differences that remain can be or have in fact been overcome. That no doubt would still leave the fundamental theological problem, a problem not so much of how we understand and explain Christianity in theory as of how we live it out in practice: how we can encourage and support the otherness of other people without experiencing it as a threat to our own identity, how we can live in peace and communion with those whom, for whatever reason, we see as menacing our wellbeing − in other and more biblical words, how we can love our enemies. And, since the invention of atomic weapons, that has become an urgent practical problem for the sheer survival of mankind.

Justification has, of course, turned out to be the first on a series of theological works from Hans Küng's pen which have played an important part in helping Catholics to see things in a fresher and, one would hope, more Christian perspective, and in helping other Christians to take a different and more sanguine view of the Catholic Church. But things could have been otherwise: the blow that fell twenty-two years later could have fallen then (and in a harsher form), and Küng's career as a theologian could quite easily have been blighted before it had really begun. The year of the book's publication – 1957 – was also the year that the Holy Office in Rome started a Küng dossier with the number 399/57/i. Yet, although the book was delated to Rome, Küng did not see his theological opus one end up on the Index – though he himself rated its chances of doing so at about fifty-fifty (*Way*, p. 142). That list of forbidden books, which includes Descartes, Berkeley, Locke, Hume and Kant (but not Hegel) among philosophers some or all of whose works were banned, as well as Balzac, Stendhal, Hugo, Flaubert and Zola among novelists, along with a mass of happily forgotten polemical works of the seventeenth and eighteenth centuries, was still very much a going concern. It had just been enriched by the addition of Simone de Beauvoir's *The Second Sex* and *The Mandarins* in 1956 and, a month before the publication of *Justification*, by the addition of Miguel de Unamuno's *The Tragic Sense of Life* and *The Agony of Christianity*. The Index was not to be formally abolished until 1966, as part of the reform of the Church's administrative machinery following the Council and immediately after the reorganization of the Holy Office as the Congregation for the Doctrine of the Faith in December 1965, although as far as I am aware the last book to be placed on the Index was a four-part work by Henry Dumery on 4 June 1958.

If Küng's first book had been placed on the Index, he would not have been in a position to take up a career as an academic theologian. Quite possibly he would not even have been properly rehabilitated in the wake of the Council. What as far as I know is the one book to have been placed on the Index and later rehabilitated is Rosmini's *The*

Five Wounds of the Church, which was published in a new
and officially approved edition in 1966, the same year that
the Index was abolished; but there was no great public
announcement to the effect that the Church was correcting
one of its past blunders. Most probably if *Justification* had
been condemned Hans Küng would today be parish priest
of some Swiss town or village – 'something that no doubt
would make many people in Rome and elsewhere sleep
more peacefully', to quote his own comment (*Way*, p. 142).

How the book succeeded in avoiding condemnation he
has himself explained (*Way*, pp. 141–2):

> In fact people from the Holy Office told me at the
> time that numerous denunciations had come in to
> Rome with regard to this book. But it was in part
> external circumstances that protected my book from a
> condemnation. My former teachers at the Gregorian,
> and particularly Fr Sebastian Tromp, who together
> with Fr Franz Hürth played a decisive role in the
> Holy Office, took me under their wing. Fr Tromp
> used to tell anyone who would listen that what my
> book was concerned with was a possible interpretation
> of the Tridentine decree on justification, even if one
> didn't therefore have to agree with everything in it.
> My professors at Paris, too, especially Louis Bouyer,
> my supervisor for my doctorate, and Guy de Broglie,
> who taught half the year in Rome and the other half in
> Paris and was held in high regard in Rome, shielded
> me from the cruder attacks through their public
> statements in the book's favour that were printed on
> the cover. I think the decisive thing was that I myself
> knew and had mastered the official Roman doctrine
> and had gone to endless trouble to adduce, as Barth
> said, a cloud of witnesses from the Catholic tradition
> to support my view. As a result even traditional-
> minded Catholic theologians could not deny that what
> was involved was a view that could not *a priori* be
> dismissed as un-Catholic.

The meticulous attention to detail had paid off.

Within the pages of *Justification* are to be found a number of themes which Küng was to develop more fully in later works. But, revolutionary as his conclusions are in this first work, they are expressed within a suitably conservative and cautious framework. Due gestures of obeisance, for example are made towards *Humani generis* (pp. 97–8); one passage (p. 206) implies acceptance of the Pauline authorship of the pastoral epistles, in contrast to the doubts he was to express later (cf. *The Church*, p. 19); and on doctrinal development he accepts a theory of explication, of making explicit what is already implicit in earlier formulations, that may well strike the reader as unsatisfactory, even if Küng warns that seeing the development of dogma as 'no more than a harmless and organic flowering' would be 'too simple' (*Justification*, pp. 97–8).

But alongside this natural and understandable deference towards the accepted wisdom of his mentors *Justification* contains the germ of many of its author's future preoccupations. What however singles it out is the way Küng has chosen to develop what might be termed ecumenical theology rather than the polemical or controversial theology of the past. Instead of setting out to prove the Protestants wrong and Catholics right – an exercise from which truth all too often emerges the victim – he is concerned to listen to what Protestants are saying and to use this as the occasion and basis for a Catholic examination of conscience. Explaining the reason for listening so carefully to what Barth had to say, Küng writes (*Justification*, p. 89):

> In this way we hoped to have arrived at one thing, that is, to have understood what his questions are in regard to Catholic teaching. Even this is not altogether easy. It is easy to understand these questions as reproaches but it is difficult to understand these questions as questions. Reproaches invite counter-attack. Questions invite self-appraisal. We have by now

sufficient material for self-appraisal and with that the goal of our first part is essentially attained. Barth was to confront us with a mirror so that we, in the mirror of the Gospel of Jesus Christ, could understand more deeply the Catholic answer. This is why we permitted ourselves to be questioned.

From this perhaps slightly defensive but certainly eirenic approach it is but a short step to pointing out, as he does in *The Council and Reunion* (pp. 138–9), that the renewal of the Church means meeting all that is justified in Protestant demands and criticisms and doing justice to the demands of the Reformers. Nor does this mean soft-pedalling legitimate criticism of the Protestant Churches and of Protestant theology. Indeed, he was later to express his astonishment that *The Council and Reunion* had had no Protestant counterpart 'in which, soberly and without any "catholicizing", a list of the justified *Catholic* concerns in the light of the gospel in relation to the Protestant Church would be provided and substantiated by a competent, authoritative Protestant theologian' (*Truthfulness*, p. 124).

Above all *Justification* represented a break with the attitude that was automatically suspicious and fearful of any doctrinal convergence with the other side – an attitude that no doubt underlay many of the delations of the book that came winging in to the Holy Office in Rome and that at a popular level welcomed practices like a Latin liturgy and a celibate clergy because they so clearly marked Catholics off from the others. Instead, Küng offers an approach that gratefully welcomes genuine doctrinal convergence and dares to hope that such convergence might come to embrace all the essential issues.

In this way Küng's concern to operate always within an ecumenical context, instead of succumbing to the temptation to withdraw into some kind of Catholic theological ghetto, antedates the experience of finding himself teaching Catholic theology at Tübingen alongside colleagues in the parallel Protestant faculty of theology such as Ernst Käsemann (among the older generation) and Jürgen Moltmann, or even his year as a research assistant at Münster, another university with Catholic and Protestant faculties of theology side by side. Nor is he open merely to his fellow-professionals across the confessional divide but within the common discipline of theology. Throughout his work – with the partial exception of *Justification*, which in places can seem very technical to the lay reader – there is an insistence on expressing what he is saying in language that can be understood by the reasonably well-educated man or woman in the street, instead of being confined to experts at home in a hermetic jargon designed to baffle the outsider.

The implication here is that theology is not just something that concerns ordinary Christians but something which they should be invited and encouraged at their own level to take part in. Again, there is a break with prevailing attitudes, those that saw theology as a technical science the fruits of which would be fed through to ordinary members of the Church via their pastors whom it was its duty to serve. From this point of view, a lay person needed to know and know about theology as much or as little as he or she needed to know about the computer technology that was responsible for servicing his or her bank account. In contrast to this, Küng has throughout been concerned to encourage the ordinary lay man or woman to think about and reflect on what he or she believes.

Küng's re-assertion of the tradition of conducting theology in a language understanded of the people is an achievement all the greater when we consider the temptations that lie in store for any theologian writing in German. That language enjoys two of the advantages of classical Greek: a complex (though much less flexible) syntax, and the ability freely to form new compounds in order to express new shades and distinctions of meaning.

The temptation for the user of German when grappling with ideas right at the limits of the human understanding – and that after all is where much of the raw material of theology is to be found – is to burrow ever deeper into a thicket of obscurity, perhaps even to discover distinctions the validity of which is called into question by the fact that they can virtually only be expressed in German. The deformation of German as a language of theological discourse is well exemplified by Karl Rahner, who can write simply and clearly when he wants to: his brother Hugo is widely quoted as having expressed the wish that someone would translate Karl's books into German. But in Karl Rahner's defence it can justly be argued that his complex and tortuous style meant that all the qualifications needed to balance any statement could be included within the one sentence – thus making it virtually impossible for anyone to detach statements of his from their context and delate them to the Holy Office in Rome.

More specifically, *Justification* enunciates a number of themes which Küng was to develop more fully later. There was his transcending of the distinction between natural and supernatural which, as we have seen, was probably what bothered him most of all about the Roman theology he was presented with as a student (pp. 137–8). There was the realization of the Church's ambiguous nature. Variations in translation hide from the English reader the fact that already in *Justification* we meet his classic distinction between the Church's nature and its unnature (p. 234):

> This, then, is the Church as she is – the holy Church of Jesus Christ, the holy bride of Jesus Christ, but simultaneously, as the Church of sinners, the sinful Church. Sin does not belong to her being but to what in her is the opposite of being [*nicht zu ihrem Wesen, sondern zu ihrem Unwesen*] – as the guilt-laden contradiction of the innocence decreed for her by her Lord. This is the great and unfortunate ecclesiological

implication of the '*simul*' – that the *ecclesia* is *simul
iusta et peccatrix*.

In the first section of *The Church* (pp. 3–39) this is
developed into the realization of the inseparability of the
Church's true nature [*Wesen*] from its 'un-nature'
[*Unwesen*] which in all its historical forms accompanies it
like a dark shadow (*The Church*, p. 28).

There was, too, an insistence on the primacy of scripture
(*Justification*, p. 106):

> The well from which Catholic doctrine and Catholic
> theology draw is the Word of God. The Word of God,
> in the *strictest* sense, is *Sacred Scripture* alone.

Scripture thus has 'an absolute precedence which no other
theological argument can whittle away' (ibid.). And
tradition has to be seen in connection with scripture (p.
108):

> Sacred Scripture can be rightly read only within the
> Church. Sacred Scripture and the Church belong
> together. This means Sacred Scripture and the
> tradition of the Church belong together.

In all this Küng is anticipating what Vatican II was to say
more than eight years later in its constitution on revelation,
when it stated that 'sacred tradition and sacred Scripture
form one sacred deposit of the word of God, which is committed to the Church' and added that 'sacred tradition,
sacred Scripture, and the teaching authority of the Church
. . . are so linked and joined together that one cannot stand
without the others' (*Dei verbum* § 10).

Finally, there was the central question of reconciling
continuity and change in the Church's teaching. How do
you reconcile the Church's claim to be an authentic witness
of the faith which was once for all delivered to the saints
with the elaborations, reformulations, fumblings, if not

actual mistakes, that have marked its history? Do you claim that the Church has been right all along and that any apparent mistakes are the result of misunderstanding what it was committing itself to and the extent to which it was doing so, or do you assume that here too grace does not displace nature and that the Church, like all other human institutions that survive, learns by its mistakes?

In *Justification* there was of course no question of tackling this question head on, but already there are hints towards the solution Küng would eventually propose to the problem of infallibility, and already he was aware of this problem in the sharpened form in which it had been put by Karl Barth (*Church Dogmatics*, IV/1, p. 626):

> A Church which maintains that its official decisions are infallible can commit errors which are irreformable. It has more than once done so.

In *Justification* Küng notes that 'the Church, whose "official decisions are infallible", never looked at these decisions as rigid and frozen formulations, but rather as living signposts for continued research into the inexhaustible riches of the revelation of Jesus Christ' (p. 96). The majority of dogmatic definitions were polemic formulations pronounced against heresies (p. 98), exposing the dark spot where divine revelation is in jeopardy to the brightest possible light with the effect that (p. 99)

> other areas move out of the bright cone of the beam – though not into total darkness – back into what, at least for the human eye, is twilight or even obscurity. These hidden truths are not lost to the Church but continue to be and to be believed as before. It is only that they no longer shine so brightly until the human eye, once it has adjusted to the new light, recaptures the full view and value of what surrounds and supports these truths.

Already these is an awareness of the distortions that can arise from the polemical nature of doctrinal definitions, even if the rather Berkeleian idea of hidden truths in the mind of the Church does not seem very satisfactory, while the image of the shifting spotlight was later to give way to the idea of every expression of error containing a kernel of truth and every expression of truth being accompanied by a shadow of error (cf. *The Living Church*, pp. 308–13, *Structures*, pp. 350–351, *Infallible?*, pp. 140–1).

From one point of view *Justification* thus marks the beginning of Hans Küng's long search for some more suitable set of criteria for judging what is and what is not essentially Christian than the reach-me-down criterion Catholics were encouraged to use before Vatican II – the latest papal (or curial) pronouncement. As Küng had come to realize as a student in Rome, papal pronouncements have too often in the Church's history reflected the partial views of harassed, well-meaning but short-sighted curial officials and theologians, instead of expressing, as they are intended to do, the consensus of the Church as a whole. Already in *Justification* the process is beginning whereby ecclesiastical and theological statements and pronouncements are tested against the touchstone of Christ himself – though of course the very attempt to do just that raises some formidable problems of interpretation. Official statements are not in this first book treated as settling the issue in the sense of blocking any further questions. Instead, they are interrogated in order to tease out their meaning and to discern the precise witness they were intended to bear to the gospel.

But for the moment the working out of these and other themes lay a long way ahead. Present reality for the twenty-nine-year-old Hans Küng was pastoral work as an assistant priest attached to the Hofkirche in Lucerne. He was now doing what he had seen as his vocation when he went to Rome nine years earlier to become a student at the Germanicum and what he had been ordained to do three years earlier in St Peter's. Even though he was not to do it for long, there was no change in his pastoral intentions, as he insisted at the press conference he gave to mark the publication of *On being a Christian* – a press conference which by chance was held at the Frankfurt Book Fair on exactly the twentieth anniversary of his ordination (*Challenge*, p. 346).

The eighteen months he spent at the Hofkirche thus provide a key to his work as a theologian by having laid the essential practical foundation for it. The basic question to which Küng as a theologian is responding is 'Is it true?' But all the time he is keenly aware that Christian truth, the truth of the gospel, is something that makes practical demands. What he is concerned about is to make this truth accessible to people and to help them work out how they can and should respond to it. His central concern, he was to say in December 1979 after the failure of his appeal to the pope to rescind the sanctions taken against him, was 'to make the message of Jesus Christ understandable to the men and women of today' (*Fall*, p. 152).

This gives much of his writing the tone of preaching, not in the derogatory sense too often attached to that word but in the positive sense of someone arousing his audience's interest and going on to give that newly awakened interest solid nourishment. It is the tone of someone who believes passionately in the gospel of Jesus Christ and who wishes to share that belief with others, explaining clearly and patiently what is at issue, answering the questions and difficulties they raise, helping them to find and keep their balance as they weigh up the often apparently conflicting claims of God and man, Church and world, past and present, tradition and contemporary reality.

The response Küng's writings have met with shows that he has the gift of speaking to the condition of the men and women of today: he has been able to listen to what they are saying, to their fears and questions and anxieties and hopes, and to help them to build some kind of constructive – and truthful – answer. Over the past two decades the audience Küng has been reaching has widened considerably from the congregation of one parish in a Swiss city of just under 70,000 inhabitants; but it was there that the foundations were laid. And, when the opportunity arose of working as an academic theologian, Küng was able to see this not as a betrayal but as a fulfilment of his primary pastoral vocation.

Here, too, there is yet another parallel with Barth, who at the end of his life found joy and satisfaction in the fact that a large number of pastors were using and reading the dozen volumes of his *Church Dogmatics* and who was happy that his readership consisted of 'a considerable number of pastors, a good collection of non-theologians – and Roman Catholics'. Barth's career had, of course, started in the pulpit. At Safenwil he saw as his principal task the writing of a Sunday sermon every week, a task which often involved a great deal of sweat and labour, even though 'his sermons demanded a great deal of intellectual effort from the congregation', according to his close friend and fellow-pastor Eduard Thurneysen.[3]

Hans Küng has stated that these eighteen months at Lucerne were 'sufficient to enable me to have a clear picture throughout my entire life of the practical problems, anxieties and needs of the pastoral clergy' (*Way*, p. 151):

> I saw how important a good theological preparation is for pastoral work in practice, for proclaiming the word, for preaching, for giving instruction. I also saw – and this, you will recall, was before the Council – how relatively easy it is to carry out reforms in worship, in the structure of the parish, in religious instruction, and in the life of parish organizations, provided one at the same time offers positive solutions alongside all the negative criticism that may be necessary, and provided one does not go over the

heads of the people involved but draws them into co-operating in the project.

He was lucky, too, in having a very good parish priest with whom he had an excellent relationship and with whom he is still very much on friendly terms. The decision to switch from the pastoral to the academic life was, however, taken at a comparatively early stage in Küng's brief career as an assistant priest. It was in the autumn of 1957 that for the first time he took part in a meeting of the association of German-speaking dogmatic and fundamental theologians. On the advice of such eminent theologians as Heinrich Fries (whom in under three years he was to succeed at Tübingen), Karl Rahner, and Hermann Volk (whose research assistant he was to become), he decided to enter for the *Habilitation* – the examination that qualifies someone with a doctorate for a university teaching post. That decision led in 1959 to his becoming research assistant at Münster in Westphalia to Hermann Volk, then a professor of theology approaching his fifty-third birthday but shortly to be appointed Bishop of Mainz in 1962 and in 1973 to become a cardinal. At the same time pastoral concerns were not forgotten. Küng became spiritual director of a student hostel, the College of St Thomas More.

As it happened, Küng never had time while at Münster to present his dissertation for his *Habilitation*. It would have been his study of Hegel's theology of the incarnation, which he had started on while still at Paris and which was to emerge one or two revisions and ten years later as *Menschwerdung Gottes*, a book that so far has defied at least three attempts to translate it into English (a reflection not on Küng but on Hegel). But without having gained his *Habilitation* Küng found himself in 1960, at the age of thirty-two, invited to Tübingen to succeed Heinrich Fries as professor of fundamental theology. This showed the impact *Justification* had made. It does not in fact seem that uncommon for a scholar without a *Habilitation* to be appointed to a chair in the German-speaking academic world when his reputation has been solidly established by a suitable piece of work. Once again, there is a parallel with Barth, who on the strength of the first edition of *Romans* was appointed to a special professorship at Göttingen when he had neither doctorate nor *Habilitation*. The British parallel would be the way a doctorate is a normal but not an essential qualification for appointment to a university teaching post: it may have become less common than it used to be, but it is still possible for someone to be appointed with simply a very good first degree.

[1] Arnold J. Toynbee, *A Study of History*, Oxford University Press, London, New York, Toronto, [2]1935, vol. i, p. 91, vol. ii, pp. 285–288.

[2] Peter Chirico, SS, *Infallibility: The Crossroads of Doctrine*, Sheed and Ward, London, 1977, p. 215. The letters after his name refer to membership not of the Nazi *Schutzstaffel* but of the Sulpician Fathers.

[3] Eberhard Busch, *Karl Barth: his life from letters and autobiographical texts*, SCM Press, London, 1976, pp. 488, 61.

5

Explaining the Council

Hans Küng brought with him to Tübingen not just the obvious qualifications for the post he was to take up: a reasonable grasp of the western theological tradition and an ability to make some personal contribution to our understanding of it and even to that tradition itself are qualities that one ought to be able to take for granted in such an appointment, and in this case certainly can. Technically he was well-equipped by a thorough grounding in the official theology that predominated in Rome, and in *Justification* he had launched himself on what was to be the first in a series of progressively bolder forays beyond the confines of that intellectual citadel. He had, too, as we have seen, an impressive command of most of the languages a theologian is likely to need these days. But beyond all this he brought with him a number of striking advantages. He was young: just over thirty, rather than approaching forty. His career had not suffered any major interruptions or frustrations but had unfolded in what could seem a natural progression, one stage succeeding another just at the right moment. And the new atmosphere of John XXIII's pontificate meant the time had come when a young theologian could publicly point to aspects of the Church's doctrine and history that his elders had had to handle with much greater circumspection.

The university at Tübingen, a small town on the upper reaches of the Neckar in south-west Germany, was founded in 1477 by Count Eberhard V of Württemberg – 'the bearded'. At the Reformation Lutheranism was imposed by Duke Ulrich – the rulers of Württemberg had already started moving up the social scale – and the university became a centre of Lutheran orthodoxy. Catholic theology returned to Tübingen in 1817, when the Catholic university founded five years earlier at Ellwangen, sixty miles to the north-east, by King Frederick I of Württemberg was incorporated into the older foundation as a Catholic faculty of theology alongside the existing Protestant one: Württemberg had emerged from the redrawing of the German political map following the Napoleonic wars no longer a Protestant duchy but enlarged to a kingdom roughly twice its previous size and with both Protestant and Catholic subjects enjoying equal rights. Tübingen thus shared with Münster, where Küng had just been working, and with two other German universities at that time the distinction of having both a Protestant and a Catholic faculty of theology side by side. (There are now seven such universities as well as two other institutions of higher education where this situation is to be found.) But, although this encouraged theology to become ecumenical through the presence of colleagues of the other confession, it was still studied on a denominational basis, unlike the situation in Britain where a non-denominational pattern is now developing in what used to be a strictly Anglican or Presbyterian preserve, as with the appointment of Nicholas Lash to the Norris-Hulse chair at Cambridge in 1978 and of James Mackey to the Thomas Chalmers chair at Edinburgh in 1979.

Among its students Tübingen had numbered the philosophers Hegel and Schelling, the poets Hölderlin (who went mad and spent the last thirty-six years of his life in a carpenter's house with a tower, now known as the Hölderlinturm, beside the Neckar), Uhland and Mörike. The Protestant faculty of theology had housed F. C. Baur and his perhaps more famous pupil D. F. Strauss, whose *Life of Jesus* was a pioneering effort at demythologization that brought its author's academic career to an abrupt end when it appeared in 1835–36. More recently it had housed G. F. Kittel, whose name means to biblical scholars and theologians the *Theological Dictionary of the New Testament* that he edited. The Catholic faculty is best known for J. A. Möhler, who with Rosmini and Newman was one of the outstanding figures in a nineteenth-century theological renaissance the full benefit of which was only felt at Vatican II and after.

The old town of Tübingen clustered round the castle that stood on top of a hillock by the Neckar; but already in the nineteenth century it was spreading on to the level ground to the north-east, and the twentieth century has seen both town and university colonizing the hills beyond. But despite the urban sprawl one hill by the Neckar, the Österberg, though built up all round, has kept a meadow where to this day sheep may safely graze: it must be rare for pastoral theology to be taught within sight of the real thing. The town's population, barely 20,000 in the 1920s, had risen to just over 73,000 by 1979; but the rise in the student population has been much greater and has had a marked effect on the whole character of the place by turning the student body into what can only be described as a dominant minority. From about 2200 in 1914 the number of students rose to 5000 in the 1950s, reached 10,000 in the mid-1960s, and by 1979 was approaching 20,000. In addition, the whole Neckar Valley from Rottenburg seven miles to the south-west downstream to Stuttgart twenty miles to the north (but nearly double that distance following the river) is threatening to become no longer a chain of separate towns and villages but a linear conurbation. Surprisingly enough, however, considering how attractive an old town it is with buildings dating back to the Middle Ages, Tübingen is off the organized tourist track. Apparently the old university town on the package tour itinerary is Heidelberg, seventy miles to the north where the Neckar is on the point of flowing into the Rhine.

For Hans Küng Tübingen had and has an additional advantage: relatively speaking, it is near home. Sursee is only just over a hundred miles away to the south-east; and though the roads may be narrow and winding – the motorway from Stuttgart to Schaffhausen and Constance is still being built – there is not that much traffic.

When at Easter 1960 Hans Küng arrived in Tübingen he brought with him the first copies of the book that was to do for him in the world at large what *Justification* had already done in academic circles: establish his reputation as the rising star of Catholic theology, as someone who could start from impeccably orthodox premises to reach refreshingly radical conclusions. The book was *The Council and Reunion*, which he had written in 1959 at Münster and, during the vacation, at Sursee. He had gone ahead with publishing it despite strong objections from Cardinal Julius Döpfner, then Bishop of Berlin, and his professor at Münster, Dr Hermann Volk. But support came from Vienna, whose archbishop, Cardinal Franz König, supplied a brief introductory message describing it as 'a happy omen' to find a theologian responding to the stimulus provided by Pope John XXIII when he announced the holding of an ecumenical council; while the French translation, which like that into English appeared the following year in 1961, had a message from Cardinal Achille Liénart, Bishop of Lille, underlining the work's ecumenical contribution.

For Catholics and non-Catholics alike Pope John's action in summoning the Council was a radical new departure; and Hans Küng's book spelled out what they could legitimately hope for from this bold initiative. Quite how much of a shock Pope John's announcement was is something it can be difficult for us to grasp now that the Council is safely part of history. But at the time – 25 January 1959, barely three months after John XXIII's election – it was not the kind of idea that would spontaneously occur to

people as the right way to follow the long and apparently
successful pontificate of Pius XII. The First Vatican
Council – then still simply the Vatican Council – had
surely settled where power and authority lay in the Church.
Indeed, papal infallibility itself had been defined not so
much by the Council as by the Pope with its advice and
consent: 'with the agreement of the Council we teach and
define' is the language of its decree (DS 3073). Hans Küng
was to note in his next book but one that 'the view generally
held by Catholic theologians today is that the Catholic
Church could do without ecumenical councils altogether'
(*Structures*, p. 7). It was not therefore surprising that
according to one report the papal secretary of state,
Cardinal Domenico Tardini, thought John XXIII had gone
'temporarily mad' when he first broached the idea.[1]

Many Catholics were equally bewildered by the prospect
of the Council and could not grasp the possibilities it
opened up. Others saw it as an opportunity to do for
Catholic teaching what Browning's grammarian did for the
doctrine of the enclitic $\delta\epsilon$ – give it 'dead from the waist
down' – and they exercised a dominant influence on much
of the preparatory work. Others again were able to look
forward to the ending of the siege mentality that for so long
had determined papal and curial policy.

For Christians not in communion with Rome there was a
happy coincidence between John XXIII's aims and the new
meaning the technical term 'ecumenical' had taken on in
the non-Catholic world. The Council was announced as an
ecumenical council, meaning simply a general council
representing the Church throughout the inhabited world.
But outside the Roman communion the adjective
ecumenical had, since the World Missionary Conference
held at Edinburgh in 1910 and the coming together of the
Life and Work and Faith and Order movements to establish
the World Council of Churches in 1948, come to be applied
to the striving towards Christian unity that had increas-

ingly marked Christian life in the twentieth century. Consequently, when John XXIII announced the calling of an 'ecumenical council' the announcement at once to non-Catholic ears carried overtones of a new and welcome Roman openness to Christian unity even before the Pope explained that this was the compelling motive behind his decision.

But it was not to be a reunion council on the lines of those at Lyons (1274) and Florence (1438–45) which were more on the lines of negotiations for reunion between the Latin and Greek Churches. It was to be a council only of the Church or Churches in communion with Rome, but with the intention of that Church putting its own house in order as an indispensable preliminary step before there could be any serious talk about reunion.

It was this programme that *The Council and Reunion* expounded. What was new and refreshing about the book was that it demonstrated what had been all too rare among Catholics: a passionate concern that all should be one and the clear perception of Christian disunity as the scandal it is, in place of the smug complacency that all too often flowed from the knowledge that one belonged to the one true Church. Küng was indeed merciless towards such complacency on both sides of the Reformation divide (*Reunion*, p. 57):

> Schism is a scandal. But it is perhaps an even greater scandal that a majority of Christians in all communions, even today, and including theologians and pastors, are profoundly indifferent to this scandal; that they feel the division of Christendom at most as a deplorable imperfection, not as an immeasurably crippling, gaping wound which absolutely must be healed; that they are deeply concerned over a thousand religious trivialities, but not over our Lord's desire just before his death 'that they may all be one'. Will the words and actions of the Pope be enough to awaken these sleepers?

Against this background Küng first of all establishes that reform is not only possible but essential; goes on to sketch the process whereby the Catholic Church came to be in particular need of reform (apart from the constant need of reform that enables Catholics to appropriate the Protestant slogan of *ecclesia semper reformanda,* the Church always needing to be reformed); and concludes by setting out the kind of issues the forthcoming Council would have to tackle if it were not to turn out yet another abortive effort at renewal.

The first part can be seen as a further development and application of ideas already worked out in *Justification,* particularly with regard to the realization that the Church is *simul iusta et peccatrix,* the awareness that the ambiguity of being at one and the same time holy and sinful is something that applies not just to the individual Christian but to the Church as a whole (cf. pp. 71–72 above). In this part Küng establishes the permanent necessity of renewal, pointing out among other things that 'the idea of the holy Church, distinct from her often unholy members, mentally hypostatized into a sort of pure substance, is a dangerous abstraction' (*Reunion,* p. 45).

He then explores the possibilities and limits of Catholic renewal in a section which begins with a surely deliberate echo of the title of Yves Congar's pioneering study by remarking: 'There is true reform and false reform' (*Reunion,* p. 53). While Catholic reform is limited to the sphere of what is relative and cannot take place in what is absolute, the two are so intertwined that we cannot *a priori* deem certain areas of the Church's life to be sacrosanct and immune to reform (*Reunion,* pp. 77–78);

> From this it is clear that we cannot simply speak of 'irreformable areas' of the Church, as though there were two storeys of a building, one on top of the other, of which one was reformable and the other irreformable; as though it were possible adequately to

separate off the irreformable essence of the Church's institutions, as established by God, from the concrete working-out of them and the living structure given to them by men in the history of the Church. It is rather that the essence is embedded in the human working-out in history somewhat as the plan, and the permanent principles of architecture and engineering, enter into the actual concrete building. Every part of the building, even the innermost room in it, or the most important or the most valuable, is, basically, liable to need renewing and can therefore be reformed and renewed. Only, the plan as expressed in any particular part of the building, and the laws of construction, as they apply to it, must not be set aside; no part of the building must become simply something else, or collapse altogether. Every institution, even the very holiest (the celebration of the Eucharist, or the preaching of the Gospel), every aspect of organization (even the primacy of Rome, or the episcopal government of the Church) can, through the historical process of formation and deformation, come to need renewal, and must then be reformed and renewed; only, the basic irreformable pattern given by God through Christ must not be set aside.

It is worth noting that Küng's metaphor of the two storeys of a building is clearly linked with the theory of the relation between natural and supernatural that he reacted against while still a student in Rome: Küng's German expression for what I have translated as the two-tier theory is *die Stockwerktheorie*, literally the 'storey theory', in other words seeing grace and nature as separate floors of a building.

The second part of *The Council and Reunion* demonstrates the strength and validity of the historical approach Küng had already used in *Justification*. Understanding how the Church got into the state it is now in can help us both to understand (and love) the Church as it is at the moment and to discern what is demanded of it (and thus of ourselves) by the gospel. Much of what Küng has to say about the flexibility and adaptation that marked the Church in the first centuries of its existence, in contrast to the rigidity and unresponsiveness that set in particularly from Trent onwards, is the kind of thing that nowadays most Catholics take for granted, thanks to the Council and the radical shift that brought about in the way Catholics see and understand the Church. But at the time this was new and revolutionary knowledge that helped to make this shift of perception possible. It was a time when Latin was still being staunchly defended as 'the language of the Church' by Catholics seemingly unaware of the pluralism of rites that, in however truncated a form, existed among Christians in communion with Rome, so that from the point of view of a Catholic living in Kerala or Galilee it would be equally true to speak of Malayalam or Arabic as 'the language of the Church'. It was a time when Catholics were appallingly ignorant of the apparently forgotten tradition followed by the early Church of almost automatic adaptation to the language and culture of the people to whom it was bringing the gospel. All this Küng brought out in his book, though oddly enough he does not point out that the crucial change in policy which led the Western Church to cling to and later to impose Latin as its liturgical language seems to have occurred with the evangelization of Ireland. For whatever reason – the role of Latin in British society at a time when Britain was the last surviving outpost or remnant of the Roman Empire in the West, so that it was natural for British missionaries to use and import a liturgy not in their own vernacular, or perhaps even Patrick's own exaggerated respect for the language through having missed his formal Latin education by being captured by pirates and becoming a slave in Ireland – the Irish were given a liturgy not in their own language but in Latin;[2] and subsequently in Western Europe (and beyond) this became the normal pattern, helped initially by nostalgia for the vanished stability and unity of the Roman Empire.

A key point in Küng's account of the often chequered history of renewal in the Church is the tension during the sixteenth century between the forces of renewal and the forces of restoration, between Catholic reform as a positive response and Catholic reform as a negative reaction to the Protestant revolt. With the idea of restoration rather than renewal gaining the upper hand there was a 'dangerous hardening' of Catholic attitudes from the time of Paul IV onwards (*Reunion*, pp. 113–5). All this led to what can be seen as a deformation rather than a reformation of Catholicism (*Reunion*, p. 116):

> Thus the position was reached in which the Church was confronting Protestantism in an irreconcilable opposition, and the unlovely accompaniments of this type of restoration-reform are all too familiar to us: negative polemics, narrowmindedness, violent elimination of abuses and defence of the purity of doctrine by inquisitorial methods; political denominational manoeuvrings in the secular sphere; and, worst of all, 'religious' wars. The fact that we can match each of these items from the record of anti-Catholic Protestantism is no consolation to us.

Küng, however, is determined not to give Church history yet another polemical slant. He pays handsome tribute to the benefits of the restoration carried out by Paul IV, the former Cardinal Caraffa, and his reforming successors (*Reunion*, p. 120):

> It hardly needs stressing here that, for all their limitations, these acts of restoration were productive of immeasurable good. It is thanks to them that the Church of the Baroque period displays a purity and strength very different from the Church of the Renaissance.

Similarly the strengthening of papal authority between the sixteenth and nineteenth centuries is seen as 'stringently necessary' on account of the stormy times the Church was passing through, with one wave of attack succeeding another from Lutheranism and Calvinism at the beginning of the period to atheistic materialism, liberalism and socialism at its end. Yet despite the Church's great and undoubted achievements even in 'the much despised nineteenth century' (*Reunion*, pp. 121, 122–3)

> most of what happened in the Church during this period bore heavy traces of being primarily a defensive, rearguard action against the overpowering assaults of the spirit of the age. It was realized all too little in the nineteenth-century Church that even revolutions become normal in time, that they have their positive, permanent kernel, and that the Church stands not only to lose but also, as the future was to show, to gain from them.
>
> It seemed from outside as though the Catholic Church were against not only what was false and pernicious in modern movements but also against the *goodness* and *truth* that they contained: as though she were against even what was *true* in modern philosophy, literature and science; against even what was *good* in democracy . . . and in the national movements . . .; against even the *valid* aspirations in liberalism . . . and in socialism . . ., and so forth. Ultimately, this was not the case, as the sequel was to show. But it is impossible to deny that there was much that seemed to indicate it.

From one point of view Küng's latest book, *Does God Exist?*, in which he grapples with the whole intellectual development of the Western world from Descartes onwards, can be seen as an attempt to heal precisely this breach that grew up between the static outlook that the Church seemed concerned to preserve and defend and the ferment of ideas going on in the world outside, and to heal this breach precisely by taking these movements of though seriously and trying to do justice to their aspirations.

Indicative, however, of the time when *The Council and
Reunion* was written is the way in which at the end of this
section Küng jumps abruptly from Leo XIII to John XXIII
(*Reunion*, pp. 132–3). There is no attempt to tackle the
modernist crisis and its aftermath, the period of panic
reaction by the Church authorities to what they saw as the
corrosive threat presented by the application of modern
scholarship to the biblical data. In 1960 any fair and
impartial treatment by a Catholic scholar of the modernist
crisis was almost certainly impossible without reactivating
the entire apparatus of suppression which that crisis had
brought to its final pitch of development. Modernism was
held out as the great danger one was liable to fall into in
trying to come to terms with the contemporary world,
while the very fact that it was so ill-defined and amorphous
a heresy made it loom all the greater as a threat. Moreover,
very many of those in positions of power in the Church
were emotionally committed to their precedecessors who
had initiated and policed the drastic measures thought
necessary to extirpate modernism from the Church. Few
indeed were those like Archbishop Michele Pellegrino of
Turin who were willing to face up to the injustices committed in the name of orthodoxy; and as we have seen his
intervention came only in 1965. Even today modernism
remains a touchy subject for Catholic scholars to handle,
while 'modernist' remains a handy label for denigrating
those whose speculations are considered too daring a
departure from the received wisdom of the past century.

Apart from this one understandable lacuna, Küng is concerned to present a balanced picture of the Church as it is,
or rather as it then was at the time just before the Council.
He notes the deformations that had overtaken it in the
course of its long and complex history. He notes, too, the
continuous and remarkable success with which despite all
these deformations it lived up to the mission with which it
had been entrusted. In all this he can be seen as fulfilling

the description he was to give later as the aim of 'a sober, realistic and scholarly theology' (*Church*, p. 29) – 'to see the Church as it really is: its "nature" together with its historical "form" and at the same time its "nature" together with its "un-nature" '.

The forthcoming Council's response to the demands thus presented by the tension between the gospel and the Church's historical development would, Küng suggests, centre on restoring the episcopate to its full value, together with a decentralization of many administrative decisions that over the centuries had become centralized in Rome. He then goes on to indicate some of the detailed reforms that could follow: the liturgy, above all; the obligation of celibacy; the Church's law on marriage; and censorship and the Index. Some of these reforms Vatican II was indeed to carry out, and others followed in its wake; but others remain an unfulfilled hope and seem hardly likely to be realized in the foreseeable future given the present temper of papal policy. Moreover, the central question of the proper balance between the bishops and the pope, between periphery and centre, has still not been adequately settled more than fourteen years after the Council. Indeed, there remains an uncomfortable grain (and more than a grain) of truth in the observation Küng made on this point (*Reunion*, p. 238):

It is pointed out, rightly, in the Curia that the episcopal office would be at once restored, to quite a significant degree, if all the bishops would have sufficient sense of responsibility to exercise *the rights they already have*, fully and entirely, instead of appealing to the Curia for answers and action in cases where they could, as bishops, give the answers and take the action themselves. This is indeed a general problem, and a basic one, in the ecclesiastical decentralization for which Catholics often clamour; what is needed is the courage to take responsibility at every level, in bishops, priests and layfolk.

Crises like those aroused by *Humanae vitae* in 1968 or by the Dutch pastoral council's proposals for an end to compulsory celibacy in 1970 show almost a conditioned reflex among bishops in their haste to assent to Rome's view of the situation. The Pauline example of withstanding Peter to his face is one that is all too rarely followed. Nor is this something for which the bishops alone can be blamed, though some part may be played by the fact that, Switzerland excepted, the appointment of bishops remains firmly under Roman control. It is rather that Catholicism tends if anything to reinforce the common human tendency to look to others to save one from the agony of acting and deciding oneself. Catholics thus tend to look to the pope to initiate policy, to provide an almost exclusive leadership that is then mediated downwards to the ordinary Catholic in the pew, rather than seeing the pope much more in the role of an umpire or referee, someone whose task it is not to produce the ideas and stimuli that the Church is continually in need of but rather to ensure that the ferment they engender when produced by others does not tear the Church apart, to ensure that the tension is creative rather than destructive.[3]

In calling for the episcopate to be restored to its full value, Küng was one of a number of theologians making the same point and thus preparing the way for Vatican II's emphasis on collegiality. But this was not so much a new departure as the rediscovery of an old and forgotten tradition. Nor was the tradition that had been forgotten necessarily that old. Küng made considerable use of the declaration the German bishops drew up in 1875 on the status of bishops in the Church in response to the manifold misinterpretations which were current following Vatican I's definition of the papal primacy and in particular of his full and supreme power of jurisdiction over the universal

Church, which was decreed to be ordinary and immediate over each and every Church and over each and every pastor and member of the faithful (DS 3064). These misinterpretations were taken up by Bismarck in a circular published in 1874: the German Chancellor's conclusions and the German bishops' reactions to them were similar to the conclusion drawn by Gladstone to be answered by Newman in his *Letter to the Duke of Norfolk*, also published in 1875.

In their declaration the German bishops simply amplified and expounded what Vatican I had already stated, that far from obstructing the individual bishop's power of jurisdiction the pope's universal immediate jurisdiction existed to strengthen and defend it. Among the misinterpretations they had to rebut was that the bishops had been reduced to the status of the pope's tools, mere officials without responsibility of their own. The German bishops' explanation of what Vatican I had really meant won the explicit approval of Pius IX himself and could thus be regarded as the official interpretation of that Council. Yet over the next eighty to ninety years it was if anything the misinterpretations they were at pains to counter that held the field, both inside and outside the Church. It was symptomatic that it was only after 1962 that their declaration was included in Denzinger (DS 3112–3117). Küng had meanwhile helped to bring the document to public notice by printing it in full as an appendix to his book. Rahner had already referred to it and quoted from it in studies appearing at about the same time.[4]

Besides dealing with practical questions of Church reform that would continue to remain matters of controversy even after the Council and would crop up again in Küng's writings, *The Council and Reunion* also touched on a central issue around which so much of his subsequent theology was to revolve: how to discern a criterion for disentangling what is permanent and essential from what is conditional and changing in what the Church is saying.

What is the ultimate criterion by which we must test any statement that claims to express what we believe before we can accept it as faithfully expressing what we as Christians are committed to believing? What is the ultimate criterion by which our behaviour as the Church must be measured? The form in which Küng poses the question, and the answer he gives, are as follows (*Reunion*, pp. 78–79):

> But according to what *norm* shall action for the renewal of the Church be measured? There is only one norm whose authority is adequate. There is no ordinary human norm which can measure every institution in the Church, Pope, bishops, priests and laity, the whole Church of yesterday, today and tomorrow. The norm to which we can keep looking, in all our action, is Jesus Christ, the Lord of the Church, who speaks to the Church of every century in his Gospel, making his demands upon her.

For those many Catholics who were worried that the Church seemed to be coming between them and Jesus Christ, between them and the gospel, this was (and is) a refreshing and encouraging stand. But it is an answer that immediately raises some formidable problems of interpretation, and Küng at once goes on to suggest the lines along which these should be tackled (*Reunion*, p. 79):

> The tradition of the Church will help us to understand the Gospel of Jesus Christ aright; and it is the apostolic Church, which was especially near her Lord, which gave us the canon of Scripture, the Scriptures themselves and Church government in its first form, which, through an understanding of Christ's Gospel, will provide us in a special sense with a model (though not one to be mechanically copied) for renewal of the Church.

Lurking here are the questions that will preoccupy Küng in *Structures of the Church*, *The Church*, and *Infallible?* as he sets out to pin down more closely what should be the ultimate guiding principle of the Church's behaviour and belief.

The Council and Reunion could be classified among Küng's 'popular' rather than 'academic' works, in much the same way that Graham Greene used to describe some of his books as novels and others as entertainments. Such a classification does not of course imply any lowering of standards. All it means in Küng's case is that the argument is not continually buttressed with footnotes and detailed examination of subsidiary issues.

It was, too, the first of his books to be published in English, and was thus the book that established his reputation in the English-speaking world, even if at the same time permitting the occasional patronizing reference to him as a paperback theologian. Catholics in the English-speaking world were perhaps more bewildered than most as to what the forthcoming Council was about, and Küng provided a much-needed concise account of the prospects and possibilities it opened up. Beyond that his book awakened the reading public to what the academic world already knew: that here was someone worth taking notice of, someone who was not prepared to let the apparatus and pretension of scholarship get in the way of communication, someone who was saying out loud what many Catholics had begun dimly and uncomfortably to become aware of but were not yet capable of articulating – and who was saying it in a way that did justice both to common sense and to the strength and wisdom of the Church's tradition. The book sold well, even if best-seller status was something that strictly speaking Küng was to attain only fourteen years later with the publication of *On being a Christian*. The English edition had to be reprinted four times in its first year of publication.

The book's success showed that Küng had found his

public, the audience he would address later in *Truthfulness*, in *Why Priests?*, in *On being a Christian*, in *Does God Exist?* It was what may be termed a 'lay' audience, though it included many priests and not a few bishops, and a non-academic one, though much of Küng's appeal to it lies in the way he consistently refuses to talk down to or to patronize those outside the narrow charmed circle of academic theology. The existence of this audience reflected the emergence of the laity from the subservient position in which too often they had been held, regarded almost as some kind of optional extra on the fringe of the Church. Newman may have remarked that the Church would look rather foolish without the laity,[5] but one suspects that Monsignor George Talbot, Pius IX's adviser on English affairs, was exceptional merely in the blunt and unqualified way he put things:

> What is the province of the laity? To hunt, to shoot, to entertain. These matters they understand, but to meddle with ecclesiastical matters they have no right at all . . .[6]

– and no doubt to Monsignor Talbot's mind laity lower down the social scale than the gentry had even fewer rights. Vatican II was to vindicate what Newman wrote at the conclusion of his essay *On Consulting the Faithful in Matters of Doctrine*:

> I think certainly that the *Ecclesia docens* is more happy when she has such enthusiastic partisans about her as are here represented, than when she cuts off the faithful from the study of her divine doctrines and the sympathy of her divine contemplations, and requires from them a *fides implicita* in her word, which in the educated classes will terminate in indifference, and in the poorer in superstition.[7]

In Britain at least, an important factor in the formation of the kind of well-informed laity Newman was looking forward to was the expansion of secondary and university education after the Second World War. From what had been predominantly a working-class community whose only educated members tended to be clergy there emerged a generation of educated lay Catholics. There thus existed in larger numbers than before a new class of intelligent, well-educated and concerned Christians who wanted to be able to live their lives as Christians by the same standards of honesty and responsibility and intellectual integrity as they applied to their secular lives. They were no longer prepared to live a schizophrenic Christianity with one set of standards for application to normal day-to-day secular life and another more indulgent set applied to Church affairs. Nor were they prepared to keep their faith at a childish level, as if what they believed was something that did not bear thinking about. They were looking for theologians who would take their aspirations seriously; and in Hans Küng they found one.

With his next book Hans Küng addressed this audience at its crucial formative stage: the young people who made up the Church of the future. Brought up as Catholics, often with Protestant friends, neighbours and school-fellows, they were experiencing enormous difficulty in reconciling what the Church was saying to them with what they were encountering at school and later at college or university, as well as at work and in the world at large. To young people such as these Küng addressed a series of articles in the separate boys' and girls' monthly magazines of the German Catholic youth movement – beginning, interestingly enough, with the whole business of talking things over honestly with Protestants and going on in the next to deal with whether Catholics were expected to defend everything the Church had done, crimes and blunders included. These articles, in the form of letters trying to help a young person sort out the difficulties he or she was encountering, began appearing at the start of 1961, and the following year they were collected together for publication in book form under the title *That the World May Believe*. They add up to a short but powerful work of apologetics for young people, informed by a sense of ecumenical urgency and an underlying need to expound Christianity as the only possible ultimately satisfactory explanation of the world as it is as well as the only possible ground for hope and trust. They are marked, too, by an awareness that Christianity can only appear at all credible to a disillusioned generation if it is rigorous in maintaining standards of intellectual honesty and truthfulness.

The book thus looks forward not only to Küng's subsequent essay on this theme of truthfulness but also to the major works of the 1970s – *On being a Christian* and *Does God Exist?* The two aspects are linked, because what had made apologetics such a dirty word was the way it had been allowed to degenerate into a systematic presentation of plausible but ultimately unconvincing excuses for the Church's past mistakes and misdeeds. With that tradition Küng's approach represented a welcome break.

[1] E. E. Y. Hales, *Pope John and his Revolution*, Eyre and Spottiswoode, London, 1966, p. 100.
[2] For Church life in fifth-century Britain and the beginnings of the Irish Church see John Morris, *The Age of Arthur: A History of the British Isles from 350 to 650*, Weidenfeld and Nicolson, London, [3]1975, pp. 335–355.
[3] Cf. the view put forward by Robert Markus and Eric John, *Papacy and Hierarchy*, Sheed and Ward, London and Sydney, 1969.
[4] Karl Rahner and Joseph Ratzinger, *The Episcopate and the Primacy* (*Quaestiones Disputatae* 4), Herder, Freiburg-im-Breisgau, Nelson, Edinburgh and London, 1962, pp. 29–30 and p. 66: the first quotation comes in a paper originally published in 1959.

[5] J. Derek Holmes, *More Roman than Rome: English Catholicism in the Nineteenth Century*, Burns and Oates, London, Patmos Press, Shepherdstown, Pa, 1978, p. 115.

[6] Quoted by John Coulson in his introduction to John Henry Newman, *On Consulting the Faithful in Matters of Doctrine*, Geoffrey Chapman, London, 1961, p. 41.

[7] *On Consulting the Faithful*, ed. cit. p. 106.

6

The Awkward Facts of History

If Hans Küng's reputation as a theologian was established by *Justification*, it was confirmed in 1962 by *Structures of the Church*. Despite some misgivings, Karl Rahner included the book in the series *Quaestiones Disputatae* that he was editing, a series of monographs which, like the French series *Unam Sanctam*, was busy exploring what were emerging as the major issues to be tackled by the forthcoming Council. The subject of the book was the same as that of Küng's inaugural lecture at Tübingen: the theology of general councils. It was a subject that had aroused little interest until the summoning of a general council made it not only topical but urgent in a new and unexpected way. Much of the surprise John XXIII created was because his announcement cut across the common assumption that general councils were a thing of the past, that Vatican I had settled where the power and authority lay in the Church. Merely by summoning a general council the pope had called this accepted ecclesiology into question.

Küng's book helped to shake a few more commonly held assumptions about the Church's structure and nature. Its great merit was that Küng allowed history to put questions to theology instead of manipulating the often embarrassingly awkward facts of the Church's history to fit in with a particular theological interpretation. *Justification* can be regarded as having side-stepped the non-historical orthodoxy[1] that held sway in Rome. *Structures of the Church* represented a direct attack, and on its most vulnerable point – its neglect or manipulation of history.

Küng's starting point is indeed the sharp contrast between the view of ecumenical councils presented by the code of canon law and that which emerges from the Church's history. Canon law prescribes that an ecumenical council must be convoked by the pope, who presides over it, whether in person or through delegates, fixes its agenda, brings it to a close and confirms its decrees (CIC § 222). But, of course, this is precisely what did not happen at the first ecumenical councils (*Structures*, p. 4). This discrepancy between theory and practice is even more blatant in the case of the Council of Constance, consideration of which occupies nearly half the book.

For the moment Küng goes on to consider ecumenical councils not as an exercise of the Church's machinery of authority, which is how the code of canon law would seem to regard them, but as intended to be an authentic and credible representation of the Church. The latter he sees as 'truly the ecumenical council convoked by God himself' (*Structures*, p. 14) and an ecumenical council as 'the representation, presentation and actualization of the Church' (*Structures*, p. 15). At an ecumenical council the Church must therefore be credibly represented with regard to its classic four marks – unity, catholicity, holiness, and apostolicity.

On this basis Küng now develops a number of major themes. There is first of all a long debate with Lutheranism on the role and function of bishops in the Church. This establishes a degree of common ground which may be thought surprising in view of the virtual disappearance of bishops from Lutheranism and their supersession by state bureacracy; but a surprising degree of doctrinal convergence is perhaps just what is to be expected from the author of *Justification*.

There is an excursus on the problem of early Catholicism in the New Testament, the way in which signs of what to Protestant eyes appears as Catholic decadence are to be found in some at least of the New Testament writings and the barrier this presents to setting the New Testament up as a criterion against which the Church's later excesses can be judged. The discovery of 'Catholic' traits in the New Testament led to the search for a canon within the canon, for some standard whereby the more primitive and authentic witness could be distinguished from later developments. Küng tackled this subject in an article in the Tübingen *Theologische Quartalschrift* (142 [1962], pp. 385–424, available in English translation in *The Living Church*, pp. 233–293). The question is the extent to which we can pick and choose among the diversity of theological positions to be found in the New Testament. As against his Protestant colleague at Tübingen Ernst Käsemann, who selected Paul as purveying the true gospel against which the other New Testament writings could be scrutinized and if necessary disregarded as unevangelical, Küng insists on acceptance of the whole New Testament in its entirety and diversity. Later, as we shall see in discussing *The Church* (pp. 166–168 below), he seems to move closer to Käsemann's position and somewhat away from his original acceptance of the theological pluralism built into the New Testament witness.

There is a discussion of the extent to which in emergency situations ministries can be exercised by those not formally ordained or commissioned to them. There is, finally, a thorough analysis of the balance in the Church between pope and bishops and of the paradoxical fact that the legitimacy of the papacy from the beginning of the fifteenth century onwards depends on the Council of Constance, which decreed the supremacy of a council over the pope – whatever the code of canon law may now say about there being no appeal from the pope to a council (CIC § 228).

The link between the last two themes is the distinction that can be drawn between what happens normally and what needs to happen in an emergency. The first theme –

the possibility of doing without actual ordination in an emergency – is further developed in *The Church*, and is one of the three points to which the Doctrinal Congregation, the former Holy Office, took exception in its declaration of 15 February 1975 that brought to an apparent close its long-drawn-out tussle with Küng over *The Church* and *Infallible?* In the present book Küng concentrates on the views of the Lutheran theologian Edmund Schlink, who is arguing towards accepting ordination in the continuing succession of the laying on of hands by a bishop as a sign of the apostolic succession and of the unity and catholicity of the Church, but who at the same time is arguing that this normal means of transmission of office in the Church cannot be the only means, since situations arise when it is quite out of the question. For the moment Küng treats this as a question legitimately asked of Catholics rather than one they can begin to answer (*Structures*, p. 184):

> Will the door some day be opened to the possibilities of reaching an extraordinary route to ecclesiastical office? That cannot be predicted at the present time. What is certain, however, is that the definitions of the Trent decrees are completely valid for the normal case; normally admission to office occurs as it was laid down at Trent; namely, through the ordination of the officeholder. Schlink too considers this to be the ordinary procedure. In regard to eventual extraordinary ways, on the Catholic side, no more can be said at present than this: the question must be examined afresh in the light of the present state of the problem. The reception and the dispensation of Sacraments *in voto* has been theologically thoroughly investigated only with respect to Baptism.

Just as awareness of the vast masses of people who could never have heard of Christ and his gospel had led theologians from the end of the Middle Ages onwards to grasp what was involved in the doctrine of baptism *in voto*, so too,

Küng argues, the ecumenical encounter, with closer
relationships being developed with Churches which had
allowed episcopacy to lapse (as with the Lutherans) or for
which bishop tended to be a dirty word (as with many of the
Free Churches), could bring into focus the possibility of
ecclesiastical office being reached by other than the normal
means of ordination. Where others had seen Trent as
having closed the question, Küng sees that it can hardly be
taken as having answered questions that at the time had
barely begun to emerge.

While we shall take another look at this issue of
emergency substitutes for ordination when we come to deal
with *The Church*, where Küng tackles it more fully, it is
worth noting that neither in *Structures* nor in *The Church*
does he mention what seems to be the one indisputable case
of this kind of substitute-ordination having taken place.
This was during the early years of the Church in Korea, a
country which at the end of the eighteenth century was
totally cut off from the outside world apart from an annual
embassy to the Chinese capital Peking where a Catholic
presence still persisted despite the negative effects of
Rome's refusal to countenance the efforts of Matteo Ricci
and his colleagues and successors to adapt the Church's
customs to Chinese culture. Through this embassy the first
Korean was converted to Christianity in 1784, and from
Peking he brought Christian literature home with him and
converted others. Because Korea was cut off from the outside world it was impossible for this newly formed
Christian community to be supplied with priests in what
was then regarded as the normal way – by missionaries
coming in from outside. With their numbers growing –
one account puts them at four thousand within five years –
the Korean neophytes read their New Testament and did
the only thing possible to enable them to live as a Church:
they elected their own bishops and priests. In the words of
a pre-war standard history of the missions:[2]

At first they proceeded, in an excessively democratic fashion, to elect a bishop and priests to celebrate and administer the sacraments; but in 1790 they entered into communication with the Franciscan Bishop [Alexander de] Gouvea of Peking, and asked him for missionaries.

It was not until 1794 that a Chinese priest was able to enter the country, and as far as clerical manpower was concerned the infant Korean Church survived on a hand-to-mouth basis until the establishment of a regular mission vicariate by Rome in the 1830s. To claim that these first 'illegimate' ordinations carried out by the Korean Church were somehow invalid would demand a theory of apostolic succession that would reduce the sacrament of holy orders to a magic power handed on by physical contact from bishop to bishop and from bishop to priest.

The last of the four themes I have listed – the papacy – can be regarded as the major subject of the book, occupying as it does very nearly the final half of the work (*Structures*, pp. 201–351). Like many other theologians at this time, Küng reminds his readers of the limitations that in fact hedged round Vatican I's definition of the papal primacy, limitations that had too easily been forgotten in the aftermath of 1870. But, while a theologian like Karl Rahner was content to point out that there were no jurisdictional but only moral constraints on the abuse of papal power and that the ultimate safeguard was the protection of the Holy Ghost,[3] Küng goes on to tackle the awkward question of how conflicts between pope and Church should be dealt with and how the Church could get rid of a pope when in such a case of conflict he was in the wrong.

For this Küng went to the manuals of canon law 'which', he notes (*Structures*, p. 230), 'even after the [First] Vatican Council, treat of cessation of the power of the Roman pontiff in a more or less thorough fashion'. He lists the five cases when, according to the canon lawyers, following a

tradition going back to Bellarmine and Suarez, the pope
loses his office and ceases to be pope: death; resignation;
mental illness; heresy; and schism (*Structures*, pp.
230–236). But except in the case of death we are still left
with the practical problem of recognizing that such a state
of affairs has come about (*Structures*, p. 236):

> In a conflict between the whole Church and a
> heretical, schismatic or mentally ill pope the Church
> not only has the possibility but also the duty to take
> action against the pope . . .
>   According to what has been said, in such a conflict
> the pope would be morally obliged to resign of his
> own free will, as has happened in Church history. And
> the Church would be morally obliged to induce such a
> pope to resign of his own free will, as has also come to
> pass. If such a pope were to oppose a voluntary resig-
> nation then the Church must look for redress else-
> where. But there is the difficult question: Who
> judges?

The answer given by Suarez is a general council. But what
if a heretical, schismatic, or mentally ill pope refuses to call
a council? In an emergency it could, again according to
Suarez, be summoned by the college of cardinals or by the
consensus of the episcopate. But – and this is the twist
which enables the canon lawyers to maintain the ultimate
supremacy of pope over council – such a council in such a
situation would not bring it about that the pope ceased to
be pope. It would instead be declaring that certain conditions had been fulfilled – mental illness, heresy, or schism
– which had the effect that the pope was no longer pope.
Its sentence, though authentic, would be merely declara-
tive, not a verdict which brings about what it states but
merely one which declares publicly and authoritatively
what is the case – just as a death certificate is not the cause
of death but merely establishes that death has occurred
(*Structures*, pp. 236–240).
   The relevance of all this to the Church here and now lies

in the Council of Constance, which met in 1414 when there were not two competing popes but three. Its solution was to persuade one to resign and to depose the other two in order to clear the way for the eventual election of Odo Colonna as Martin V. In doing so it asserted not a general superiority of council over pope, a radical conciliarism which would have made the council the Church's parliament and the pope its executive, but a certain 'control function' both in the actual emergency it was dealing with and in any similar emergency in the future (*Structures*, pp. 254–255). At the same time Constance decreed that the holding of councils at frequent intervals was the best way of ensuring that the Church was run properly. It laid down that the next council should take place in five years' time, the one after that in seven, and that thereafter councils should be held at intervals of ten years at the most. Within half a century this decree had become a dead letter. Martin V convoked a council at Pavia in 1423, five years after Constance concluded: this moved to Siena because of an outbreak of disease and was brought to an end the following year. The Council of Basle met in 1431 after the statutory interval of seven years and had rather a chequered career: an anti-papalist rump lingered on in Basle itself and was eventually excommunicated, while the officially recognized council moved first to Ferrara and then to Florence, where it engineered the short-lived reunion with the Greeks, before finally concluding in Rome in 1445 or later. But there was a gap of over half a century before the Fifth Lateran Council met in 1512, and that council notoriously failed to provide any remedy for the grievances that were about to erupt in the movement of protest which Luther sparked off in the very year it ended, 1517. Nearly thirty years were to pass before Trent met in 1545 in response to that crisis, while between the conclusion of Trent in 1563 and the assembling of Vatican I there was a gap of three centuries.

For the dedicated advocate of a one-sided papalism the

Council of Constance is as tricky and awkward to handle as is the case of a heretical pope like Honorius. As Küng points out, if we accept the present papacy we have to accept Constance (*Structures*, p. 242):

> The (traditionally understood) legitimacy of Martin V and all other subsequent popes up to the present day depends on the legitimacy of the Council of Constance and its procedure in the question of the popes.

Nor can we evade the difficulty by arguing that the Council was providing merely a momentary expedient without consequences for the later Church (*Structures*, p. 254):

> The binding character of the decrees of Constance is not to be evaded. The whole Church and the pope stood behind these decrees at that time with a great unanimity. Indeed, on the basis of these decrees the Church was able to settle the question of the three competing popes, and Church unity (at least in the West) was again restored. On the basis of these decrees the new pope was elected. On the one hand, the legitimacy of the new pope depended on the legitimacy of these decrees; on the other hand, according to the usual view, it is in turn the premise for the legitimacy of the popes in the last five hundred years. The Council was convinced that with the decrees it had provided a solution which had to be valid not only for this conflict between pope and Church, but also for future councils.

The answer Küng sees in trying to establish the proper balance and in recognizing the necessary tension between the two poles of pope and council (*Structures*, pp. 279–280):

> The history of the Church fluctuates over and over again, ever between the problems posed by Vatican I and the problems posed by the Council of Constance. Both are councils of the same Church; both teach what is necessary and exhibit the essential structures of the Church. Both can be wrongly understood and, instead of interpreting structures constructively, they

can work destructively against their very intentions. If both these councils are understood in terms of the whole ecclesiastical reality, they manifest the fruitful tension between Peter and the community of the apostles, between Peter and the Church, the centre and the 'periphery'. If they are selectively (heretically) understood and absolutized, they do not express a fruitful living contrast but a contradiction having fatal effects for the Church.

Relying exclusively on Constance means one ends up not with the Petrine office as this can be deduced from scripture but with at best 'the chief official of a democratic-parliamentary Church association'.[4] Relying exclusively on Vatican I means one ends up not with a picture of the people of God as a Spirit-filled royal priesthood but with at best 'an ecclesiastical subject people ruled in a totalitarian fashion by an absolute monarch (or his apparatus of officials)'. Küng continues (*Structures*, p. 280):

> The Council of Constance and Vatican I are respectively different emphases of the two poles to which all structures of the Church are directly or indirectly drawn without its being possible to trace them back either to the one or to the other: pope and Church.

The answer is thus not the 'either/or' that out human limitations so often seem to drive us into but a 'both/and', a creative paradox of unresolved tension that is but one of a number of similar paradoxes in which Christianity abounds.

In all this discussion of the relation between council and pope and the ability of a council to over-rule a schismatic or heretical pope there is a surprising lacuna. In 1409 a council convoked by the joint action of cardinals of both the Roman and Avignon popes met at Pisa. It enjoyed the support of the greater part of Christendom. In order to bring to an end the schism that had been debilitating European Christianity ever since the disputed election of Urban VI in 1378 and the subsequent election of his rival

Clement VII later that year, the council of Pisa declared both Benedict XIII (Avignon) and Gregory XII (Rome) notorious schismatics, notorious and obdurate heretics, and notoriously guilty of perjury, and went on to depose both of them. In their place it elected the Cretan Peter Philargis as Pope Alexander V. Unfortunately he died a year later, and his successor John XXIII's character was such as to wreck the chances of this Pisan line being universally recognized as the true succession of Peter. As we have seen, the Council of Constance had to meet five years after Pisa to get rid or the three competing claimants to the papal throne.

Küng is of course aware of the council of Pisa, but he mentions it only very briefly and then as an example of the representation of the laity at a general council (*Structures*, p. 78). What he passes over is its role as a council which genuinely tried to act for the Church, and with the backing of the greater part of the Church, in the kind of emergency he has been discussing in his book. True, the tendency has been to write Pisa off, and the line of popes it gave rise to are dismissed as anti-popes by the official list of popes to be found in the *Annuario Pontificio*. But at the time it was not so simple, and historically it is surely an open question who the true pope was in 1409 and 1410 − or indeed whether there was one at all.[5] Pisa may not be recognized today as an ecumenical council, least of all by the school of theology predominant in Rome, but it is at least worth asking whether it ought not to be. Certainly one might have expected from Küng some discussion of Pisa if only as an example that failed to do what Constance succeeded in doing.

Given, however, Küng's bipolar model of the Church balanced between pope and council, one question remains quite apart from whether it is pope or council that ultimately decides: the binding authority that attaches to their decisions. To this question Küng devotes the concluding section of his book. Once again, his method is to engage in friendly discussion with leading exponents of the Protestant view, in this case for the most part Calvin and Barth. The fallibility of Councils on this particular point or that was something of which the Reformers had become keenly aware. Luther found it impossible to follow Constance in its condemnation of Jan Hus, and this provided the context of the famous statement attributed to him at Worms (even though in that setting he may only have uttered the last three words): 'I can do no other; here I stand; God help me.' Councils, as far as he was concerned, were only to be followed when what they said had the backing of scripture or the evidence of reason. Similarly article 21 of the Thirty-nine Articles, which in piquant contrast to the code of canon law only allows general councils to assemble by 'the commandment and will of Princes' (which in fact was how Nicaea and the other early councils were convoked, as indeed was Constance), says of them:

> And when they be gathered together, (forasmuch as they be an assembly of men, whereof all be not governed with the Spirit and Word of God,) they may err, and sometimes have erred, even in things pertaining unto God. Wherefore things ordained by them as necessary to salvation have neither strength nor authority, unless it may be declared that they be taken out of holy Scripture.

Calvin, again, who as summarized by Küng shows a high regard for councils, was concerned that because they were capable of error we should not accord them blind obedience but should rather test them to see whether they were composed of true rather than wicked shepherds (*Structures*, pp. 306–313). The question at issue is not so much the essential inerrancy of the Church but whether that inerrancy is inevitably articulated in the doctrinal statements of councils. The real point of controversy, Küng writes (*Structures*, p. 313), 'does not at all concern . . . the con-

tinuation in principle of the *Church* in truth, but rather the
continuation of the individual *councils* in the truth'.

We are thus very close to the key issue Küng will tackle
eight years later in *Infallible?*: how we can reconcile the
Church's essential indefectibility with the mistakes in detail
that it makes from time to time. For the moment Küng is
content merely to expound the criticisms of Calvin and
Barth, and then against these to set out all the limitations
with which papal (and *a fortiori* conciliar) infallibility was
hedged about at Vatican I. Beyond this very careful exposition of the provisos and conditions which that council laid
down, not only explicitly in its decree but also implicitly in
what was taken for granted, as expressed by such
spokesmen as Bishop Gasser, Küng does not offer very
much in the way of a positive answer to the Protestant
critique of infallibility. Rather it is left as a series of
questions Catholics have to come to grips with. Perhaps he
already sensed that meeting these questions meant either
retreating behind a hermeneutical smokescreen, ready to
produce a fresh twist of re-interpretation whenever the
Church's past commitments seemed on the point of
throttling its response to present needs, or adopting the
position he was to reach in 1970 – that 'the Church will
remain in truth in spite of all the errors that are always
possible' (*Infallible?*, p. 144).

Meanwhile Küng is able to tackle the widespread miscon-
ception that would see the Church as somehow being in
control of the word of God which has called it into being
and which it is its duty to serve and preach (*Structures*, p.
323):

> The Church never 'possesses' the word of God, pro-
> claiming itself in human utterance, as her property.
> Rather, the Church remains under the word of God,
> precisely thereby remaining the possession and the
> property of the Lord, precisely thereby remaining the
> κυριακή, belonging to the Lord. Despite the unity

existing between the Church and Christ, the Church in juxtaposition to Christ, therefore, remains as the pupil to the master, the servant to the lord, the flock to the shepherd, the earthly body to the heavenly head.

Hence the teaching authority of the Church is never of a directly original character, but only one that is mediated through and derived from Christ and His word. The ground and, at the same time, the limit of the Church teaching authority is the word of God proclaiming itself in a human utterance. The exercise of Church teaching authority also can be understood only as an actualization of obedience *vis-à-vis* the superordinated word of God. God and His word above, the Church and her word below: here no reversal is possible – all commissioning, authorization comes from above. Nor is absorption of the word of God by the Church possible. God's authority can never be simply appropriated by the Church. The obedience of the Church can never become an obedience to herself, towards her own teaching authority. God's authority exclusively is autonomous, the Church's authority is and remains heteronomous. The Church could wreak no greater damage on her authentic teaching authority than to want to divinize and transcendentalize it. If this authority no longer has God and His word about it, it is therefore lacking in source and ground, and it cancels itself out. The Church cannot strengthen her teaching authority better than by subordinating her authority again and again, in the concrete, humbly, modestly and gratefully to the authority of God's word, by seeking simply to hear, to proclaim, to realize, not her own word, but God's.

It is in this context, Küng argues, that papal infallibility can be understood 'not as a self-glorifying appropriation of divine revelation but as a humble, obedient, non-partisan service of interpretation, directed and protected by the Holy Ghost, that remains a human interpretation'

(*Structures*, p. 324). This context of the Church's relative and provisional nature is something we shall meet once again in *The Church*, particularly with regard to avoiding any confusion between the Church and the eschatological kingdom proclaimed by Jesus.

In his final pages Küng develops his views on the ambiguity inherent in doctrinal statements, which are normally polemical in form because they are made to settle some particular controversy that has arisen. Any statement of error, Küng holds, thus contains a kernel of truth, and any statement of truth has attached to it a shadow of error (*Structures*, p. 350):

> A truth pronounced for polemical reasons borders particularly on error, since it is directed against a specific error which it is attempting to destroy. Since every error, no matter how great, contains the kernel of some truth, a polemically oriented utterance is in danger of striking not only at the error but also at the error's kernel of truth: namely at the erroneous opinion's legitimate demand . . .
>
> A statement of truth having polemical intent is in danger of regarding itself as a mere denial of an error. By so doing, however, it necessarily neglects the authentic kernel of truth inherent in the error. This statement of truth is then a *half* truth: what it asserts is right, what it passes over in silence is also right.

This can all too easily lead to a dialogue of the deaf, with each side seeing merely the truth of its own assertions and the error of the other's without being aware of the truth hidden in the other's statements and the erroneous implications lurking in its own.

The concluding section of *Structures* thus provided part of the foundation on which Küng was later to build *Infallible?*, and in turn Küng's rejection of a black-and-white concept of infallibility had its roots in his discovery in *Justification* of common ground despite the mutual condemnations. Indeed, the example of an orthodox and a heretical interpretation of 'by faith alone', with the result that the Catholic condemnation of the heretical interpretation was understood by Protestants as a condemnation of the orthodox interpretation, crops up first in *Structures* (p. 350) and then eight years later (put more clearly and succinctly) in *Infallible?* (p. 141).

This illustrates once again the remarkable consistency of Küng's development as a theologian. There are no false starts, no time-wasting explorations of blind alleys. Instead, he is able always to build on previous work, elaborating and correcting earlier views where necessary but never forced totally to abandon them. Not only is there a consistency of subject-matter but also a consistency of style. Küng's books have the air of arguing with their reader, of trying to arouse in him or her the same passionate concern with the things of God and with the truth about the things of God that animates their author. In *Structures* this is amplified by the way so much of the book consists of friendly but candid debate with Protestant theologians, from Luther and Calvin through to Barth and Küng's own contemporaries. But the keynote of the book is above all its insistence on facing up to the awkward facts of history instead of using preconceived theological theories in a vain attempt to explain them away. 'It is without doubt the first time in contemporary Catholic theology that a theologian has loyally accepted these incontestable historical data and tried to interpret them,' said the Belgian Benedictine Paul de Vooght of Küng's willingness to grapple with the implications of the Council of Constance and its decrees.[6] When this historical realism is coupled with a similar willingness to let the biblical data speak for itself, as it is in Küng's case, the result can best perhaps be described as empirical theology.

[1] This useful description we owe to Michael Novak, *The Open*

Church: Vatican II, Act II, Darton, Longman and Todd, London, 1964, pp. 52–56.

[2] Joseph Schmidlin, *Catholic Mission History,* edited by Matthias Braun, SVD, Mission Press SVD, Techny, Illinois, 1933, pp. 496–7. Other histories of the missions preferred to pass over this embarrassing episode in silence: e.g. the contribution by M. A. Launay to J.-B. Piolet, SJ (ed.), *Les Missions Catholiques Françaises au xixe siècle,* Paris, n.d., vol. iii, pp. 385–6.

[3] Cf. Karl Rahner and Joseph Ratzinger, *The Episcopate and the Primacy,* Herder, Freiburg-im-Breisgau/Nelson, Edinburgh and London, 1962, pp. 129–132.

[4] This is the kind of phrase that is virtually guaranteed to be offensive to many Catholic ears. Both criticism and alarm were aroused at the January 1970 meeting of the Dutch Pastoral Council when a vaguely similar phrase was used in the draft report on the ministry in its discussion of the need for greater decentralization in the Church: 'Perhaps we must gradually become used to the idea of the pope as "president or secretary general of the united Catholic Churches throughout the entire world", keeping closely in touch with similar figures in other Christian Churches and in other human movements at the world level.' The report went on to make it clear that it was not thinking in terms of merely a Catholic equivalent of the secretary general of the World Council of Churches: 'Just as at their local level all office-holders represent the believing community in service to the gospel, so the pope too would be the representative and "president of the community of love", but in this case with relation to the "catholica" dispersed over the entire world.' Cf. *Herder Correspondence,* March 1970, vol. 7 no. 3, p. 77, and p. 51 of the draft report.

[5] For the decline in the standing of the Pisan line of popes as mirrored in successive Catholic encyclopaedias, see Francis Oakley, *Council over Pope?: Towards a Provisional Ecclesiology,* Herder and Herder, New York, 1969, pp. 123–126.

[6] '*Le conciliarisme aux conciles de Constance et de Bâle (Compléments et précisions)*', in *Irénikon* 36 (1963), pp. 73–75, quoted by Francis Oakley, *Council over Pope?,* p. 121.

7

Pope John's Revolution

In *Structures of the Church* Küng had pointed to the need to redress a balance within the Church that had become dangerously tilted in favour of the papacy. This was the achievement of the Council Pope John had so surprisingly summoned. The crucial first step in redressing the balance may have been Pope John's action in convoking the Council, but the success or failure of the whole enterprise hinged on the response of the bishops assembled in St Peter's. The decisive turning point came at the very first business session. According to the agenda the bishops were to vote at once for members of the various commissions that would handle the Council's business and draft its decrees. The only list of candidates they had was a list of the members of the various preparatory commissions – who had, of course, all been appointed by the Curia. If they had gone ahead with these elections there and then, the Council would have become virtually a rubber stamp for the Curia's decisions, and things in the Church would have gone on very much as before. But this the Council fathers refused to do. They insisted on, and got, a three-day breathing space to consult each other about suitable candidates before proceeding with these elections.

This episode illustrates precisely what it was a key factor in bringing about: the shift away from a centralization of power at the centre of the Church and a realization of the corresponsibility of the bishops (and of the local Churches over which they preside) for the affairs of the Church as a whole. Theologically this shift was expressed in the doctrine of collegiality, the view that the bishops with the pope form a collegial body in the same way as did Peter and the other apostles. The Council thus stated that together with the pope (and never without him) the college of bishops possesses full and supreme power over the universal Church (*Lumen gentium* § 22).

For the bishops present the Council did not just provide an opportunity for them to share collectively in giving the Church a new impetus in a new direction. It was also a remarkable education. In their own dioceses they tended to be isolated individuals treated with an outmoded deference. Someone meeting a bishop would normally greet him by genuflecting and kissing the episcopal ring on his right hand; and a bishop would of course be addressed as 'My Lord'. (Some still are.) In Rome bishops were lost in the crowd: there were over 2,300 of them at the first session of the Council. Probably for the first time since their consecration, they were able to enjoy the luxury of being treated as human beings.

At the same time they were able to catch up with a theological education which for many of them had not only been a long time ago but had left a great deal to be desired. According to the late Cardinal John Carmel Heenan, theological education in his time at the English College – 1924 to 1930 – consisted of finding out the precise degree with which the Church had committed itself to some dogmatic statement or had condemned some heterodox opinion. It was a question of discovering the right theological note to be attached to each thesis. 'Only after the student discovered the theological note was he encouraged to search the scriptures and the fathers for light and inspiration', commented Cardinal Heenan. 'That is why I did not find the study of theology so enthralling as the study of philosophy.'[1]

Beyond this, theological education tended to be thought of as something to be got over during one's student days.

The Council was the focus in spreading and encouraging the idea that theological education was something that needed to persist right through a Christian's life. Regular in-service training for the clergy, adult Christian education for the laity, are ideas now accepted as normal when in earlier generations theology was something a priest 'did' as a seminarian and the catechism was something a Christian learned as a child.

Much of the credit for this shift in consciousness must go to the educational process to which the bishops were subjected at the Council. A great part of this came from the work of the Council itself, from listening to the various arguments being propounded and from having to weigh these up and to decide what should be done. But a great part also came from the opportunity of meeting and listening to virtually all the world's Catholic theologians of any significance. They were in Rome as *periti* attached to the Council, expert consultants to help it in its work. Many of them gave lectures for the benefit of both bishops and journalists to help them understand what was at stake in the various questions before the Council. And of course the theologians themselves were learning all the time. Being involved in the revolutionary change which the Church was making in its understanding of itself and in its pattern of behaviour meant that they too were able to see things in a new light and were continually having to revise and develop the ideas they had brought with them to Rome.

Hans Küng was not among the first list of 195 *periti* named by Rome at the end of September 1962. Nevertheless he attended the first session of the Council as the private theological adviser to Bishop Karl Joseph Leiprecht of Rottenburg, the diocese which includes Tübingen. By the end of the first session the omission had been made good and Küng jointed such eminent colleagues as Congar, Daniélou, de Lubac, Jungmann, Rahner and Häring as one of the official *periti*.[2]

The theologians may have had an invaluable contribution to make to the work of Vatican II, but the responsibility for the change brought about in the Church's life rests firmly with the bishops. To see the Council in terms of bishops led astray by avant-garde theologians would be a ludicrous distortion of the educational process that took place. Most of the bishops were shrewd enough to be able to sift theological wheat from theological tares. They were well aware, too, of the practical realities awaiting them back in their dioceses, and had no wish to replace the imposition of one abstract theology on the Church's life by the imposition of another.

Nor, however revolutionary the change it brought about in the Church's consciousness, was the Council a total victory for one theological outlook over another. Sometimes views were definitely discarded, as with the idea that 'error has no rights'. More often old and new were juxtaposed, and the unresolved tensions between them left for the Church to disentangle over the coming decades. One example was the reaffirmation of papal primacy, as defined by Vatican I, along with the rediscovery of episcopal collegiality.

There remained, moreover, pockets of strong resistance to the new outlook. After all, people were being asked to change what they had been brought up to believe unchangeable. And this resistance was if anything encouraged by the new pope. Paul VI can be regarded as having been elected to bring to a successful conclusion what John XXIII had begun. But often he gave the impression of going out of his way to accommodate the tiny disgruntled minority who could not come to terms at all with what the majority of bishops had come to see as the more Christian way of seeing and doing things.

Paul VI thus intervened in the Council's business in order to placate this diehard minority, as with the addition of the *nota praevia explicativa* to *Lumen gentium*, the constitution on the Church, so as to make quite clear that collegiality did not infringe papal primacy, or with the nineteen last-minute amendments to the decree on ecumenism. He prejudged the whole question of clerical celibacy by withdrawing it totally from public discussion by the Council and telling the bishops that he not only intended 'to maintain this ancient, holy and providential law to the extent of our ability but also to reinforce its observance'. He also withdrew from the Council any competence to decide the question of birth control, even if that was at least debated in St Peter's with a number of outspoken contributions from various bishops which helped to reshape Catholic attitudes in the Church at large.[3]

In this way Paul VI fostered a hesitant and negative reaction to the work of the Council. But it would be unfair to make him a scapegoat for the Council's failure to live up to many of the more radical hopes it had inspired. To a considerable extent he was merely reflecting the hesitations and difficulties felt by his contemporaries. They had been brought up under the old system, and their conversion to the new freedom and openness they experienced at the Council represented a very remarkable achievement indeed. Naturally, there remained some of the old fear of what might happen when rigid controls were relaxed.

Perhaps the bishops and Catholics in general would have responded to bolder leadership. But bold leadership from the papacy was surely the last thing the Church needed at a time when what needed to be broken was the old habit of waiting passively for Rome to take the initiative. The whole body of the Church had to become aware of its responsibilities after having for so long been encouraged to rely on being spoon-fed by papal encyclicals and allocutions for it merely to assent to and implement. The Hamlet-like indecisiveness which throughout his pontificate Paul VI was labelled with can be seen as providential for the Church.

Nor were the benefits of Paul VI's leadership merely

negative. One of the greatest of the many anxieties that weighed on this naturally anxious man was that he should not preside over any rupture of the Church's unity. Previous general councils had tended to confirm or to occasion a schism: even if opponents of infallibility eventually accepted Vatican I's decrees precisely in order to safeguard the Church's unity, nevertheless that council ended with about 150,000 Catholics in the German-speaking world breaking away under the leadership of theologians and Church historians such as Ignaz von Döllinger (though Döllinger himself warned against raising altar against altar and did not join the Old Catholic Church that gave institutional expression to this schism). Paul VI was determined that no such consequences should attend Vatican II. This explains the leniency with which he treated the rebel French Archbishop Marcel Lefebvre. It also explains why, although a handful of theologians were disciplined in the 1970s, no formal measures were taken against Hans Küng in 1975 over *Infallible?* or over *On being a Christian* in 1977. It was only John Paul II who was willing to risk the disruptive effects such measures would inevitably have on Catholic morale.

For the moment, however, the future hid the controversies that would mark Paul VI's pontificate, particularly the row over birth control sparked off by his encyclical *Humanae vitae* in 1968 and the isolation of the Dutch bishops over celibacy in 1970 when their national pastoral council advocated a change of policy. But the roots of these controversies were to be found in the blurring of issues that was the price the Council paid for simply juxtaposing old and new ways of thinking. Thirteen years later Küng was to comment on the Lefebvre case (*The Times*, 28 August 1976):

> Many council documents were in fact compromises imposed on the majority by the conservative curia which controlled the machinery of the council; it was

then possible only to warn and to demand consistent solutions.

Compromises are liable to interpretation in different ways by the different parties: a fact which has contributed substantially to the confusion and polarization in the post-conciliar Church.

It was because he did not want any part in this blurring of issues that Hans Küng turned down Karl Rahner's suggestion during the second session that he should attach himself to the doctrinal commission. He could see no likelihood of the commission being reconstituted to reflect more accurately the view of the Council majority and of its being given a president other than Cardinal Alfredo Ottaviani, who held the post in virtue of his position as head of the Holy Office (*Way*, p. 168):

> During the second session I drafted an assessment that was concerned particularly with the election of a fresh doctrinal commission and the replacement of Cardinal Ottaviani by a president to be elected by the council. This assessment was handed over to Paul VI personally by the Melkite Patriarch Maximos IV Saigh. The result of this and many similar initiatives was merely that a few more members were elected on to the commissions, a second secretary was appointed, and other steps were taken along these lines. For the rest, however, everything stayed as it was. This made it clear that there could be no thought of recasting the fundamental conciliar constitution on the Church [*Lumen gentium*] to place it on a more solid biblical basis. In particular, no decisive change would be possible in what is now the third chapter on the Church's hierarchical structure which confirmed Vatican I with its problematical definitions of the papal primacy and infallibility without introducing any differentiation and even partly extended this to the episcopate. This was the reason why I was not ready to take part in the work of this commission . . .

In addition, Küng felt the commission should be drawing

on the services of more and better biblical scholars. 'The German critical school of exegesis was in fact not represented at the council,' he said (*Way*, p. 168).

It was thus a question of Küng's own personal theological integrity, not some vendetta against Cardinal Ottaviani: Küng has always done his best to prevent the theological disputes he has been involved in degenerating into personal squabbles. Had he joined the commission he would have found himself committed to a text he regarded as a theological curate's egg – excellent in parts, but with some sections to his mind gravely defective. Under Cardinal Ottaviani's chairmanship, and with as secretary Father Sebastian Tromp, the Jesuit who had taught Küng fundamental theology at the Gregorian, the commission was committed to precisely the non-historical orthodoxy that Küng was reacting against, and he saw no chance of it being able to adopt the kind of scripture-based understanding of the Church that he was working towards.

By sheer coincidence Küng became involved with the Holy Office at the same time as he was refusing to join the doctrinal commission under its secretary's chairmanship. *Justification* may have led to the opening of a dossier on Küng, but *Structures of the Church* led to his being summoned to a hearing. This took place at the Bishop of Rottenburg's residence in Rome in 1963 with in the chair Cardinal Augustin Bea, the Jesuit from Swabia whom Pope John had appointed to head the Secretariat for Promoting Christian Unity he had established in 1960. Present at the hearing were professors from the Gregorian and the bishops of both dioceses with which Küng was connected, Basle to which he was (and is) formally attached as a priest, and Rottenburg where as a Tübingen professor he was working.

Küng's crime had basically been to point out that several of the developments that had led to the centralized papacy of the nineteenth and twentieth centuries were not irreversible but could be, and in many cases should be, reversed. 'Much that traditional dogmatic theology and traditional canon law declared to belong to the papacy by divine right and thus to be unalterable now appeared as an at least problematical historical development – if not indeed as a false development when seen from the point of view of the original Christian message,' was how Küng summed up this book's doctrinal conclusions, conclusions that from the point of view of the Roman school of theology were 'not inoffensive' (*Way*, p. 157).

Cardinal Bea did all he could to ensure that the hearing went smoothly and was clearly concerned to avoid a conflict arising (*Way*, p. 158):

> Well, it was the period of the Council, and so I was forgiven a certain amount. At all events a solemn session took place in Rome with Cardinal Bea in the chair . . . I had to answer various questions that had been drawn up in the Holy Office. Later I had to repeat my answers in writing and in Latin. Without a doubt it was thanks to Cardinal Bea, whom I had got to know during my first years in Rome when he was visitor of the German College, in the days when he was still a simple Jesuit priest and Pius XII's confessor, that the proceedings came to a happy conclusion and in fact were discontinued without any obligation of any kind being laid upon me.

As he realized, Küng was lucky in his timing. Any harsher treatment of someone who was already one of the Church's best-known theologians would have been a political impossibility at this juncture, with the Council now well into its stride and the Church as a whole becoming used to hearing out loud what previously would only have been whispered in corners if uttered at all – and non-Catholic Christians and the world in general watching with amazed delight a Roman Catholic Church that seemed suddenly to have turned human.

There was, of course, nothing inevitable about the way in

which the Council was developing. The changes it introduced could have been purely cosmetic, leaving the old
order more firmly entrenched; or they could have been
even more far-reaching. A sense of opportunities missed
underlies the disappointment Hans Küng felt at what
actually happened in the Church under Paul VI. While he
cannot be accused of blaming Giovanni Battista Montini
for not being another Angelo Roncalli, certainly Paul VI
was unable to arouse in the Swiss theologian the same
loyalty and devotion awoken by John XXIII. Küng had
indeed met Paul VI on a number of occasions, the first time
when the future pope was simply Archbishop Montini of
Milan and not yet a cardinal, and long before any actual
meeting he had had a mutual friend in Dom Anselm
Fellmann, a fellow-native of Sursee and guest-master of the
Benedictine monastery of Engelberg, twenty-eight miles to
the south-east, where Monsignor Montini used to spend his
holidays. Often enough those who met Paul VI privately
came away full of an admiration that was not always shared
by those who had merely observed his public appearances.
It seems to have been only in a face-to-face setting that this
pope could exert the kind of magnetic charm that his predecessor and two successors were able to radiate at public
gatherings.

Even if personal encounter did not convert Küng into a
fervent partisan of Paul VI, relations between the two seem
to have been cordial. Küng recalls that Cardinal Montini,
as he then was, was extraordinarily friendly when they met
in Rome just before the Council and discussed *The Council
and Reunion*. In December 1965, despite all the pressures
involved in the Council's conclusion, Küng was grateful for
a long private audience. Nevertheless it was the public man
and his policies that came under scrutiny, and Paul VI was
judged very differently from John XXIII. How differently
can be seen by comparing the panegyric Küng wrote on the
latter's death[4] with the scathing indictment of papal policy

during and after the Council that forms the foreword to *Infallible?* As Küng made clear, it was not a question of personalities (*Infallible?*, pp. 12–13):

> Paul VI is a man of integrity, who suffers under his load of responsibility and perhaps feels overburdened by it. Personally he is motivated by a selfless desire to do only the best for the Church and for humanity, and he sincerely believes he must act accordingly. Where he does not feel bound by dogma or Church policy he has shown this plainly, as in his initiatives for world peace and disarmament, social justice, the Third World and development aid, the continuation of liturgical reform and a limited reform in the personnel and structure of the Roman Curia, and so on. In comparison with some high Curial advisers, he must be described as a moderate. Though to many in the Church and in the world he seems to be of the extreme right, to many inside the Vatican ghetto he is a man of the left. Just as John XXIII was not without his faults, so Paul VI is not without his strong sides. No one should dispute or belittle all this. And yet – would it help the Church to pass it over in silence? – it is impossible to go on shutting one's eyes to the fact that, in spite of his and his advisers' best intentions, the longer the teaching office is exercised by this pope and his curia, the more damage is done to the unity and credibility of the Catholic Church; and, yet again in history, this damage is done from within Rome itself.

The indictment is thus based not on Paul VI's character but on what he had done and what he had left undone. During the Council he gave more and more support to 'the backward-looking, unecumenical, traditionalist Curia, that thinks in terms of nationalism and power politics' (*Infallible?*, p. 13). On such sensitive issues as birth control, mixed marriages, celibacy, the structural and personal reform of the Curia, and an effective local voice in the appointment of bishops, 'the firm, strong, hopeful spiritual

leadership provided by John XXIII was lacking' and in its
place came 'a growing stream of sometimes very sombre
warnings, jeremiads and imputations' (*Infallible?*, p. 16).
Küng's central accusation was that 'the greater the Pope's
efforts to take his teaching office seriously, the more they
seem to take place at the expense of the credibility of that
office and the inner cohesion of the Church' (*Infallible?*,
p. 20).

The Second Vatican Council in this way formed a
turning-point in Hans Küng's development as a theologian,
and this in two different ways. It was first of all a turning-
point in that it did not represent a total sweeping victory for
the approach and attitudes he and many of his fellow-
theologians shared. The more the old style of centralized
authoritarianism reasserted itself in the central government
of the Church, the more he found himself forced into the
role of His Holiness's loyal opposition. The changes inaugurated by Pope John and the way the first session
developed offered a background against which Hans Küng
could be seen to emerge as a theologian uniquely well
qualified to interpret, expound and defend what the
Church was doing at this central, official level. The increasing hesitation and misgiving that crept in under Paul VI
made this no longer possible. There was a gradual fading of
the hope that Catholics might find themselves living in a
Church for which they would not continually be having to
make unnecessary excuses. It was at the second session that
the pattern was fixed, and Hans Küng was perceptive
enough to realize from the start what was happening.

Secondly, it was a turning-point for him in much the
same way that it was for everyone else caught up in this
extraordinary event. It marked a new beginning, a new
reference-point from which he could start his explorations,
a new encouragement to take the Church seriously. After
the end of the third session he wrote that, despite the
ambiguous judgement that could be made of what the

Council had done, there stood to its credit the fact that no doors were closed, that innumerable doors were opened, that a new spirit had been brought to life in the Church, and that substantial positive results (such as the reform of the liturgy) had been achieved.[5] The ferment of ideas that Vatican II represented went on working through the decades that followed, while the two or three months each year the Council was in session gave theologians an unrivalled opportunity to meet each other and spend long hours putting the Church to rights.

The Council thus contained the germ of much of Hans Küng's future work. *Truthfulness* came out as a book in 1968, but it started life as a lecture he gave at the Dutch centre in Rome in October 1964. *The Church*, published in 1967, has its roots in the second session: the way things were going then, and particularly his dissatisfaction with the doctrinal commission's approach to the subject, made him decide to write his own analysis and vision of how the Christian community was constituted. Together with such colleagues as Rahner, Schillebeeckx, Congar and Metz he joined in founding *Concilium*, a theological journal launched with the aim of providing a platform for the kind of theology that emerged at the Council and designed from the start to be international: one aim was to ensure that after the Council was over and everyone had gone home again theologians would remain in touch with what their colleagues in other and different parts of the world were thinking. The first issue appeared in January 1965, published simultaneously by eight publishers in six languages (Dutch, English, French, German, Portuguese, and Spanish): there was also from the start a partial edition in Italian, with a full edition from 1967 onwards, while later in 1967 a partial edition was begun in Japanese and one in Polish in 1970. Throughout Küng has edited the section on ecumenism and has been a member of the central editorial board.

Vatican II thus meant a great deal of hard work for Hans Küng. He gave lectures to various bishops' conferences, though not to the German bishops: perhaps they found him too young and brash. Like other theologians, he drafted bishops' speeches for them. Together with Yves Congar and Daniel O'Hanlon he edited a selection of the speeches made during the second session arranged so as to bring out the dominant ideas of the Council. He wrote articles and gave talks explaining what was happening in Rome for the benefit of those unable to be there. Much of this occasional writing was collected in book form (*The Living Church* and *The Changing Church*, originally published in German in 1963 and 1964).

All this work still had to be combined with his duties as a professor at Tübingen as well as with an increasing number of invitations to lecture from all over the world. The academic year at Tübingen may start a little later than is normal in England, in mid-October rather than at the beginning of the month, but for each of the four years the Council met there was an overlap of the best part of two months when ideally Küng needed to be in two places at once. But it meant he was able to keep his students at Tübingen in touch with the extraordinary ferment going on in Rome and Council circles in touch with a significant part of Catholic opinion outside.

There was a change, too, in his circumstances at Tübingen. In 1963 he moved from the chair of funda-mental theology he had held since 1960 to the newly created chair of dogmatic and ecumenical theology. It did not seem to make very much difference to the range of subjects he pursued in his writings, though it meant a change in subject-matter for his university lectures: funda-mental theology covers questions which in England would often be classified under the philosophy of religion, while dogmatic theology is concerned to analyse the doctrinal structure erected on this basis. Books like *Structures of the*

Church and *The Church* would fall under the latter heading, *Menschwerdung Gottes* and *Does God Exist?* under the former.

At the same time the Institute for Ecumenical Research was set up at Tübingen with Küng as director. Among other things this gave him a team to work with. As a professor he was entitled to a research assistant, but the establishment of the Institute includes not merely a research assistant but two other posts at the level of what in English terms would be lecturer and senior lecturer. This helped to ward off the danger of working too much on his own as a theologian by ensuring that others would bring their questions and criticisms to his work. At the same time Küng has always been concerned to avoid the Institute forming a clique. He insists on openness to what others are saying and on the proper presentation of somebody's views as an essential preliminary to any critique of them, while when appropriate outsiders are invited to take part in joint seminars.

The Institute also serves a social purpose by acting as a centre for Küng's doctoral and other students. What is apparently an innovation in the German academic world is the custom inaugurated in 1978 of inviting past students back for a day's meeting to report to each other on the work they had been doing as well as to enjoy each other's company: the translation, perhaps, into the serious language of Tübingen of an Oxford gaudy.

Besides its library, the Institute's facilities include a catalogue of theological books and articles published since 1945 classified according to subject-matter. This enables the student in any field to see what the relevant literature is and where he needs to start reading. By mid-1978 it had reached a total of 168,000 entries, with new cards being added at the rate of about 12,000 a year. The Institute's archives include thirty dossiers of material supplied at Vatican II to the Council fathers and official *periti* –

successive drafts of the various Council documents along with explanations from the commissions as to why they did or did not accept the various amendments proposed – along with supplementary material. There are, too, eighteen dossiers devoted to the infallibility debate sparked off by Küng's book in 1970, and in 1979 a new set of dossiers had to be started to document the row that broke out with the sudden announcement of the withdrawal of Küng's *missio canonica*. The Institute's library includes what is understood to be the only complete set of *Concilium* in all its nine languages available outside the journal's central secretariat in Nijmegen.

Meanwhile the years of the Council saw Küng's first major lecture tour, the start of a series of travels that were to take him all over the globe. The invitation to visit the United States came from an American Jesuit, Father Frank Sweeney from Boston, whom he met at the party held by his English publishers to launch *The Council and Reunion*. The whole trip, which concluded with a shorter visit to England, occupied six weeks in the March and April of 1963. There were some sour notes. Along with three native American theologians – Father Godfrey Diekmann, OSB, Father Gustave Weigel, SJ, and Father John Courtney Murray, SJ, the latter being one of the chief architects of the Council's declaration on religious freedom – he was banned from lecturing at the Catholic University of America in Washington, DC. The lecture he was to have given on 3 April at the University of California in Los Angeles had to be cancelled, apparently because he or the tour's organizers had been too late in applying to the arch-diocesan authorities for permission to speak. But as a whole the tour was an enormous success. The impact Küng made on his American audiences has been described by Michael Novak:[6]

Philadelphia, San Diego, and St Paul quietly refused

to let him speak. Los Angeles tried to keep him out,
but even there a large-scale tea was given him. But in
other cities, four, six, and eight thousand people came
to hear him. The tension in the halls was electric. In
his clear, forceful voice, his blond hair shining in the
lights, Father Küng brought the careful, strong
theology of Europe to American audiences caught up
in the enthusiasm of Pope John's *aggiornamento*. He
created an impact no American could, for Catholic
America somehow still depends upon Europe for its
imaginative life. We receive, John Updike says, 'our
supernatural mail on foreign soil' – or from foreign
lecturers. Dr Küng (he does not like to be called
'Father') spoke about freedom and lack of freedom –
coining a new word 'unfreedom' which Bishop Ahr of
Trenton confessed publicly he couldn't understand at
all – in accents which American Catholics, caught up
in a highly juridical, authoritarian, smoothly run
Church, were thrilled to hear.

In England his audiences may have been numbered in
hundreds rather than thousands but were equally
enthusiastic – if perhaps less overtly so in keeping with the
English reputation for avoiding emotional display. *The
Tablet* (11 May 1963, p. 510) remarked that he had been
described as the most notorious German theologian since
Martin Luther, but for its part received the overwhelming
impression of someone providing rational milk without
guile. There was, it noted, 'a pleasantly deflating irony in
the way he would let some minor depth-charge fall and then
wait, looking up quickly from his notes, for the explosion of
delighted laughter from his listeners'; and it recorded that
his proposals about the Index (abolish it) and mixed
marriages (recognize the validity of those solemnized at a
non-Catholic ceremony) 'each brought a cheer from the
young people in the audience'. The tour also gave Küng an
opportunity to visit Oxford and Cambridge: in the latter
city he and his hosts became so absorbed in looking at the

colleges that they had to run for Küng to be on time to deliver his lecture.

The lecture on 'The Church and Freedom' with which he toured the United States and England duly appeared in print the following year as the sixth in the series of 'Theological Meditations' that had started to appear under his editorship from the Swiss publishing house of Benziger and initially at any rate in translation from associated publishing houses abroad. The aim of this series was to combine spirituality and theology, to provide as it were, a theology that could be prayed and a spirituality that was not an insult to the intelligence. The books that make it up are short, usually nearer fifty than a hundred pages, and for this reason the series never did well in England, where only the first nine titles came out from Sheed and Ward in two batches in 1965 and 1967: in America Küng's first four contributions to the series were brought together in a single volume under the title *Freedom Today* in 1966. The German reading public, however, is used to the short book. A *Novelle* or long short story like Thomas Mann's *Tonio Kröger* is normally published on its own, even though in one edition it fills only 108 pages – and that is a little long for the genre.

Certainly the series of 'Theological Meditations' has continued to flourish in the German-speaking world, with Karl Rahner and Hans Urs von Balthasar among the thirty-one authors to have contributed the forty-eight titles published by the end of 1978: of these eight are by Küng himself, with a ninth – one of the two pieces of writing in which he broke his silence on infallibility – following in 1979.

The brevity of the format enables a theologian either to make a preliminary sketch of a subject he intends to deal with at greater length and in greater detail later, or to tackle an isolated topic that for the moment at least would not justify any more extended treatment and does not link up easily and naturally with other topics to make a longer book. In this way what Küng had to say on the problem of evil (*Gott und das Leid*, published in 1967) can be seen as a preliminary sketch for two sections of *On being a Christian*, that on 'God and suffering' (precisely the same title as the earlier work) and that on 'Coping with the negative side' (*Christian*, pp. 428–436 and 570–581): the same line of argument is followed, the same phrases occur in passages that are newly written with modifications, condensations and expansions to suit the new context in which they find themselves. Similarly his discussion of confirmation (*Was ist Firmung?*, published in 1976, and available for American readers in *Signposts*, pp. 178–204) can be seen as working towards the study of the theology of the sacraments that he has long promised himself (and others) that he will write.

[1] John C. Heenan, *Not the Whole Truth*, Hodder and Stoughton, London, 1971, p. 59.

[2] *The Tablet*, 6 October and 8 December 1962, pp. 943 and 1205.

[3] For the *nota praevia explicativa* see Xavier Rynne, *The Third Session*, Faber and Faber, London, 1965, pp. 240–252; for the amendments to the decree on ecumenism, ibid. pp. 263–266; for the withdrawal of celibacy, Xavier Rynne, *The Fourth Session*, Faber and Faber, London, 1966, pp. 148–9; and for the Council's debate on birth control, *The Third Session*, pp. 153–170. On the last two issues see also Peter Hebblethwaite, *The Runaway Church*, Collins, London, 1975, pp. 93–94.

[4] 'Servus Servorum Dei: Why Pope John was Great', *The Tablet*, 8 and 15 June 1963, pp. 630–632 and 645–646, reprinted (in a new translation) in *The Changing Church*, pp. 1–19.

[5] 'The Council – End or Beginning?', *The Changing Church*, pp. 120–152, especially pp. 136–140.

[6] *The Open Church*, Darton, Longman and Todd, London, 1964, pp. 14–15. For reports of some of the things Küng was saying see *The Tablet*, 27 April 1963, p. 468.

8

The Church Discovered

If, as I suggested earlier, *Structures of the Church* could best be described as an example of empirical theology, that label applies even more clearly to *The Church*. It was a book that had its roots in Küng's own experience of the Second Vatican Council. As we have seen, the decision to write it dates back to the second session. He had long wanted to write something along the lines of the classic work by Karl Adam, one of his predecessors at Tübingen, *The Spirit of Catholicism*. 'But now the time seemed to have come to write a book about the nature and essence of the Church in what is indeed a very different fashion,' he said (*Way*, p. 169). He started a private contest to finish his book by the time the Council concluded. In the event the Council won by a year. The book was completed by the end of 1966 and published in 1967.

Throughout, *The Church* breathes the new atmosphere created by John XXIII with his symbolic opening of windows to let some fresh air blow through the Church. Before Vatican II, dubious reasons and intellectually shoddy arguments were indeed things Catholics would question, but now they were things they would no longer even put up with. This more vigorous attitude Küng not only shared but had done a great deal to propagate, and it was fully reflected in his book. It meant a new confidence not just that he could pursue the truth wherever it might lead him without risking any harm to the Church, but that precisely by pursuing the truth wherever it might lead him he would be doing the Church the greatest service he could.

There is, too, a new confidence displayed in the book's actual writing and structure. *Justification* may be an exceptionally good example of an often dispiriting genre, but it is still fundamentally a doctoral thesis and was planned more to satisfy the examiners than to beguile the reader while convincing him. *Structures of the Church* still reflects something of the approach university teachers are tempted to adopt when faced with a captive audience and only a limited time to fill them up with facts. But from the start *The Church* sets out to woo the reader. In it Küng demonstrates that scholarship and readability need never be in conflict. Many would rank it as his masterpiece, a judgement English-speaking readers are further encouraged to make by its being probably the best translated of his works.

When it appeared *The Church* marked a break with the tradition in Catholic ecclesiology that saw the Church in ideal and idealized terms and that thus was tempted to regard it as somehow sacrosanct and beyond criticism. There was so much stress on the Church's divine nature as to blot out its human imperfections. This tendency was boosted by the terminology that spoke of the Church as a 'perfect society'. This terminology had its roots in the medieval attempts to vindicate the Church' independence over against secular society, but in modern parlance the adjective 'perfect' naturally brought with it overtones of being beyond criticism and irreproachable.

Küng's starting point was thus to apply to the Church Luther's insight that the Christian was at one and the same time justified and a sinner, something which, as we have seen, he had already done in *Justification* after a painstaking demonstration that what was habitually taken as a Protestant slogan also made sound orthodox Catholic sense. The Church's true nature, he now writes, is inseparably accompanied by its 'un-nature' as by a dark shadow. The Church in splendour, without spot or wrinkle, holy and without blemish, is the eschatological goal towards which

the Lord is leading his people and which will be truly
revealed only at the end of time. Küng thus strikes a note of
historical realism that insists on taking the Church as it was
and as it is and that points out that precisely in this
necessarily imperfect Church God can be discovered at
work in human history. The negative aspects which rightly
provoke criticism are the expression of the Church's evil
'un-nature'. They represent the illegitimate side of the
Church, the perversion of its true nature. They arise not
from God's will but from the failings of the men who make
up the Church (*Church*, p. 28):

> In all its historical forms the true nature of the
> Church is accompanied, like a dark shadow, by its
> 'un-nature'; the two are inseparable.
>   Not that the discovery of an 'un-nature' in this
> Church made up of human beings can serve as an
> excuse for all the dark corners of the Church's history.
> It should rather serve as a reminder to admirers and
> critics alike that this dark and unnatural side of the
> Church is something that we should reckon with from
> the start. Since we are dealing with a Church com-
> posed of men, it should surprise neither admirers nor
> critics. It is impossible to discern the permanent
> nature of the Church, which survives all changes,
> except through the changing historical forms of the
> Church; and in the same way it is impossible to
> discern the positive nature of the Church except
> through its negative 'un-nature'. Permanent nature
> and changing forms are inextricably interwoven; and
> in the same way good and evil, positive and negative,
> true nature and 'un-nature' in the Church are inter-
> dependent things which cannot ultimately be worked
> out by human calculations. Even the most essential
> things can change. Even the essentials of the Church's
> true nature are subject to the effects of 'un-nature'.
> Sin is possible even in the area of the most holy. All
> ecclesiology must take as one of its bases, not merely
> the historicity of the Church, but the fact that the

Church is historically affected by evil; and this fact must be accepted from the start without false apologetics and always taken into account. For this reason ecclesiology can never simply take the *status quo* of the Church as its yardstick, still less seek to justify it. On the contrary, taking once again the original message, the Gospel, as its starting-point, it will do all it can to make critical evaluations, as a foundation for the reforms and renewal which the Church will always need.

With this last sentence Küng brings in what can be seen as the major theme not just of this book but of his theology as a whole: the gospel as the criterion by which the Church's later development must be judged, the norm against which it must always be measuring and correcting itself, the standard by which ultimately all Christian behaviour and all Christian doctrine must be guided.

Coupled with this is Küng's insistence that the Church is utterly dependent on the will of God. The Church stands or falls by its links with its origins in Jesus Christ and his message, he writes (*Church*, p. 15). It remains permanently dependent, for the ground of its existence, on God's saving act in Jesus Christ. Again this can be seen as an application of ideas first worked out in *Justification*. Salvation is God's work, not man's, and man can only respond in faith to God's gracious call: as soon as he is tempted to rely on his own strength, on his own abilities (which in any case are not his own but given to him by God), he is doomed to failure and disaster. Applied to the Church this means a decisive shift away from the Church in itself towards the message it is preaching. Nor should the debt to Barth be overlooked. There is an awareness of the Church standing always under God's judgement, a realization that God's thoughts are not our thoughts nor our ways his ways.

The way in which the Church tended to be seen as an ideal that was exempt from criticism had its roots in two

misconceptions which Küng tackles head-on. One was an
uncritical acceptance of the idea that Jesus founded the
Church as if he spent the time between the resurrection and
the ascension dictating the 1917 code of canon law to the
apostles. The other was too close an identification of the
Church with the kingdom or reign of God which it is its
duty to preach and to prepare the way for. Küng indeed
starts his chapter on the relation between Jesus's preaching
and the Church by asking if we are forced to agree with the
comment which, he notes, Loisy meant as a positive statement but which is always taken the wrong way in a negative
sense: 'Jesus proclaimed the kingdom of God, and what
came was the Church' (*Church*, p. 43). The answer the
reader deduces is that we must – provided we take it in the
right way as seeing the Church as essentially founded on
and governed by the preaching of Jesus, as indeed the indispensable means of bringing us into contact with that
preaching. Küng uses the findings of New Testament
scholars to establish that in the period before his death
Jesus did not found a Church but by his preaching and
ministry laid the foundations for the emergence of the
Church after his resurrection; that the Church has existed
from the time of faith in the resurrection; and that the
origins of the Church do not lie solely in the intention and
the message of Jesus in the pre-Easter period but in the
whole history of his life and ministry (*Church*, pp. 70–79).
In this way we can, if we want to, talk of Jesus founding the
Church provided we realize that what is involved is
something subtly different from what we mean when we
talk of George Fox founding the Quakers or John Wesley
founding the Methodists.

There is in fact a very close connection between Jesus's
preaching and the Church. Küng is able to take the five distinctive perspectives discernable in the former and apply
them to the Church. Jesus's preaching of the coming reign
of God that is at once 'not yet' and already at hand thus lays

down certain imperatives which the Church ignores at its peril. Jesus preached that the reign of God is a decisive, future, final event at the end of time; so the Church should not pretend to be an end in itself but should instead point from the fulfilled reign of God in Christ to the coming reign of God, should not forget that it is something temporary, provisional, and interim, awaiting the consummation of the history of mankind in the kingdom of God. Jesus preached that the reign of God is an all-powerful act of God himself; so the Church must not imagine that it is it itself which makes the decisive moves and can out of its own strength inaugurate and build up the kingdom of God, but must instead trust in God's decisive act. Jesus preached the reign of God as a purely religious reign; so the Church must not adopt the style and methods of political power but must instead remember that it is called to the selfless service of mankind, of its enemies and of the world. Jesus preached the reign of God as a saving event for sinners; so the Church should preach not warnings of doom but the message of salvation, not menaces but the joyful good news, remembering that it is composed of sinful men and exists for sinful men, aware of its guilt and sin but living in joyful assurance of forgiveness. Jesus required for the reign of God that man should make a radical decision for God; so the Church too must not be distracted by anything from its radical decision for God, must avoid pretending that its own rules and regulations are God's commandments or are equal or even superior to God's will as revealed in Jesus Christ (*Church*, pp. 96–104 with pp. 47–54).

The Church is thus seen not as a preliminary stage but as an anticipatory sign of the final and definitive reign of God (*Church*, p. 96), not as some quasi-divine hypostasis interposed between God and man but as us, as the fellowship of its believing members (*Church*, p. 130), not primarily as a hierarchy but as a community, as the new people of God. It is in fact only some three-quarters of the way through the

book that Küng starts discussing specific 'official'
ministries in the Church. This mirrors the approach of
Vatican II, which in its central constitution on the Church
discusses first 'The mystery of the Church' and then 'The
people of God' before devoting its third chapter to 'The
hierarchical structure of the Church, with special reference
to the episcopate'. Küng indeed is able to use quotations
from this Council document (and from the decree on
ecumenism too) to punctuate and sum up his argument.

Again, the Church's four classic dimensions – the term
Küng prefers to 'notes' or 'marks' – of unity, holiness,
catholicity and apostolicity are seen more as a challenge to
the Church than as qualities it is irrevocably possessed of
(*Church*, p. 269):

> What is truly decisive is not the formal presence of
> certain characteristics, but their use and practice. The
> word of the Gospel must truly be preached, heard and
> followed, the sacraments must really be used, oneness,
> holiness, catholicity and apostolicity must be lived by
> living men in a living Church, and the *notae Ecclesiae*
> must become in one way or another *notae Christi-*
> *anorum*.

Küng's discussion of the Church's unity thus turns into an
analysis of how the Churches became divided and what can
be done towards bringing them together again. Nor is
catholicity seen as just a matter of the widest geographical
extension, of having the greatest numbers, of embracing the
widest variety of cultures and societies, or of temporal continuity. Negatively, it is not the particular but the particu-
larist Church which is un-catholic. Positively, Küng writes
(*Church*, p. 302):

> It is an all-embracing *identity* which at bottom makes a
> Church catholic, the fact that despite all the constant
> and necessary changes of the times and of varying
> forms, and despite its blemishes and weaknesses, the
> Church in every place and in every age remains un-

changed in its essence, whatever form it takes: this must be its aim and its desire. In this way the unchanging essence of the Church will be credibly preserved and confirmed and activated anew 'always and everywhere and by all men'. Only if this identity is present does the Church appear as the undiminished entire Church, as the undiluted universal Church, as the undivided total Church, as the truly Catholic Church. If a Church at any time or place or in any form renounces this identity, if it allows itself to be absorbed into any nation, culture, race, class or social phenomenon, then it becomes uncatholic; it becomes heretical if it takes on a different, foreign nature, or apostate if it consciously rebels against its proper original nature. Catholicity is that which links together all the local Churches into one entire Church, that which distinguishes them from any debased form of Church. Identity is the *basis* of catholicity.

And in discussing the way in which the label 'catholic' has become exclusively associated with the Church or Churches in communion with Rome he suggests the illuminating and helpful analogy of seeing the relationship between the Catholic Church and all the other Churches which in the course of history have broken with it on the lines of the relationship between a mother and her daughters who have quarrelled with her (*Church*, pp. 307–311). There can thus be no turning back of the clock, no reversion to an earlier and perhaps more innocent state of affairs, no trying to pretend that the Reformation never happened, just as a quarrel between a mother and her daughters cannot be settled by the latter reverting to an infantile role and the former treating them as if they were still children but instead by the former recognizing that they are now mature and grown up and the latter realizing that their mother represents a fundamental and formative part of their own lives and one they cannot run away from.

Holiness and apostolicity receive similar treatment. In a section much of which can be read as a concise summary of *The Council and Reunion*, Küng points out that we cannot escape from the dilemma of the sinful Church either by setting its 'holy' members apart or by distinguishing between a 'holy' Church and its sinful members or even by distinguishing between 'holy' and sinful parts of the individual Christian. The Church is a Church of sinners, and these sinners are undivided and indivisible human beings, while 'in actual and real terms there is no ideal Church floating above the human world, there is no such thing as a Church without members' (*Church*, pp. 322–323). Yet the Church is 'holy': which means set apart by God for his mysterious purposes. But, Küng notes, there has been a shift between the Old and New Testament understanding of holiness (*Church*, p. 325):

> In comparison with Old Testament usage, the New Testament significantly leaves the material element out of account. There is no reference to holy places or objects specially set apart. Even baptism and the Lord's Supper are not referred to as 'holy'. They do not of themselves create holiness in a magic or automatic way, but are totally dependent on a holy God on the one hand and the human response of faith on the other. The New Testament knows nothing of institutional sanctity, of a sacred 'it'; it does not speak of a Church which invests as many of its institutions, places, times and implements as possible with the attribute 'holy'. The only kind of holiness at issue here is a completely *personal* sanctity. It is the believers who have been set apart from the sinful world by God's saving act in Christ and have entered a new Christian existence who make up the original '*communio sanctorum*'; they constitute the Church of the saints and hence the holy Church. The Church is holy by being called by God in Christ to be the communion of the faithful, by accepting the call to his

service, by being separated from the world and at the same time embraced and supported by his grace.

Holiness, too, is in this way a challenge to the Church rather than something it can lean back and luxuriate in the possession of: a Church that is at one and the same time justified and sinful, that from patristic times has been called a chaste whore, is inevitably a Church that stands in continual need of reform and renewal.

The condition for these first three dimensions of the Church can only be found in the fourth: 'The Church can only be truly one, holy and catholic if it is in all things an *apostolic* Church' (*Church*, p. 344). But the apostolic office as a whole is 'unique and unrepeatable' (*Church*, p. 354): 'The decisive thing about the apostles is their personal meeting with the Lord, whom they all, in one form or another, knew as someone who had been dead and was alive again.' From this point of view there can be no successors to the apostles in their role of direct witnesses and messengers of the risen Lord. But though the apostles themselves are dead the apostolic mission and the apostolic ministry remain. To the question: 'Who are the followers or successors of the apostles?' there can only be one basic answer: the Church. 'The whole Church, not just a few individuals, is the follower of the apostles' (*Church*, p. 355). Once again, Küng insists on seeing the Church first as a community before looking at the differentiation of function and role and ministry within that community (*Church*, p. 356): 'The Church is apostolic, is a true follower of the apostles, when it preserves in all its members continuing agreement with the witness of the apostles, and also preserves a vital continuity with the ministry of the apostles.'

This need to preserve continuity with the original apostolic witness and ministry provides the basic justification for the emergence of the various forms of ministry in the different Churches: bishops and deacons in the Pauline Churches with their Gentile Christian communities, elders or presbyters in Jewish Christian communities. The two traditions coalesced to give us the classic ministerial structure of bishop, presbyter and deacon which, aided by the powerful advocacy of Ignatius of Antioch, fairly quickly established itself as the norm. With the realization that it was not just a question of a brief period of existence before its risen Lord returned but that it would live on with its origins becoming more and more distant in time, the Church needed to remain determinedly faithful to the original apostolic testimony in order to avoid the danger of losing touch with its origins and becoming absorbed into the all-absorbing world of syncretistic Hellenism (*Church*, p. 425):

> Any factors which could help to preserve the original tradition and to preserve contact with the origins of the Church took on a new importance in this new situation. These included not only the original gospel writings, but also the special commissioning of ministries intended to preserve the original apostolic testimony. Such ministries could make a vital contribution towards preserving and bringing to fruition in the post-apostolic communities the original tradition of the Gospel of Jesus Christ; something which was especially important at a time when heretical confusion was widespread, when the communities were growing in size, but many of their individual members were losing their original zeal.

But these pastoral ministries, as Küng prefers to call them (*Church*, p. 428), were not and are not exercised in a vacuum. Earlier in the book he has drawn attention to the continuing charismatic structure of the Church, to the fact that the Spirit bestows a variety of gifts which serve to build up the community (*Church*, pp. 179–191). The word 'charismatic' all too easily conjures up the weirder and more emotional phenomena recorded in the New Testament and fostered by the charismatic movement in our own day; but the charisms listed by Paul include such everyday gifts as service, teaching, helping and administration – who on earth would describe an administrator as charismatic? – while the 'still more excellent way', the best and greatest of the charisms, revealed by Paul at the conclusion of his list of charisms turns out to be 'the least sensational, the most everyday of gifts: love' (*Church*, p. 183).

The job of the Church's pastoral ministries thus turns out to be not to suppress or ignore the charismatic ministries exercised by all the members of the Church but to maintain them in harmonious order, to prevent the Spirit-fed ferment within the Church from spilling over into the kind of unholy dissension that meant Paul had to intervene at Corinth – and that a generation later or even sooner, depending on one's dating of the documents, led to the intervention of the Church of Rome with the letter we know as 1 Clement. These ministries, in particular the ministries of bishops and priests, ministries to which people are commissioned or ordained by the laying on of hands (which of course ought as a rule to involve the recognition of an existing charism), are thus seen as normal but not absolutely necessary, in the sense that in certain emergency situations the Church could dispense with them (*Church*, pp. 442–443):

> Our examination of the Pauline constitution of the Church showed that a charismatic ordering of the community without any special appointing of ministries (such as ordination) is perfectly possible; in Corinth there were neither *episkopoi* nor presbyters, nor ordination, but, apart from the apostle, only freely expressed charisms. Despite this, the Church at Corinth was a community provided with everything that was necessary, equipped with the preaching of the word, baptism, the Lord's Supper and all kinds of ministries. At the same time, as we have seen, there

are good reasons why at a relatively early stage there were *episkopoi* and deacons in the Pauline communities, and, after Paul's death, appointed presbyters, with the result that the presbyterial-episcopal Church constitution soon established itself throughout the Church as a whole. By speaking here of other ways into the pastoral ministry and into this special apostolic succession, it is not of course suggested that we should overthrow the whole existing constitution of the Church and go back to Corinth.

And yet one thing must be stressed: the later Church cannot simply and totally exclude the Pauline constitution. While it is unlikely ever to become a norm for the Church, this view of the Church might, even today, be of importance for certain missionary situations.

As examples Küng cites a concentration camp, a remote prison from which there is no possibility of escape, or an extreme missionary situation such as that of Communist China (at a time when it was most hostile to outside contacts and influence). But, as I have already noted (pp. 104–105 above), he does not mention the one example when something like this seems to have happened – the formation of the Church in Korea at the end of the eighteenth century. Admittedly, the Koreans did not adopt the Corinthian model of what on Küng's account seems to have been ministerial anarchy or a free-for-all, but instead chose to appoint and ordain their own bishops and priests without any contact (because no contact was possible) with the Church's official ministry. This historical example would no doubt have sharpened the questions Küng puts as to the validity of the sacraments celebrated by a Christian who steps in and acts as a pastor in the absence of officially ordained ministers. 'These are at least debatable questions,' he comments in a surprisingly mild conclusion. But Rome did not seem to think so. In its 1975 declaration which was then understood to have brought to an end the proceedings

against *The Church* and *Infallible?* the Doctrinal Congregation remarked that 'the opinion suggested by Professor
Küng in his book *The Church* whereby the eucharist can at
least in cases of necessity be validly celebrated by those who
are baptized but lack ordination to the priesthood cannot be
reconciled with the teaching of the Fourth Lateran and
Second Vatican Councils'.

The emergence of the classic threefold ministry of
bishop, priest and deacon came about comparatively
rapidly, even if Ignatius of Antioch should perhaps be read
as evidence more for how it was felt the Church should be
organized than for how it was actually organized at that
time. But the emergence of the papacy takes us that much
further from the Church's origins. The Petrine ministry in
any unambiguous form only developed a very considerable
time indeed after the New Testament period. The
questions surrounding it, as Küng notes, are historical
ones, the solving of which 'is going to be a fairly exacting
task': 'Are there grounds for assuming the primacy of
Peter? Was the primacy of Peter something that was to
continue? Is the bishop of Rome the successor of the
primacy of Peter?' (*Church*, pp. 462 and 456). While
Orthodox and Protestant theologians may remain uncon-
vinced by Catholic arguments on these questions, they
cannot, according to Küng, dispute that the ministerial
primacy of a single person is not contrary to scripture
(*Church*, p. 462).

What is decisive, however, is the pragmatic, empirical
question: 'Does it work?' Küng writes (*Church*, p. 463):

> The decisive thing is not the historical aspect of a
> proven succession, however valuable that may be.
> The decisive thing is succession in the Spirit: in the
> Petrine mission and task, in the Petrine witness and
> ministry. If someone could prove conclusively that his
> predecessor and the predecessor of his predecessor
> and so on backwards were ultimately successors of
> Peter, even if he could prove that the original pre-

decessor of all his predecessors had been 'appointed' by Peter himself and invested as Peter's successor with all rights and duties, and yet on the other hand he completely fails to fulfil the Petrine mission, if he does not carry out the task it implies, if he does not give witness or perform his ministry, what use to him, what use to the Church is all the 'apostolic succession'? Conversely, if there were someone whose succession, at least in its earliest years, were difficult to establish, whose 'appointment' two thousand years ago was not at all documented, but who on the other hand fulfilled the Petrine ministry as described in Scripture and performed this ministry for the Church, would it not be a secondary, if still important, question whether this real servant of the Church had a regular ancestral tree? He might not have a commission through the laying-on of hands, but he would have the charism, the charism of governing, and that would basically be enough.

The point we are trying to make is this: it is not the claims, the 'rights', the 'chain of succession' as such which are decisive, but the exercise and carrying out of a ministry in practice, service in action.

What the world saw in John XXIII was not someone with a legitimate claim to be the successor of Peter but someone who fulfilled the Petrine ministry. 'And this kind of legitimacy,' comments Küng, 'is more decisive for the Petrine ministry than any other.'

Above all Küng is concerned with the ecumenical implications of the question (*Church*, p. 464):

It is an absurd situation that the Petrine ministry, which was intended, as Catholics in particular see it, to be a rock-like and pastoral ministry, preserving and strengthening the unity of the Church, should have become a gigantic, apparently immovable, insuperable and impassable block of stone barring the way to mutual understanding between the Christian Churches.

Devoting even more effort to the scriptural and historical aspects of the problem is not likely to bring about any greater agreement unless there is already greater agreement about the role of the papacy. In other words, Küng seems to be arguing, if the model of the papacy we wish to justify is that of Pius IX we shall not get very far, but if it is that of John XXIII there is hope.

The question thus becomes whether there is a way forward in finding the way back from the primacy of dominion which in practice the papacy has become to the old primacy of service and ministry which it originally was and which is in keeping with the gospel. This would involve a voluntary renunciation of the power that has become associated with the papacy (*Church*, p. 472):

> Without this reununciation of power the reunion of the divided Christian Churches is as impossible as a radical renewal of the Catholic Church according to the Gospel.

Once again, reunion and reform go together as they did in John XXIII's programme for the Council. And this renunciation is only possible if we grasp what the message of Jesus is about, and particularly the challenge of the sermon on the mount.

Revealingly, Küng here presents Paul as the model of the apostle who understood this aspect of what is demanded by the gospel. He suggests it would be a tremendous gain both for the Church and for the Petrine ministry if the latter could take Paul as its exemplar. Indeed, in his view one reason for the Petrine ministry degenerating into a Petrine dominion has been because Paul has not been regarded as highly as Peter. Moreover, the image of Peter too has become distorted by forgetting that the three great promises to him recorded in the gospels are each balanced by three serious failures on his part. These, he suggests, should be written up in gold on black in St Peter's in Rome to balance the promises inscribed there in black on gold (*Church*, pp. 474–475).

But the question remains whether the kind of Petrine ministry Küng is describing is so far removed from what actually happens in Rome that he has taken off into the realm of fantasy. 'Are we here describing an ideal?' he asks. 'Have we finally ceased to talk about the *real* Church? Is the real Petrine ministry not still, as it has always been, a Petrine dominion?' His answer, given 'with all due caution', is that once again the primacy of service is now being realized (*Church*, p. 477). But even in the warm after-glow of the Council there is still a formidable list of reforms he would regard as necessary to restore the humility, simplicity, brotherliness and freedom demanded by the gospel. These questions of practical reform are spelled out in greater detail in two subsequent works which can be read as pendants to *The Church*: *Truthfulness* and *Why Priests?* For the moment he is concerned with establishing the Petrine ministry not as the obstacle to unity it can now appear but as the focus of unity. But, he warns (*Church*, p. 480), however much the Petrine ministry may be a rock for the Church, its unity and its coherence, it cannot be turned into a criterion for deciding what is Church and what is not Church, just as tradition cannot be a dividing line between orthodoxy and heterodoxy nor the Bible be turned into a quarry for stones to be hurled at others.

9

The Struggle Begins

In general *The Church* met with a warm and enthusiastic welcome. For many Catholics it came as a refreshing confirmation that a scriptural and common-sense view of the Church was legitimately Catholic. It provided a firm theological basis for the understanding of the Church that had been implicit in the more radical achievements of Vatican II. For non-Catholics it was equally refreshing. It suggested that the fundamental theological agreement that is essential if organic Christian unity is ever to come about might in some respects be closer than anyone had dared hope. Nowadays we have got used to the discovery by the Anglican/Roman Catholic International Commission of 'substantial agreement' on such issues as the eucharist, ministry and ordination, and even to a remarkable degree on authority in the Church. But at the time Küng's book appeared such issues still loomed as apparently insuperable doctrinal obstacles to closer relations between the Catholic and Anglican communions, and a similar situation prevailed in ecumenical relations between Rome and other non-Catholic Churches. Küng indeed dedicated the English edition of his book to Dr Michael Ramsey, then Archbishop of Canterbury. 'This will record my humble hope that there lies within the pages of this book a theological basis for a *rapprochement* between the Churches of Rome and Canterbury,' he wrote in his preface to the English edition (*Church*, p. xii). However, Küng's book does not seem to have played a direct part in the deliberations of ARCIC, even though it is still significant for that

153

commission's work because of its achievement in expressing the ecclesiological climate of opinion which made ARCIC's work possible. Thus the new emphasis on the local Church, expressed by Küng by saying that the local Church is not the whole Church but none the less fully represents it (*Church*, p. 85), changed the whole ecclesiological picture in a way that could much more easily be reconciled with Anglican traditions.

Naturally, there were those who had their misgivings about the book. In particular, it aroused the suspicion of the Doctrinal Congregation, the former Holy Office, in Rome. The German edition of *The Church* appeared in April 1967, and the Dutch translation shortly afterwards. At the end of November the Doctrinal Congregation decided that the diocese of Rottenburg should be rebuked for having given the book an *imprimatur* and that the author should be asked to stop further distribution of the book and its translation into other languages until he had had talks with representatives to be named by the Congregation. This decree was communicated to the Bishop of Rottenburg on 19 December, and from Rottenburg it reached Hans Küng (by express letter sent to him both at Sursee and at Tübingen) two days after Christmas. His reaction was to get on the 'phone the next day to his publishers in Paris, London and New York to urge them to speed up publication of the French and English translations: the English and American editions are indeed dated 1967, though they actually appeared early in 1968. The French translation was published in 1968, as was the Spanish; and the Italian in 1969, followed in due course by a Portuguese version. The Roman authorities were thus not very successful in putting a stop to the book's diffusion, though in 1971 the nunciature in Seoul was able to prevent a Korean edition appearing.

In May 1968, in the middle of the univerity term, Küng received an invitation to attend a discussion of his book at the Doctrinal Congregation in Rome at 9.30 a.m. five days hence. The letter, dated 30 April, reached him on a Saturday, 4 May, and the date the Congregation had fixed was 9 May. Küng decided to teach the Roman authorities a lesson about expecting university teachers to drop everything in mid-term and rush off to Rome at less than a week's notice. He waited until the day before he was due in Rome to send a telegram: 'Sorry can't make it letter follows.' The telegram clearly stung. It was reproduced as exhibit 2 in the thick wad of documentation (weighing two and a half pounds) issued by the German bishops on 18 December 1979 to justify the withdrawal of Küng's *missio canonica*.

The unhealthy interest the former Holy Office was taking in Küng's work was one of a number of symptoms of the rather febrile atmosphere prevailing in the Church at that time, corresponding to the student unrest and general social tension that came to a head in France in the disturbances of May 1968 that came close to toppling de Gaulle's Fifth Republic. 'Progressives' were afraid that the gains of the Council were being nibbled away, 'conservatives' that 'progressives' were diluting the faith to the point of dissolution. 1968 may have begun with the appointment of the 62-year-old Archbishop of Zagreb, Cardinal Franjo Šeper, to succeed 77-year-old Cardinal Alfredo Ottaviani at the head of the Doctrinal Congregation. But it was also the time of increasing dispute over the Dutch Catechism. It was the year when Cardinal Giacomo Lercaro was sacked from his see of Bologna when other, more 'conservative'-minded bishops who had likewise passed the recommended retiring age of seventy-five years were left in possession of their sees. It was the time when the Doctrinal Congregation began investigating the Flemish Dominican Father Edward Schillebeeckx, most probably as a way of getting at the Dutch. It was above all the year when all these tensions and mutual suspicions in the Church exploded in the dispute over *Humanae vitae*, Paul VI's reaffirmation of the traditional condemnation of 'artificial' birth control.

The letter Küng had promised the Doctrinal Congregation duly followed on 30 May. He began graciously enough by welcoming the invitation as demonstrating 'a decisive advance over the procedures that were formerly customary'. He remarked that it was normal for the date for this kind of meeting to be fixed by agreement between the two parties. In his case his workload was such that he had had to turn down an invitation from a Catholic university in the United States to receive an honorary degree. Any meeting would therefore have to be held during the university vacation. But first of all there were six conditions which he felt would need to be met if such a meeting were to be fruitful: the right to see the dossier on him and all the documents in the case; the scrapping of the November 1967 decree calling for a halt to further diffusion of his book; a list of the detailed questions at issue; the names of those who would be taking part in the talks; the talks to be conducted in his native language, German; and the Holy Office to reimburse his expenses – though if they jibbed at that he was quite willing to place his house at Tübingen at their disposal for the meeting. (It is a pity this offer was never taken up. There would have been a pleasant irony in the former Holy Office grilling a theologian in a house where the first thing to strike the visitor's eye on entering is a paperback thriller entitled *Unfehlbarkeit kann tödlich sein* – 'infallibility can be lethal'.)

Some of these demands were conceded. The Congregation implicitly disavowed its November 1967 decree in its 30 April invitation, in which it said it was examining Küng's book, using the present tense and thus implying the process was still going on, whereas in November it spoke of having examined it. In July the Congregation asked Küng to suggest suitable dates and said it would pay his expenses, but refused to let him see his dossier. For his part Küng

said he would be ready to conduct the discussion in any of
the modern languages he spoke, not just in German. Moreover, he was willing to postpone consideration of his
demand to be allowed to see his dossier and all the documents in the case – something the Congregation dismissed
as irrelevant because what was involved was not a trial but a
discussion – until it had been settled whom he would be
talking to and what precisely they would be talking about.
In August he learned who would be taking part in the
discussion: the Belgian Jesuit Edouard Dhanis, one of the
fiercest official critics of the Dutch Catechism; the Dutch
Jesuit Jan Witte, a professor at the Gregorian specializing
in Protestant and ecumenical theology; and the American
Passionist Barnabas Ahern, a scripture scholar who was
associated with *Concilium* and who is a founder-member of
the international theological commission formed in 1969
and attached to the Doctrinal Congregation. He was
assured that the subjects to be discussed would be communicated to him 'soon'.

But he heard nothing more. Meanwhile the fact that he
was being investigated became known. Indeed, as he had
complained to the Congregation, right-wing Italian papers
considered to have very close relations with certain circles
of the Roman Curia had been saying that what was being
investigated was his alleged heretical attitude. The following year Bishop Carlo Colombo, who was widely regarded
as Paul VI's personal theologian, was under the impression
that Küng had rejected talks with the Congregation and
that this alleged rejection was a well-known fact – imputations Küng indignantly refuted in a letter to the head of the
Concilium organization, a copy of which was passed on to
the Doctrinal Congregation. In response to this Cardinal
Šeper admitted in January 1970 that the fact that the talks
had not yet taken place was due to a number of reasons for
which Küng was not responsible. But he rejected Küng's
suggestion that the Congregation should publicly announce

it was calling a halt to its investigation of *The Church*. Küng
had argued that the investigation had in practice ground to a
halt and that as a gesture of goodwill he was prepared to
forego any more detailed official refutation of the calumnies
circulating against his good name as a Catholic theologian.
Instead Cardinal Šeper promised Küng he would hear more
once the Congregation had published its rules of procedure.

Those did not appear for another year, and it was only in
May 1971 that Küng was sent a copy of them along with
the Congregation's analysis of the difficulties it felt his
book had raised. While acknowledging the book's considerable merits and praising its author's deep learning, powers
of exposition and ecumenical spirit, the Congregation
objected to two points: one concerning the unity of the
Church, the other the necessity of ordination for a valid
celebration of the Eucharist. The first point centred on the
Council's crucial substitution of 'subsists' for 'is' so that it
no longer simply identified the one, holy, catholic and
apostolic Church confessed in the creed with the Catholic
Church in communion with Rome but said that the former
'subsists' in the latter, while recognizing that 'many
elements of sanctification and of truth can be found outside
of her visible structure' (*Lumen gentium* § 8). The Congregation queried Küng's translation of the Latin *subsistit* by
the German *existiert* – the official German translation
approved by the German bishops has *ist verwirklicht*, 'is
realized' or 'is embodied', while the point for English
readers is obscured by the fact that the English translation
of Küng's book (*Church*, p. 283) uses 'subsists' – and his
apparent identification of the ecclesial elements to be found
elsewhere with the (non-Catholic) 'Churches or ecclesial
communities' referred to later in the Council's constitution
(*Lumen gentium* § 15). This, the Congregation felt, could
easily lead one to say that the Church of Christ exists as far
as its principal element is concerned in the Catholic
Church but as far as other elements are concerned in other

Churches or ecclesial communities. It argued that the
'elements' referred to were not the Churches or ecclesial
communities themselves but such things as certain
sacraments or various revealed truths. It thought the idea
whereby the Church of Christ whose unity was broken persisted in all the Churches and ecclesial communities could
appear to have inspired Küng's chapter 'The Church is
One' (*Church*, pp. 263–296).

In other words, the Congregation was accusing Küng of
watering down the Church's exclusive claim to be the one
true Church. But in turn it seemed to be placing insufficient weight on the Council's deliberate shift away from
this exclusive claim as it had been presented in the past by
refusing any longer simply to identify the one Church of
Christ with the Catholic Church. This went along with the
Council's recognition of the churchly character of other
Christian bodies, in place of the former insulting attitude
which tended to regard the Churches of the Reformation as
mere associations of individual heretics. Coupled with the
Council's recognition of the Catholic share in responsibility
for the Reformation and for the schism between East and
West, as well as the new sharp awareness of the sheer
scandal of Christian disunity, these new emphases
developed at Vatican II gave ample legitimation to Küng's
approach to the difficult question of the Church's unity.

The second point, about the possibility of a valid
eucharist being celebrated in an emergency by someone
who had not been ordained, we have already looked at in
connection with its first appearance in *Structures of the
Church* (pp. 102–105 above) and Küng's further treatment
of it in *The Church* (pp. 147–149 above). Remarking that
it was aware that other theologians had followed Küng in
asking whether this might not be possible, the Congregation said, in language that would be closely followed by its
formal public declaration in 1975, that his arguments did
not strike it as valid and that it thought he should have con-

sidered what the magisterium taught on this issue, particularly at the Fourth Lateran Council, Trent, and Vatican II. Trent, interestingly enough, is not mentioned in 1975.

Both points raised by the Congregation were answered by Küng in a letter to Cardinal Šeper dated 21 June 1971. His interpretation of *subsistit* by *existiert* was based on the interpretation he had elicited at the Council from Mgr Gérard Philips of Louvain, who was second secretary of the Council's doctrinal commission. In support he quoted Aloys Grillmeier from the standard German commentary on the Council documents. On the second point he stressed the historical datum that there seemed to have been no ordained priests in the infant Church at Corinth (which, as we know from Paul's epistle, certainly celebrated the eucharist), and said he would be grateful for any serious proof of the presence of an ordained presbyter in that city. Again he quoted the standard German commentary on the Council documents, this time Joseph Feiner on the decree on ecumenism talking about the need to regard neither Catholic nor Protestant understanding of the sacraments as something final and complete.

But from the point of view of the future development of his dispute with the Congregation what was more important was his profound dissatisfaction with the Congregation's rules of procedure. 'Despite improvements in detail which I gladly recognize,' he wrote, 'these are in no way free from the spirit of the Inquisition and in any case lag far behind the very moderate demands put forward by 1360 professors of theology from all over the world in their statement calling for freedom for theology.' Under the Congregation's procedure, it would normally appoint two experts to examine suspect writings or speeches, and the report of their findings would then be passed on to a *relator pro auctore*, another expert appointed by the Congregation to put the author's case: all this would then be discussed and voted on by the Congregation's consultors before being passed on to one of the regular meetings of the cardinals attached to the Congregation. If false or dangerous opinions were discovered, the author's bishop would be informed and the author asked to provide an answer within a month, with the possibility of his being invited to a discussion with representatives appointed by the Congregation. Any final decision by the Congregation in response to all this would need to be approved by the pope.

For their part the 1360 theologians had stressed the need for the Congregation not to appear biased in favour of one particular theological school. They called for its consultors to be appointed from among professional theologians generally acknowledged as outstanding, and for a limited term of office. Any examination of somebody's writings should be based on the authentic original publications in the author's own language. A *relator pro auctore* should be appointed by the Congregation right from the start. The author should be informed in writing of all the doctrines objected to or disapproved of, together with all relevant documents, and should reply in writing. If his answer was not satisfactory, the question should be examined by a team of two or more distinguished professional theologians, half of whom would be appointed by the author himself. If after all this a discussion with the author were thought necessary, he was to be informed in good time who he would be talking to and what they would be talking about and be given the complete texts of all relevant reports and documents: he was to be allowed to speak in whichever language he chose and to bring a fellow-theologian as his stand-by and support. Nor could he be bound to secrecy. If after all this the Congregation thought it had been proved unambiguously that the doctrines objected to clearly contradicted the Church's genuinely binding formulations of belief and jeopardized many people's faith, then 'the Congregation must publicly refute these doctrines and repel them by argument'. Finally, any administrative or economic measures taken against authors and publishers, over and above such a public refutation, should be avoided as being usually useless 'or even harmful' (*The Tablet*, 4 January 1969, p. 21). The statement was originally drawn up and signed by thirty-eight theologians associated with *Concilium*, among them, besides Küng himself, Chenu, Congar, Metz, Rahner, Ratzinger (later as Cardinal Archbishop of Munich to emerge as one of Küng's chief opponents but then still dean of the theological faculty at Tübingen), and Schillebeeckx.

The difference between the Congregation's and Küng's views of how it should conduct its proceedings proved unbridgeable. Comparing the Congregation's rules of procedure with those normal in states acknowledging the rule of law showed that the Congregation's procedures must still regrettably be described as inquisitorial and discriminatory, Küng wrote to Cardinal Šeper. 'I regard it as my duty formally to maintain and reaffirm my fundamental misgivings about such a procedure,' he added.

There was thus never any question of Küng refusing to go to Rome. Indeed, he was even willing to take part in a discussion quite apart from any formal investigation of his work, if the Congregation were willing to follow his suggestion and formally bring to an end the proceedings they had started, he wrote in his letter of 1 June 1970 to Cardinal Šeper. But what he was concerned about was being given a fair hearing if he went to Rome. The Congregation might say it was merely a discussion, but as far as he was concerned his book and his orthodoxy were on trial. Nor was there much ground for optimism about how such a discussion or trial would be conducted. The late 1960s saw one of those periodic bursts of activity by the Doctrinal Congregation that have punctuated the Church's history since the Council rather like the eruptions of some dormant volcano. Its most prominent victim was Monsignor Ivan Illich, then founder and director of the Intercultural Centre

of Documentation at Cuernavaca, Mexico, an organization
begun to train North American priests and religious for
work in Latin America. He was summoned to Rome in
June 1968 and presented with an 85-point questionnaire
which included such loaded questions as: 'What do you say
about those who say you are "petulant, adventurous,
imprudent, fanatical and hypnotizing, a rebel to any
authority, disposed to accept and recognize only that of the
Bishop of Cuernavaca"?' or: 'Do you think that the so-
called "conciliar aggiornamento" should be an overthrow,
contradiction [of] and battle against the traditional past and
against the perennial doctrine of the Catholic Church?'
The upshot was that in January 1969 the Doctrinal Congregation banned priests, nuns, brothers and deacons
from visiting the Centre and taking part in any of its
activities.[1]

Meanwhile by the summer of 1971 the Doctrinal Congregation's proceedings against *The Church* were counter-
pointed by its proceedings against *Infallible?*, which had
come out the year before, and the two sets of proceedings
now ran together. The first stage came to an end with the
publication by the Doctrinal Congregation in July 1973 of
its declaration *Mysterium Ecclesiae*, which did not mention
Küng (or indeed anyone else) by name but which was
clearly aimed at his views. The first and final sections of
this document took up the points the Congregation had
earlier objected to and asked Küng to clarify. Reaffirming
the Council's statements about the Church of Christ sub-
sisting in the Catholic Church (*Lumen gentium* § 8) and
about it being 'through Christ's Catholic Church alone,
which is the general means of salvation, that the fullness of
the means of salvation can be obtained' (*Unitatis redinte-
gratio* § 3), the Congregation reminded Catholics that they
belonged to the Church founded by Christ and led by the
successors of Peter and the apostles. It then went on, in
what is surely a very strained interpretation of what Küng

had written about the Church's unity:

> The followers of Christ are therefore not permitted to
> imagine that Christ's Church is nothing more than a
> collection (divided, but still possessing a certain unity)
> of Churches and ecclesial communities. Nor are they
> free to hold that Christ's Church nowhere really exists
> today and that it is to be considered only an end
> towards which all Churches and ecclesial communi-
> ties must strive.

The final section similarly started with positive statements
about the priesthood of all believers and the ministerial
priesthood before concluding:

> Passing over at this point questions regarding the
> ministers of the various sacraments, the evidence of
> sacred Tradition and of the sacred Magisterium
> makes it clear that the faithful who have not received
> priestly ordination and who take upon themselves the
> office of performing the Eucharist attempt to do so
> not only in a completely illicit way but also invalidly.
> Such an abuse, wherever it may occur, must clearly be
> eliminated by the pastors of the Church.[2]

This still did not answer Küng's point that priestless
Eucharists had taken place in the Corinthian Church and
that such goings-on could not simply be totally excluded by
the later Church.

The Doctrinal Congregation made Küng an offer with
this declaration: if he would subscribe to it and accept its
teaching, then it would drop the proceedings against both
The Church and *Infallible?* Küng responded with a public
statement accusing the Congregation of unfair procedures
redolent of its inquisitorial past and claiming that it had not
answered his questions and arguments. Matters dragged on
until the 1975 declaration, which mentioned only three
specific points in the two books. The difficulty the Congregation had earlier found about Küng's treatment of the
Church's unity no longer seemed to bother it. But it still

argued that Küng's suggestion of a valid 'lay' eucharist in an emergency could not be reconciled with the teachings of the Fourth Lateran and Second Vatican Councils: Trent was no longer mentioned. And besides the specific issue of infallibility it now criticized Küng's views on the Church's magisterium or teaching authority, an issue which could be regarded as applying to both books:

> In fact he does not conform to the true concept of the authentic magisterium, according to which the bishops are genuine 'doctors' in the Church, endowed, that is to say, with the authority of Christ and preaching to the people confided to them that faith which they are to apply in their practical life (*Lumen gentium* § 25). In fact 'the mission of authentically interpreting the Word of God, whether written or otherwise transmitted, is confided to the living magisterium in the Church alone' (*Dei verbum* § 10).[3]

In fact, as we shall see, this is one of the points the Congregation first raised about *Infallible?*, but what it was objecting to could perhaps be read back into the earlier book, particularly in view of his stress on the apostolic succession of the *whole* Church (and hence of every individual member) and on the succession of prophets and teachers in the Church (*Church*, pp. 432–436).

As far as *The Church* was concerned, the 1975 declaration brought matters to an end. The 1979 withdrawal of Küng's *missio canonica* was justified by reference to *Infallible?* and *On being a Christian*. But in the meantime the earlier book had been subjected to the probably more useful criticism of his fellow theologians. Their reactions naturally varied, though few shared the disappointed sympathy expressed by his former teacher in Paris, the Oratorian (and convert from Protestantism) Louis Bouyer. Yves Congar called it a 'significant' and 'original' book that made an extraordinarily rich and constructive contribution to ecclesio-

A Passion for Truth

logy (*Diskussion*, pp. 43–57, 155–175). But the praise was mingled with criticism. Two connected points stand out in particular: Küng's use of scripture; and his apparent neglect of tradition. In both cases Küng is accused of the very faults he has always been at pains to warn against. His concentration on the gospel as the ultimate criterion against which all developments in the Church's life or doctrine must be judged can give the impression that he is short-circuiting the whole messy, involved, untidy but necessary history of the Church's continual struggle to live out the message with which it has been entrusted. Accusations of neglecting tradition Küng indignantly refutes by citing his constant awareness of and reference to the Church's history and tradition. But what is more to the point is that he adopts a different attitude to the Church's past to that expected of either 'Catholic' or 'Protestant'. He does not regard the Church as bound by its past mistakes. He does not see its history as a linear ratchet-like progression where there can be no going back but only going forward on the basis of positions already reached. Instead he sees the Church's history as a continual circling around the constant focus of the gospel. This immediately makes tradition, however important, essentially secondary to the primary witness of Jesus Christ and his message of salvation. At the same time it avoids the 'Protestant' temptation of scrapping the intermediate development and trying to start again with a clean sheet, whether that clean sheet be the Church of the first four ecumenical councils or the Church before early Catholicism reared its ugly head in the New Testament. The entire past experience of the Church must be taken into account in interpreting the basic primary Christian message.

Criticism of Küng's use of scripture centred on his apparent emphasis on Paul to the seeming neglect of other New Testament writings, particularly Acts and the pastoral epistles. He was in fact accused of the very failings he had earlier exposed in his Protestant colleague Ernst Käsemann.[4] Once again, the charges seem to have left Küng more than a little puzzled and bewildered. Had he not made his position quite clear? He had, after all, laid considerable stress on the need to take the New Testament as a whole instead of picking and choosing (*Church*, p. 19):

> Only if we take the New Testament as a *whole* with *all* its writings as the positive witness of the Gospel of Jesus Christ, can we avoid the temptation to dissociate the contradictory ecclesiological statements of the New Testament, to 'purify' the New Testament message and to make a selection, a *hairesis*, all of which is an attack on the unity of Scripture and of the Church.

What was needed was 'a discriminating study in depth' which would not reject the secondary testimonies of the New Testament canon but which would refuse to attach more importance to them than to primary ones.

But the secondary testimonies tended to remain firmly secondary in Küng's eyes. The real point at issue is Küng's acceptance of the consensus of German biblical scholarship, both Catholic and Protestant. This, for example, means dating Acts between 80 and 85 AD and refusing to ascribe it to a companion of Paul, or refusing to consider the pastoral epistles genuinely Pauline. Küng can start from the conclusion that '1 Corinthians is in content nearer to the Gospel of Jesus himself than James' (*Church*, p. 19) and regard the latter epistle as 'written by a Jew with a hellenistic education probably several decades after the death of James, the brother of the Lord, in 62' and as reflecting 'the situation of a second-generation Christian community' – in contrast to 1 Corinthians (*Church*, p. 294). Yet a number of scholars, most recently the former Bishop of Woolwich, Dr John A. T. Robinson, would date James *before* 1 Corinthians[5] – which would at once give

one a very different picture of the diversity in unity
exhibited by the primitive Church.

Küng is indeed very keenly aware of the dangers lurking
in too discriminatory a handling of the New Testament. He
criticizes those who split up the Church's original history
by opting firmly for one side, nearly always that of Paul.
'And from this apparently secure position,' he writes
(*Church*, p. 416), 'they snipe carefully at Luke and Acts, at
James, at the anonymous writer of the pastoral epistles,
indeed often at Paul himself for not being sufficiently
consistent.' Küng's answer is thus that he takes the whole
New Testament seriously, just as he takes seriously all the
doctrinal formulations which have punctuated the
Church's history at moments when its faith has been
challenged. What is at issue is not whether one should
discard this New Testament writing or that as unevangelical, or this definition or that as not in keeping with the
gospel – for, as Küng has argued many a time, this would
be illegitimate, a sectarian picking and choosing, which is
what *hairesis* really means – but how we are to interpret
this often conflicting mass of testimony. We cannot simply
accept everything on the same level without trying to disentangle the contradictions: that would effectively paralyse
our understanding of this message and our response to it.
We need a guiding thread, a set of hermeneutical
principles. Küng may be open to criticism over the
particular set of hermeneutical principles he is applying,
but what he cannot be criticized for is for having chosen a
particular set.

[1] See 'The Cuernavaca Dossier', *Herder Correspondence*, April
1969, vol. 6 no. 4, pp. 110–119.
[2] Text quoted from *The Tablet*, 14 July 1973, pp. 667–670.
[3] *The Tablet*, 1 March 1975, p. 210.

4 ' "Early Catholicism" in the New Testament as a problem in controversial theology', *The Living Church*, pp. 233–293.

5 John A. T. Robinson, *Redating the New Testament*, SCM Press, London, 1976, p. 54 (1 Corinthians), pp. 135–139 (James). His case for dating the entire New Testament canon *before* 70 AD is very cogently argued and cannot be ignored by anyone wanting to preserve the accepted later dating.

10

Practical Consequences

Küng's vision of the Church was not just a theoretical construct floating free in a theologian's imagination. Not only was it based firmly on the Church's original mandate and message and how it had interpreted these throughout its history, but from time to time Küng's ecclesiology would come down to earth with practical implications of a kind that some can find disturbing. One example is his conclusion (or rather question) about the possibility in an emergency of a valid eucharist in the absence of a duly ordained priest: as we have seen, this was one of the two (or possibly three) points the Doctrinal Congregation found to object to in the book.

But for the most part the practical implications, though clearly present, are not spelled out in *The Church* quite so clearly or in so much detail as they are in two smaller works which can be thought of as pendants to the larger book: *Truthfulness*, which appeared in 1968, and *Why Priests?*, the German original of which appeared in 1971. Both books explicitly refer back to the earlier ecclesiological treatise. In the preface to *Truthfulness* Küng writes (p. 23):

> What is there [in *The Church*] developed − the programme, covered in her origin, of a church which in a new age corresponds to the gospel of Jesus Christ − is given concrete form here in the present book and applied in view of some central post-conciliar problems and of both theoretical and practical tasks.

Similarly the reader of *Why Priests?* is referred to *The*

170

Church for the 'ecclesiological bases' of the later study (*Priests*, p. 11). Both books are concerned with a practical problem: in the one case, the hindrance to the Church's credibility presented by the sheer lack of honesty and truthfulness it can too often display; in the other, the crisis in the ministry that came to a head in the late 1960s and early 1970s.

The main lines of the argument Küng presents in *Truthfulness* had been developed as early as 1964, when during the third session of Vatican II he gave a lecture at the Dutch centre in Rome on this subject, a lecture ending with a series of challenging rhetorical questions asking whether the Church would not be more honest and truthful if it adopted this or that practical reform. But over the four years since then the questions had become even more urgent as the first stages of post-conciliar depression began to set in. Symptomatic were Paul VI's handling of the celibacy issue in his 1967 encyclical *Sacerdotalis caelibatus*, which did at least try to answer the arguments for reform even if it was unable to do so with any degree of conviction, and the pretence that the Church was not considering changing its collective and official mind on the subject of birth control.

Paul VI's claim that the Church's teaching authority was not in a state of doubt but rather in a moment of study and reflection on this issue of birth control seems to have been the final example of lack of honesty that made the English theologian Charles Davis announce in December 1966 that he was leaving the Church because he could find neither concern for truth nor concern for people represented by the official Church, because to his mind 'there is concern for authority at the expense of truth', and because he had come to the painful discovery that he no longer believed in the Roman Catholic Church as an institution.[1] The shock caused by his departure was immense, and not just in England where he could justly be described as that country's foremost Catholic theologian. Küng was as shaken as anyone. He had got to know and like Charles Davis at the Council. His response appeared first as an article in the Swiss Jesuit fortnightly *Orientierung* and was then incorporated as a chapter in *Truthfulness*. But that book was not an answer to Charles Davis, he pointed out (*Truthfulness*, p. 75), even though its first part anticipated many of the English theologian's questions. The book in which unwittingly he had expounded the reasons for staying in the Church despite all the difficulties and had answered Charles Davis's concrete questions was in fact *The Church* (*Truthfulness*, p. 88).

Nevertheless, *Truthfulness* can still be read as Küng's response to what for many people, particularly in the English-speaking world, was the major issue raised by Charles Davis's departure and the reasons he gave for going: the deplorable lack of intellectual honesty and the contempt for truth and truthfulness too often displayed by the official Church and its spokesmen. The issue occurs in its acutest form when the Church changes its collective mind and at the same time pretends that it has not really done so. Küng devotes a couple of pages to setting side by side 'errors' condemned by Pius IX's Syllabus of 1864 and the assertions of Vatican II. The change is not something that can be explained as a 'development': the later teaching is hardly a more developed version of the first but rather a contradiction of it. The first example shows this clearly (*Truthfulness*, p. 171):

> The affirmation of modern progress, of modern liberal achievements and of modern civilization, by the *Pastoral Constitution on the Church in the Modern World* (1965), cannot possibly be understood as 'development' of that teaching of 1864 in which the [following] proposition was solemnly *condemned*: 'The Roman Pontiff can and should reconcile and harmonize himself with progress, with liberalism, and

with modern civilization' (DS 2980).

Similarly Vatican II's affirmation of freedom of religion is neither explicitly nor implicitly contained in Pius IX's condemnation of freedom of religion – and Küng would have made the point even more sharply if he had gone back a few years and quoted Gregory XVI's 1832 encyclical *Mirari vos* which described the idea of affirming and defending freedom of conscience as not just absurd and erroneous but raving lunacy (DS 2730). Küng asks why the Catholic Church should be ashamed of having learned something and of having changed for the better, why it should be ashamed of being capable of *metanoia*, that radical conversion of heart and mind called for by the gospel.

But does not facing up to the Church's past mistakes and admitting both that they have been made and that some of them have been serious ones, does not this somehow cast doubt on the promise of the guidance of the Holy Spirit, on the Church's essential indefectibility in the truth, on its infallibility? Küng's answer already summarizes the thesis he was to put forward two years later in *Infallible?* (*Truthfulness*, pp. 182–183):

> Infallibility in this radical sense means a *basic persistence of the church in truth, which is not destroyed by errors in detail.*
>
> Anyone whose trust in God and in his Spirit is not superficial, rationalist, but profoundly Christian, believes unshakably that the Spirit of God will maintain the church in the truth of the gospel, *in spite* of all errors and *through* all errors. This is the great miracle of the Holy Spirit of God in the church: not that no errors occur – where then would be the humanity of the church of men? – but that the church, in spite of all her defection from God, is never dropped by God, never abandoned by God; that, in spite of all sins and errors of popes, bishops, priests, theologians and laymen, she did not perish like the

dynasties of the Pharaohs and the Roman Empire of
the Caesars, but continues to be sustained by God in
the Spirit throughout the centuries and – even after
long periods of decadence – is led to ever new life and
new truth.

Already, too, the rejection of infallibility in the sense in
which it is usually understood is coupled with a passionate
belief in the essential indestructability of the Church.

Nor is it only *Infallible?* that *Truthfulness* looks forward
to. The final chapter opens up the whole question of
whether life itself makes any sense for late twentieth-
century man who is trapped in 'the contradictions of a
society which, in an unparalleled triumph of technology,
reaches for the stars and yet is still not capable of solving
the most primitive problems of the earth' such as the
glaring inequality and injustice and cruelty that prevails
over too much of the globe, and who, as Kafka had pro-
phetically described, 'feels that he is abandoned to
authorities, anonymous powers, which rule the world as
hidden and yet everywhere present, who suffers from up-
rootedness and estrangement, . . . and who can no longer
discover any meaning in paradoxical human existence'
(*Truthfulness*, pp. 208 and 209).

These questions receive a fuller treatment in *On being a
Christian* and *Does God Exist?* For the moment Küng's
concern is to point out that only a truthful Church can
hope to offer any kind of answer, not by offering modern
man merely pie in the sky, not by suggesting cheap solutions to his private or social problems, but by enabling him
to accept his responsibility and to act on it, by showing him
the reason for his responsibility and helping to banish his
fear and despair, by giving him somewhere to stand and
offering him clues as to where he comes from and where he
is going, why things are as they are and what the purpose of
it all is (*Truthfulness*, p. 213).

And for the untruthful Church to be converted into the

truthful Church there is needed a reform and renewal of its institutions and structures. The renewal called for and made possible by Vatican II must be put into practice in each individual country, along the lines pioneered by the Dutch with their national pastoral council. There must be a general renewal of theology, with complete freedom for theologians to do their work and with trust and co-operation between theologians and bishops. There must be a living reform of the liturgy along the lines laid down, not a relapse into a new form of the old rigidity. There should be a thorough and radical revision of canon law. There must be a voice for all members of the Church in the affairs of the Church at local, diocesan, national and international level, through representative bodies on the lines of parish councils, diocesan and national pastoral councils, and at the international level a council of laity parallel to the synod of bishops, but all this with 'a good system of checks and balances' and with the final authority of the parish priest, bishop and pope expressly maintained 'in order to avoid a general paralysis of the different forces'. There should be free election of the appropriate superiors, such as parish priests, bishops, and the pope, by representatives of the Churches concerned, and there should be serious consideration of election for a limited period only of, say, six or eight years with the possibility of re-election. There should be a scrapping of the obligation of clerical celibacy, which should be left to the individual's free decision, while recognizing that the place of celibacy is the religious life and that something which cannot be a universal law for the Church's ministry makes sense particularly for a religious community serving its fellow men and women. There should be a thorough reform of the Roman Curia, together with a re-examination of the need for the papal diplomatic service as at present constituted and the abolition of Vatican court titles and orders. There should be a more rational division of dioceses coupled with decentralization and reorganization, with in large cities teams of bishops each with a specific pastoral responsibility, along lines that in fact were independently followed when the archdiocese of Westminster was reorganized in 1976. There should be an upgrading of the position of women in the Church together with a serious examination of the concrete conditions for ordaining women – something against which, Küng notes, 'no biblical or dogmatic arguments can be raised'. On the ecumenical front there should be mutual recognition of baptism without reservations (something which has been the case in England and Wales since 1972), and the mixed marriage problem should be settled by recognizing the validity of *all* mixed marriages and by allowing the parents to decide in conscience which Church their children shall be baptized and brought up in. Finally, with regard to the Church's role in the world at large, Küng suggests 'deliberately unpretentious and realistic undertakings to enable Christians to contribute to the solution of important problems of the time wherever and in so far as the gospel of Jesus Christ itself is unambiguously involved (the racial question, over-population, reconciliation of nations, social distress, and so on)'. This he sees not as a question of institutionalizing everything the Church undertakes in the secular sphere but rather as 'acting as a mobile "fire-service" wherever and as long as a special effort is required' (*Truthfulness*, pp. 218–232).

A detailed programme of reform like this could leave even Küng's well-wishers feeling a little breathless and, given the yawning gap between his proposals and the Church as it actually was and is, more than a little despondent. To those satisfied with things as they were it could appear both irrelevant and irritating. In this way Hans Küng did not help his future career in the Church when he started acting on the proposals he had put forward. His intervention in 1967 when the Holy See started taking what he saw as an unhealthy interest in the election of a new bishop of Basle was seen by official circles as stirring things up to no good purpose and causing unnecessary complications. Even less popular was his reaction to *Matrimonia mixta*, the *motu proprio* Paul VI issued in April 1970 to regulate mixed marriages. That document not merely continued the tradition of according only a grudging toleration to mixed marriages but also continued to insist that to be valid a mixed marriage had to be solemnized before a Catholic priest. While a dispensation was possible from this requirement (known as the canonical form), what was not allowed was a joint Catholic-Protestant ceremony or having two ceremonies, one Catholic, one Protestant. In addition, a dispensation was still in any case required for a mixed marriage as such, and without it the marriage would be illicit – unless the non-Catholic partner had not been baptized, in which case it would be invalid. The insistence on the canonical form for validity means that a mixed marriage contracted without the Church's permission in a registry office or Protestant or Anglican church is simply not recognized as existing by the Church. Among other things this means that if the marriage subsequently breaks down the divorced Catholic partner is regarded by the Church as unmarried and there is no obstacle to him or her contracting a valid Catholic marriage: to the outsider (and to many inside the Catholic Church) this does not seem a particularly honest way of bearing witness to the indissolubility of marriage. There is, moreover, a growing number of Catholics who drift away from the Church or break with it and who contract marriages which for this reason of the canonical form are technically invalid, and this can be seen as yet another obstacle to the Church's ability to reach such people.

Küng's reaction took the form of an article in the *Frankfurter Allgemeine Zeitung* and in the *Neue Zürcher Nachrichten* advocating a do-it-yourself policy of creative lawbreaking. In the article, which appeared in translation in

Britain, France, and Italy and thus reached a wider audience than merely the Germans and Swiss, Küng argued that a fundamental solution of the mixed marriage question would have had to include the recognition of the validity of all mixed marriages, with or without the canonical form; an ecumenical marriage rite that took the other Church seriously as an equal partner; and leaving a decision about how the children were to be baptized and brought up to the conscience of the couple concerned. He disputed the right of Church leaders to decide which marriages were valid and which invalid (*The Tablet*, 30 May 1970, p. 519):

> Now, finally, the fundamental question must be raised as to the real source from which Church leaders derive the right to decide the validity and invalidity of marriages [in this way]. In the light of modern theology such a right seems impossible to substantiate.

In view of 'the millions of human beings hard-pressed in conscience and defamed by an irresponsible ecclesiastical legislation', Küng wrote, it was no longer possible to wait in patience for a solution more than ten years after the Second Vatican Council was convoked and more than five years after its close. (It was in fact just over four years since the Council concluded – one of Küng's rare lapses.) What he suggested was what so many bishops had been recommending over birth control: 'Act according to conscience, particularly since this law itself attaches so great an importance to the responsibility of conscience.' Priests were urged to exploit as much as possible the scope afforded by the law and even to go against the marriage regulations for the benefit of those getting married. He even speculated on parish priests in the German-speaking world following the practice which he said was quite common elsewhere, particularly in the United States, of simply not bothering to apply for a dispensation.

This stung the German bishops' conference into issuing a brief statement in reply. They found it incomprehensible that a Catholic theologian should have not only taken a polemical and in parts offensive stand but should not have shrunk from publicly advocating breaking the law. Acting contrary to the prescriptions of a document that corresponded to the views of the bishops of the world as well as did the *motu proprio* on mixed marriages could not honestly serve the cause of Church reform, they said.

Clearly Küng had done nothing to endear himself to the German bishops' conference. Nor did some of his fellow-theologians see eye to eye with his blunt approach. In an open letter the French Dominican Yves Congar suggested that Küng saw the jug half empty when he saw it half full: this, he said, was always the difference between the reformist and the revolutionary. After gently taking issue with him on the detailed points he raised, Congar concluded with regard to Küng's appeal to Catholics to ignore the law (*The Tablet*, 25 July 1970, p. 726):

> My dear Küng, you are very sure of yourself. Are you not pushing the valuation of your theological gift very far? Do you believe that the pastors responsible are so badly informed or retrograde on this point that they speak without a valid foundation? Or is it rather a question of ecclesiology? You bluntly suggest it. The question then takes on monumental proportions and is obviously beyond the scope of a letter and of a newspaper.

In reply Küng said that Congar too had long before been described as a revolutionary because he was not satisfied with a half-filled glass when it would have been so easy to fill it to the brim – and anyway the revolutionary did not see the glass as half-empty rather than half-full, he threw it down instead. Küng stressed that he had been speaking from his pastoral experience more than from theological reflection. Recent decisions on mixed marriages, birth control and celibacy he regarded as not just theologically false but also, and particularly, pastorally harmful. On none of these would it be possible to maintain the negative Roman decisions. But above all Küng saw these decisions and the disputes they gave rise to as diverting the Church from its proper task: 'Why have we constantly to be grappling afresh in the Church with secondary questions which torment people so grievously . . ., instead of getting involved in God's great cause with men?' he asked (*The Tablet*, 15 August 1970, pp. 782–783).

However, irritated as they may have been by Küng's reaction to the *motu proprio*, the German and Swiss bishops then went ahead and interpreted it for application in their respective countries in a way that won Küng's approval. Dispensations for mixed marriages were to be granted by the parish priest, with the right of appeal to the bishop. The promise to bring the children up as Catholics applied 'as far as this is possible in the actual circumstances of their marriage', while there was an explicit recognition of the non-Catholic's obligation in conscience 'to act in accordance with what his faith tells him is true'. The Swiss bishops were even clearer on this point: 'To do what is possible under the circumstances means expressing oneself sincerely and, while appreciating the reasons and conscientious conviction of the other partner, to make a decision which both can approve.' There was provision for the non-Catholic minister to take part in the wedding ceremony and *vice versa*. These points, Küng noted, amounted to a considerable difference from the papal decree (*The Tablet*, 21 November 1970, p. 1137):

> The bishops deserve the sincere thanks of all concerned for devoting themselves to the needs of partners in a mixed marriage and their priests, for seeking better solutions together with the Evangelical Churches in a truly ecumenical spirit and responsibility, and finally for deciding on concrete steps that

go far beyond the Roman decree and for the future
spare the partners and the priests involved the moral
dilemmas created by the Church's legal system.

But difficulties still remained. Would it not be logical, now
that dispensations were automatically given for 'mixed
religion' (a Catholic marrying a baptized non-Catholic
Christian), to scrap this impediment altogether? Would it
not also be logical to scrap the promise to bring the children
up as Catholics? This was something the partners had to
decide according to their conscience. And there were, too,
the theological difficulties about the status of marriage as a
sacrament and about the Church's ability to declare a
marriage invalid because of a defect of form.

Why Priests?, which followed in 1971, was concerned
with another of the great practical difficulties the Church
was facing: the crisis in its ministry. This became apparent
particularly in the wake of the Council. The old, rigid
pattern of priesthood now appeared unlivable and
irrelevant, and as yet there seemed to be no new pattern to
put in its place. Priests could no longer see themselves
simply as some kind of magician, as someone whose job it
was to turn bread and wine into the body and blood of Jesus
Christ by uttering the words of consecration and to pro-
nounce the forgiveness of sins. If Vatican II and its
associated theological revolution meant anything, a priest
could not be defined simply by the performance of sacred
acts. Ministry was obviously much, much more than that, a
service that reached out to people in their need; and yet so
often this very reaching out was hampered rather than
helped and encouraged by the Church's structures and
regulations. (A surprising number of laicized priests are
engaged in social work.) In all this celibacy and difficulties
over celibacy formed a symptom rather than a cause. Priests
found, gradually and painfully, that the old framework
could no longer sustain their life. Friendship with a woman
could then develop to provide a new focus and give new

meaning to their life. But usually the breakdown of the old self-sustaining priestly life came first: it does nor normally seem to have been precipitated by a need for female company. Most priests who have left the ministry have got married, but it would thus be wrong to see getting married as the cause of their leaving the ministry: rather it has been a sequel.

The exodus from the ministry became serious in the mid-1960s. In 1963 91 diocesan priests and 76 regulars (members of religious orders) asked to be dispensed from their promise of celibacy and to return to the lay state, but there were apparently no actual laicizations. In 1964 371 diocesan priests and 269 regulars asked for laicization: 200 dispensations were granted to diocesan priests, 115 to regulars. The figures rose steadily to reach 1059 laicizations of diocesan and 1237 of regular priests in 1968, a total of 2296; the following year the total went over 3000; and it reached its peak with 3728 in 1971, dropping back to 3001 in 1975, 2679 in 1976 and 2506 in 1977. Interestingly enough, the proportion of diocesan priests leaving the ministry in 1969 was highest in the West Indies (22.4 per 1000 priests), North America (15 per 1000) and South America (14.8 per 1000), with Europe losing only 3.9 of every 1000 priests. The effect of these 'defections' – the official Vatican term – was a net decrease in the total number of priests year by year.[2] The crisis may not have been more acute in the Netherlands than elsewhere, but it was much better known: the Dutch Church was virtually the only one to publish the numbers of priests leaving the ministry and to admit what was going on, whereas hierarchies elsewhere preferred not to draw attention to these embarrassing statistics and left people to rely first on guess-work and then, when in 1971 the Vatican started publishing annual figures, on their digging them out from this not always easily available source. The number of Dutch diocesan priests leaving the ministry first reached double figures in 1965 with 16, and then rose to a peak of 96 in 1970, while figures for regulars hovered around the 10 mark until they started rising in 1964, reaching 113 in 1967 and 157 in 1969 and again in 1971. Ordinations, meanwhile, declined dramatically: only four diocesan and 43 regular priests were ordained in 1970 compared with 81 diocesan and 156 regular priests in 1965.

To cope with this situation the Church's leaders did nothing except make it somewhat easier for a priest to leave the ministry (until John Paul II halted laicizations completely on his accession in 1978). In January 1970 the Dutch pastoral council voted by overwhelming majorities in favour of making celibacy optional both for new recruits to the ministry and for priests already ordained; and the Dutch bishops, who abstained on this vote in order to be free to make their own position clear, supported the idea of ordaining married men to the priesthood and, in special cases and under certain conditions, reinstating in the ministry married laicized priests. Rome's reaction was to insist on the necessity of maintaining the link between celibacy and priesthood and to drum up support for its stand from other national hierarchies. At the 1971 synod of bishops there was little enthusiasm even for the limited possibility of ordaining older married men to the priesthood: only a minority could be found in favour of this cautious proposal.[3]

It was to this situation of malaise and frustration that Hans Küng spoke in *Why Priests?* – dedicated 'to my brothers in the Church's ministry as an aid in this transitional age'. But it is not just the crisis in the Church alone to which he addresses himself. As a university teacher he was fully aware of the wave of student unrest that swept through universities in the late 1960s, a wave which in its positive aspects expressed a laudable disquiet with a society of mass consumption and high technology that seemed to leave little room for human beings, a society geared to achievement and success that seemed to have little compassion for the inevitable failures that we all are in some aspect or at some stage of our lives. Küng's first chapter thus shows how 'as a non-dominative and non-coercive community, the Church could be a model of the best possible form of democracy' and goes on to consider the Church as a community characterized by liberty, equality and fraternity (*Why Priests?*, pp. 18 and 20–24) – a posthumous canonization of the aims of the French Revolution, whose democratic slogans, as he points out, did not start out as, and were not intrinsically, hostile to the Church. Küng admittedly seems to ignore the great distinction between the Church and any secular democracy, which is that the Church is a voluntary society to which its members only belong because ultimately they want to, whereas everyone belongs willy-nilly to some particular political society and opting out of membership is virtually impossible. In this he may well be reflecting the situation of the German-speaking world, where Church allegiance is something comparatively few reject, and the vast majority continue to be officially identified as members of a particular Church and to support it financially through the institution of the *Kirchensteuer*, the system whereby a small extra percentage is added on to people's income tax to fund the Churches.

Besides pointing to the political implications of the fact that the Church is an anticipatory sign of the definitive reign of God, in this first chapter Küng also established the community nature of the Church as the background against which its ministry must be seen and understood. He then goes on to analyse the criteria which can be deduced from the New Testament for the Church's pattern of ministry and to sketch briefly how this pattern has developed in the Church's history. Finally he sets out the forms that can be taken by the Church's ministry of leadership – what is normally thought of as the episcopate and presbyterate or priesthood – and the elements that are constant and those

that are variable in this ministry. In his view it does not
have to be a full-time ministry, it does not have to be a lifelong task, it does not have to be something that confers a
superior social status, it does not demand a university
education, it does not require celibacy, and it does not have
to be an exclusively male preserve. The constants are that
ministry does not aim at domination of but at service to the
community, that it is not an autocratic form of management
which tries to absorb the other functions and ministries to
be found in the Church, that it is not meant to be a rigid
and uniform pattern but something flexible and able to
adapt itself to differing circumstances, and that it is not
something that men have at their disposal but a response to
the call of God (*Why Priests?*, pp. 54–60 and 60–64).

What emerges from this is basically a plea for genuine
leadership in the Church: the kind of leadership that does
not suppress other people's talents and abilities but enables
them to flourish and encourages them while making sure
that they do not do so at the expense of those of others.
Küng can thus be seen as appealing for creative leadership
in place of the authoritarian insistence on obedience that
too often marks its absence. In his view a good Church
leader is one 'who proclaims the word in his community
with authority', someone who 'can inspire, moderate and
animate his community', and someone who can become 'a
symbolic figure for the community' (*Why Priests?*, pp.
88–90). A lack of false modesty needs to be combined with
a selfless realism and a wholly unpretentious kind of
rectitude (*Why Priests?*, pp. 90–91):

> It is not his [the Church leader's] personal power of
> attraction that is decisive, whatever part it
> (necessarily) plays on this or that actual occasion.
> Instead his clear and unequivocal conviction, definite
> and unambiguous commitment, and greater open-
> ness and availability to the cause [of Jesus Christ] and
> to men make him a clear and shining light.

In this way, despite all his limitations, the Church leader can become a symbolic figure for the community, who not only (like a specialist or expert) arouses men's understanding, observation, experience and reason, but by virtue of an authority emanating from his whole personality – both in his requirements and his assurances – appeals to their emotions, affectivity and passions – in short, to the whole man.

At the same time every individual Church leader cannot be expected to excel in every aspect of what is demanded of him. The decisive thing, Küng remarks, is: 'Does the man at the top really believe what he says? Is he convinced that the way in which he preaches is the right way? Does he really think that the goal he puts before us is actually attainable? *Does he believe?*' It is thus only a profound personal commitment in faith that can serve as the basic principle of the ministry of leadership in the Church (*Why Priests?*, pp. 91–92).

[1] Charles Davis, *A Question of Conscience*, Hodder and Stoughton, London, 1967, p. 16. Paul VI's statement of 29 October 1966, and Charles Davis's reaction in the form of an editorial in the *Clergy Review* of December 1966, are both to be found in Leo Pyle (ed.), *Pope and Pill: more documentation on the birth regulation debate*, Darton, Longman and Todd, London, 1968, pp. 60–62 and 63–66.

[2] *Herder Correspondence*, vol. 6 no. 9, September 1969, p. 273; *Tabularum Statisticarum Collectio 1969*, Vatican Polyglot Press 1971; *Annuarium Statisticum Ecclesiae 1970–1977*, Vatican Polyglot Press 1972–1979.

[3] For the Dutch pastoral council's debate on the celibacy question and the Dutch bishops' response see *Herder Correspondence*, March 1970, pp. 73–84; for the reaction from Rome and elsewhere, ibid. May 1970, pp. 137–148; for Paul VI's highly emotional feelings on the subject, as expressed in a speech in October 1969 during the second synod of bishops, ibid. December 1969 p. 360. For the 1971 synod see Peter Hebblethwaite, *The Runaway Church*, Collins, London, 1975, pp. 51–52 and 62–64.

I I

An Infallible Mistake?

The disquiet and unease so many Catholics dimly felt at the way the Church was failing to live up to the hopes engendered by the Council came to a head with Paul VI's publication of his encyclical *Humanae vitae* at the end of July 1968. More than a decade later, it can be difficult to remember just how much of a shock he inflicted on the Church with his reaffirmation of the traditional condemnation of 'artificial' methods of birth control. 'The Church will have to learn to live with this encyclical,' remarked Hans Küng (*Infallible?*, p. 30); and for the most part that is precisely what it has done. Most lay Catholics, at least in Europe and North America, ignore the encyclical's ruling; and comparatively few clergy feel bound to correct them. It has become yet another ecclesiastical blunder that Catholics have to make excuses for.

But at the time it meant the dashing of hopes that the Church would stop being an institution its members had to make excuses for. The question had been debated fairly thoroughly within the Church, and it had become clear that a doctrine which had always been presented as derived from the natural law and therefore demonstrable on the grounds of reason alone could not be made to look remotely convincing. If the question was looked at on its merits, there seemed to be only one way the Pope could decide: in favour of recognizing that contraception could be morally justified. Indeed, in anticipation of such a verdict a number of bishops (including members of the commission the pope had set up to advise him on the question) had

187

already discreetly instructed their priests to take a
'permissive' line.

Despite all the personal anguish it cost him, Paul VI's
decision went the other way. Why? It was to answer this
question and its implications that Küng wrote *Infallible? An
Enquiry*. The common view was that on birth control the
Church was pronouncing on a matter of natural law and
not therefore on something which fell within the scope of
revelation and which would thus bring infallibility into
play. It would therefore be merely embarrassing and not
totally impossible for the Church to change its mind. The
question was whether Pius XI's and Pius XII's condemnation could still be upheld. Increasingly it had become clear,
particularly within the papal commission itself, that this
could only be done not by appealing to the 'natural law' –
which if anything would suggest that human sexual activity
is primarily for the purpose of maintaining the pair-bond
while the offspring is being brought up, and almost
secondarily for the purpose of begetting it in the first place,
and which would thus seem to raise no real objections to
contraception – but by appealing to the Church's
authority. The Church thus faced a choice of embarrassment: either the embarrassment of trying to maintain a
teaching that had lost all intrinsic authority; or the
embarrassment of publicly changing its mind with rather
greater haste than had been needed in, for example, the case
of religious liberty.

Küng, however, pointed out that the condemnation of
artificial birth control fulfilled the criteria laid down by the
Roman school of theology for the exercise of the Church's
infallible magisterium or teaching authority in its ordinary
form. Normally infallibility is thought of as being exercised
through the Church's extraordinary magisterium – by
means of a dogmatic definition by an ecumenical council or
by the pope alone acting as the spokesman for the entire
Church. But infallibility could also be exercised through

the Church's ordinary magisterium, when the pope and the
bishops had been unanimous in teaching some point of
faith or morals. Now clearly Pius XI and Pius XII and the
bishops of the time had been unanimous, not to say intransigent, in teaching the immorality of contraception, and the
consensus was only broken by the Jesuit Archbishop
Thomas Roberts in 1964. The condemnation of artificial
birth control was thus a textbook example of the infallibility of the Church's ordinary magisterium; and this was
why Paul VI disappointed so many hopes and acted the way
he did. If, Küng pointed out (*Infallible?*, p. 45), theologians
had been able to offer the pope a formula, however
specious, enabling him to present approval of artificial
birth control as a 'development' of Pius XI's condemnation
– resulting, no doubt, in an encyclical beginning: 'As the
Church has always taught . . .' – then there seems little
question but that Paul VI would have reversed the
traditional teaching. But the condemnation had been too
specific and too emphatic to allow this kind of comfortable
sleight-of-hand.

Küng's starting-point was thus that the Church had made
something like an infallible mistake (*Fehlbar?*, p. 365). It
had landed itself precisely in the position that Karl Barth
had warned against in his *Church Dogmatics* (IV/1, p. 626):

A Church which maintains that its official decisions
are infallible can commit error which are irreformable. It has more than once done so.

Küng does not quote this passage, but his study of infallibility could be read as the discovery of a Catholic sense of
what at first sight is a purely Protestant reproach – just as
in *Justification* he was able to discover a Catholic sense of
all the polemical slogans of the Reformation.

What Küng was concerned to do was to test out the
alternative that Paul VI and his advisers shied away from:
accepting that contraception was morally licit and working

out the consequences for our understanding of how the Church is maintained in the truth. The dilemma Paul VI could not solve was how it would be possible for the Church publicly to change its mind on this question without doing irreparable damage not just to the doctrine of infallibility but to the doctrine of which infallibility is a particular expression, the doctrine of the indefectibility which God had promised to his Church, the assurance that it will not be swept away by error, that the gates of hell shall not prevail against it. Of this the minority of four conservative-minded theologians on the papal commission were all too keenly aware:

> If contraception were declared not intrinsically evil, in honesty it would have to be acknowledged that the Holy Spirit in 1930, in 1951 and 1958 assisted Protestant Churches, and that for half a century Pius XI, Pius XII and a great part of the Catholic hierarchy did not protest against a very serious error, one most pernicious to souls; for it would thus be suggested that they condemned most imprudently, under the pain of eternal punishment, thousands upon thousands of human acts which are now approved. Indeed, it must be neither denied nor ignored that these acts would be approved for the same fundamental reasons which Protestantism alleged and which they (Catholics) condemned or at least did not recognize. Therefore one must very cautiously inquire whether the change which is proposed would not bring along with it a definitive depreciation of the teaching of the moral direction of the hierarchy of the Church and whether several very grave doubts would not be opened up about the very history of Christianity.[1]

In other words, if the Church were to change its teaching it would be admitting that it had not just been misleading its members but positively harming them. Catholics would have been better off listening to the Anglican bishops assembled at the 1930 Lambeth Conference. It was their cautious appröval of birth control that provoked Pius XI's encyclical *Casti connubii*.

Küng's answer was to scrutinize the dogma of papal and episcopal infallibility. The attribution of infallibility to the college of bishops was in his view based on the traditional, unhistorical theory of the bishops' direct and exclusive apostolic succession. This was not how in *The Church* he had seen apostolic succession working. Such an attribution thus 'stands exegetically, historically and theologically on feet of clay' – unless its authority were provided by Vatican I's definition of papal infallibility (*Infallible?*, p. 70). Papal infallibility in its turn he found based on foundations both meagre and brittle. It was something that most of the bishops at Vatican I took for granted before it was defined, and 'the traditional doctrine of infallibility in the Church, for all the precision of its description in the technological textbooks and at Vatican I and II, rests on foundations that cannot be regarded as secure and unassailable from the viewpoint of present-day theology and perhaps could not be so regarded even at that time' (*Infallible?*, pp. 99, 100, and 102).

Küng's doubts do not just centre on the way in which the Church's infallibility has traditionally been thought of as being expressed by the pope and the bishops. He questions the whole idea of infallible statements as such, the idea that certain propositions can *a priori* be designated infallible. It is not just that God alone can rightly be termed infallible, God who, to quote Vatican I's decree on the Catholic faith, 'can neither deceive nor be deceived' (DS 1789). It is that human propositions suffer from defects that prevent them from being able to be free from error. They always fall short of reality; they are liable to misunderstanding; it is only within limits that they can be translated; language is not static but always in a state of flux; and sentences are susceptible to ideology (*Infallible?*, p. 132):

These five observations should be sufficient for our purpose, to demonstrate the problematic nature of sentences and propositions. But, to eliminate misunderstandings as far as possible, we do not mean that sentences or propositions are incapable of stating the truth, that all propositions are equally true and false, that they cannot be measured against the reality to which they claim to refer, that understanding is impossible. All we mean is that propositions are not as clear as they seem to be, that, on the contrary, a considerable degree of ambiguity is inherent in them, that they can consequently be understood differently by different people, and that with the best will in the world all misunderstandings and misuse of them cannot be avoided.

Küng further takes up an insight that dates back to *Justification* and emphasizes that statements of truth, especially when made in a polemical context in order to defend and affirm some truth that is under attack, are half-truths. Such polemical definitions are aimed at some specific error and always run the risk of striking not only the error but also the kernel of truth it necessarily contains (*Infallible?*, pp. 139–142).

The promises of the Church's essential indefectibility on the one hand and on the other the Church's undeniable errors thus create a dilemma. Küng's solution is to define the Church's indefectibility as 'a fundamental remaining in the truth in spite of all possible errors' (*Infallible?*, p. 153). This could seem not so much like explaining as explaining away the Church's indefectibility so that there is nothing left to grasp hold of. Küng, however, insists that this is far from being the case. The promise that the Church will remain in the truth he describes as 'a challenge to faith' (*Infallible?*, pp. 154–155):

> This does not mean that the Church's indefectibility is unverifiable. That the Church of Christ has behind it a history of twenty centuries is a fact that cannot be ignored. It is a history with many, all too many,

shadows; the mistakes, the sins, the crimes in that long history are innumerable. If we look at certain centuries in the Church's history – say the tenth, that *saeculum obscurum*, or the fifteenth, the century of the Renaissance popes – we may have the impression that practically everything was done at that time to corrupt the Church and its truth. Yet it ultimately turned out to be incorruptible.

What guarantee did we have that the Church of Christ would not suffer the same fate as the Roman Empire?

The answer is that no institution and no constitution can give any such guarantee. But so far, at all events, it has not happened, and two thousand years of Christendom provide an illustration that is not to be despised (not proof) that in spite of all error and sin the Church in the last resort has not been corrupted, but has remained in the truth. All the numerous prophets of the Church's decline have so far turned out to be false prophets. It survived the tenth and fifteenth centuries, retrogression was followed by revival, and decadence by renewed knowledge of the truth.

History, of course, cannot be extrapolated to show the future. As in the past, the Church's being and truth will continue in the future to be dependent on the promise, and this cannot be demonstrated, but only apprehended by faith. As in the past it will continue in the future to depend on the living faith and love of Christians.

At the darkest periods of the Church's history, Küng adds, it was neither the 'hierarchy' nor the theologians but the simple faithful who were the true witnesses to the truth of Christ and who by their Christian life and conduct manifested the Church's indefectibility in the truth.

Before going on in the next chapter to summarize and discuss the uproar this book aroused, it would be as well to make several points clear. First, Küng's concern is to harmonize his passionate loyalty to the Church with the evidence of history and experience. His loyalty to the Church, however, is not a loyalty to the institution as such but rather to the God who sustains it and is at work through it. There is a Barthian insistence on the absolute primacy and otherness of God. The Church is there to point us towards God, it is the normal means of our encounter with God and with what he has done in and through Jesus Christ, but it must never get in the way, it must never become an obstacle between us and God.

Secondly, belief is a matter of faith, not a matter of recognizing a set of self-evident or demonstrable propositions akin to the propositions of mathematics. One section of *Infallible?* (pp. 133–139) is devoted to analysing the hankering after clarity that marks the Roman school of theology. Küng finds the roots of this attitude in Cartesian rationalism, in Descartes' efforts to reach in philosophy the clarity of mathematics. By implication, at least, Küng is concerned to emphasize that the God with whom we are dealing (or rather who is dealing with us) is the God whom on the evidence of scripture it is impossible to pin down. He is concerned to underline the fragmentary nature of our knowledge: 'we see through a glass darkly' and 'know in part' (1 Cor. 13:12). Along with an emphasis on the otherness of God there goes an emphasis on the provisional nature of human and Christian life, on the fact that it is awaiting its consummation in the definitive reign of God.

Third, this does not mean that the faith of the Church cannot be articulated in propositions. The faith of the Church, Küng writes, 'relies on confessions of faith in Christ in which that faith is comprehensively stated in summary or recapitulatory or symbolic form' (*Infallible?*, p. 118). The faith of the Church is also 'marked by polemical demarcations from the unchristian' (*Infallible?*, p. 120), in other words by statements drawn up to distinguish Christian belief from un-Christian when Christian belief is threatened in some way: most doctrinal definitions are in fact of this nature, and what is anomalous about the definitions of the immaculate conception in 1854, papal primacy and infallibility in 1870, and the assumption in 1950 is that they were gratuitous. Küng concludes that such defensive-defining propositions, 'even if they have a definitive and obligatory — and, to that extent, dogmatic — character in a particular situation, do not constitute rulings valid for all eternity, but pragmatic forms of words arising out of specific situations' (*Infallible?*, p. 121). He would thus seem to go beyond the commonly accepted position that, while the Church is not bound to the precise form of words it used to define its faith in some past crisis, it *is* bound to the belief those words were chosen to articulate: we could, for example, happily drop the term 'transubstantiation' as long as we retained the belief in the real presence which the fathers of Trent thought was most suitably described by it. In contrast, Küng seems to be saying that the Church might find that, however valid in a particular situation the implications were that it had deduced from the Christian message, they might be wrong in a different situation: the Church might be forced to deduce a different set of implications — though of course from the same Christian message. Küng thus seems to be insisting that the Church cannot and must not be shackled by its past.

Fourth, Küng is undoubtedly right in the reasons he gives for Paul VI's refusal to endorse contraception as morally licit. In the pope's eyes this would have dangerously weakened the Church's claims to be able to proclaim the gospel with any kind of authority.

Fifth, Küng is again undoubtedly right in underlining the extent to which the whole concept of infallibility bristles with difficulties. At the time Küng wrote *Infallible?* Brian Tierney had not yet published his researches into the doctrine's origins among the dissident Franciscans of the late thirteenth and early fourteenth centuries. Nevertheless,

Küng has a telling quotation from Yves Congar pointing out that it could not be said that the dogma of papal infallibility was accepted other than in embryo in the high Middle Ages, while the universally shared basic belief at the time of Albert the Great, Thomas Aquinas, and Bonaventure was that the Church itself could err, could be storm-tossed, but in the end remained faithful (*Infallible?*, pp. 151 and 150–151). Küng's case, inasmuch as it depends on Church history, rests on the incompatibility between the doctrine of infallibility and what has actually happened in the Church's history, not so much on the doctrine's dubious origins or on the extent to which Vatican I was manipulated. Indeed, he expressly rejects the assertion that Vatican I was not free (*Infallible?*, p. 107), and with it the line of attack that would argue from the unfreedom of that Council to the invalidity of its decrees. A further set of difficulties centres on the problem of recognizing when an infallible statement has been made. Küng makes it clear that according to one set of criteria Pius XI's condemnation of contraception in *Casti connubii* fulfils the conditions for an infallible statement; but this is and has been hotly disputed by probably the majority of theologians. Infallible statements have a tendency to stop being infallible once they become a real embarrassment to the Church. There have been theologians who ascribed infallibility to Pius IX's syllabus of errors. No doubt some could still be found today, but they could hardly be said to express the mind of the Church. This Pickwickian interpretation of the doctrine of infallibility has been summed up by Brian Tierney in the general principle: 'All infallible decrees are certainly true but no decrees are certainly infallible.' The other approach is to re-interpret infallible statements so as to rob them of their embarrassing sting. To quote Tierney again, 'one is reminded of the Cheshire Cat – the body of a past pronouncement disappears but its grin of infallibility persists'.[2] Nor are we ever vouchsafed an infallible interpretation of an infallible statement.

Finally, Küng can be forgiven for being surprised at the furore his book aroused. Not only had he throughout his career as a theologian been working steadily towards the position he adopted in *Infallible?*, but he had actually anticipated it in books published some years earlier. Much of the groundwork was laid in the final chapter of *Structures of the Church* (pp. 305–351) in which the concept of infallibility was analysed in the light of the criticisms made by Luther, Calvin and Karl Barth. In *The Church* he had already reached the central conclusion he was to put forward in the later book (*Church*, pp. 342–343):

> What 'infallibility' means, as the root of the word shows . . ., is that the Church is not deceiving or deceived. The trouble with the word 'infallibility' is that it suggests that the Church is 'free from error', which of course cannot apply to the Church and its representatives. It means that the Church, in so far as it is humbly obedient to the word of God, has a share in the truth of God himself, 'who can neither deceive nor be deceived' . . . If it is obedient, then all lies and deceits and deceitfulness are removed from it. 'Infallibility' therefore means a fundamental remaining in the truth, which is not disturbed by individual errors.

(This last definition is in the German word for word the same, with one insignificant exception, as that given in *Infallible?*, p. 149.)

> This infallibility is scriptural, and even the Reformers never questioned it. Whether on the other hand it has as a necessary consequence the *a priori*, unquestionable and *verifiable* infallibility of particular *statements* is something that is not directly demonstrable from the New Testament. This is a question which is much disputed between the individual Christian Churches, especially in connection with councils, bishops and the pope, and needs a new investigation on the basis given above.

Oddly enough, this passage does not seem to have aroused suspicion in Rome. Not only was it not mentioned by the Doctrinal Congregation in the objections sent to Küng on 6 May 1971, but it was not even mentioned by a Vatican theologian – thought to be Father Luigi Ciappi, OP, the official papal theologian – in a long list of what to his eyes were the book's major shortcomings (*Diskussion*, pp. 32–43).

In *Truthfulness* (pp. 182–184) Küng was even more explicit:

> Infallibility of the Church means: in so far as the Church is humbly obedient to God's word and will, she shares in the truth of the Spirit of God in the church (*Deus revelans*), who can neither deceive (*fallere*) nor be deceived (*falli*) (DS 3008). She is then far above lying and fraud (*omnis fallacia*) and all deception (*omne fallax*). Infallibility in this radical sense means a *basic persistence of the church in truth, which is not destroyed by errors in detail.*
>
> Anyone whose trust in God and in his Spirit is not superficial, rationalist, but profoundly christian, believes unshakably that the Spirit of God will maintain the church in the truth of the gospel, *in spite* of all errors and *through* all errors. This is the great miracle of the Holy Spirit of God in the church: not that no errors occur – where then would be the humanity of the church of men? – but that the church, in spite of all her defection from God, is never dropped by God, never abandoned by God; that, in spite of all sins and errors of popes, bishops, priests, theologians and laymen, she did not perish like the dynasties of the Pharaohs and the Roman Empire of the Caesars, but continues to be sustained by God in the Spirit throughout the centuries and – even after long periods of decadence – is led to ever new life and new truth. Particularly here it is strikingly evident that the truth and truthfulness of the church is not her own achievement, but the incomprehensible event of God's merciful grace. And our faith rejoices in the

thought that ultimately our own endurance in truth, although we constantly fail, is indeed important, but not ultimately decisive. What is much more decisive is the great promise of his fidelity, which God will not revoke in all eternity, in spite of our failure all along the line.

So the storm may still rage so fiercely and darkness fall; the ship of the church may toss and roll, it may lose its course and drift hither and thither utterly aimlessly with sails slackened: 'He will be with you forever, the Spirit of truth' (Jn 14:16–17). She will not succumb to the power of darkness, of lying and fraud. She is certain: by God's gracious promise, infallibility is bestowed on her. In spite of all her erring and misunderstanding, she is maintained in truth by God.

Thus we see that the infallibility of the church, from the standpoint of the scriptures (and also affirmed by the reformers), is much more than the infallibility of certain (and ultimately in fact always ambiguous, because human) ecclesial *propositions*. It is more fundamental, more comprehensive than an *a priori* indubitably ascertainable infallibility of particular propositions. This kind of infallibility cannot be directly proved from the New Testament: it is disputed among particular churches (not only in regard to the pope, but also in regard to the bishops and their councils) and at any rate on the basis described – with which Vatican I never really came to terms – it ought to be freshly examined. Whatever may be the outcome of the inquiry, acceptance in the concrete of errors in the church can never mean treating light-heartedly ecclesiastical professions of faith and definitions which have the whole church behind them. All irresponsibility here takes its revenge on the church.

From Küng's point of view, all he had done in *Infallible?* was to conduct the enquiry he had long thought necessary and to confirm and sharpen the conclusions he had already provisionally reached, spelling out their implications in fuller – and, for many, more disturbing – detail. He could legitimately ask why, if his views on the subject were so offensive, the storm had not been unleashed earlier.

[1] Peter Harris and others, *On Human Life: An Examination of 'Humanae Vitae'*, Burns and Oates, London, 1968, p. 195. All but the last sentence of this passage is quoted in *Infallible?*, p. 46.
[2] Brian Tierney, *Origins of Papal Infallibility 1150–1350: A Study on the Concepts of Infallibility, Sovereignty and Tradition in the Middle Ages*, E. J. Brill, Leiden, 1972, pp. 4 and 5.

12

A Liberal Protestant?

Infallible? was for many an offensive book. It made plausible the question that has long dogged Hans Küng: 'Is, he still a Catholic?' This degree of divergence from official accepted teaching was something new. But it was not just the fact that Küng had argued so powerfully that the official accepted teaching on this point was too riddled with absurdities to be upheld that had caused so much offence. It was also the sharply critical tone of the book's foreword, a pungent survey of the gradual disappointment and frustration of so many of the hopes raised by Vatican II. Contributing to this sharpness of tone was the lack of attention paid to Küng's earlier warnings about the way things were going in the Church, just as the book itself might not have been written (and certainly would not have been written in its present form) had his colleagues picked up and responded to all the manifold probings and questionings he had already, as we have seen, devoted to the question of infallibility. Admittedly, Küng was perhaps more aware than most of the danger of Vatican II's achievements gradually being nibbled away by bureaucratic encroachment as the Curia reasserted its power. He was, after all, fully aware of the rapidity with which the decrees of Constance had become a dead letter. And certainly, having during his students days been able to watch its operations at close quarters, he viewed the Roman bureaucratic machine with the gravest suspicion and was hardly likely to give it the benefit of the doubt. All this helps to explain why he felt it necessary to sound the alarm in order to wake the theological sleepers from their no doubt dogmatic slumbers (*Way*, p. 171).

No doubt many of his colleagues resented being woken so abruptly. But that alone cannot explain the sharpness of many of the reactions. Clearly Küng had touched on a particularly neuralgic point – for some, perhaps, unconsciously felt to be the Catholic *articulus stantis aut cadentis ecclesiae*, the essential criterion for separating papist sheep from Protestant goats. The fiercest onslaught came from Karl Rahner,[1] whom Küng revered as a pioneer of theological freedom: that the attack should come from this quarter was an especially bitter blow. As far as Rahner was concerned, Küng's thesis contradicted all Catholic theology since the Reformation at least, to say nothing of the explicit teaching of the First and Second Vatican Councils. With certain reservations, it seemed to him a contradiction of a defined truth of faith (*HPR*, May 1971, p. 13):

> To this extent one can surely raise the question whether or not there is any common ground left on which one can even talk with Küng and argue against him. One can carry on such a discussion with Küng under the given presuppositions certainly only as one would with a liberal Protestant for whom a council and also scripture are not matters that make an absolute claim on him.

That label 'a liberal Protestant' Küng would find difficult to shake off. Rahner went on to rub the point home by asserting that throughout *Infallible?* Küng was denying what up to the present had been an indisputable presupposition for an internal Catholic theological discussion (art. cit. p. 14): 'We can no longer consider the controversy over Küng's thesis, from the nature of the case, as an inner-Catholic theological controversy.'

Rahner found it impossible to understand why Küng rejected any connection between the Church's remaining in the truth and 'at least some propositions that objectively affirm this remaining-in-the-truth' (art. cit. p. 21). He went on to give a synopsis of the book he thought Küng ought to have written (art. cit. pp. 21–22):

> Küng would be right if he would emphasize (what scholastic theology often oversees) that the indefecti- bility of the propositions of Church dogma is a partici- pation in and derivation from (of course of a necessary kind since Christ) the grace-filled indefectibility of faith as the basic decision of men in the Church. Küng would be right if he demanded a better and more exact theory of error from traditional Catholic theology . . . Küng would have done us a great service if he had worked out a more precise theory of the historicity of propositions as such . . . Küng should have been able to develop a theologically deeper and more radical concept of truth in order to say what 'error' in theology really means . . . From such a foundation (at least it seems so to me) Küng could have easily proceeded from the distinction between a fundamental remaining-in-the-truth and the truth of propositions. Then he would have been able to 'define' the truth of theological propositions com- pletely as also the objectively successful realization of the original 'being-in-the-truth'.

But, of course, such a book could only be Rahner's: Küng's whole approach is different.

Gregory Baum is thus absolutely right in seeing here a clash between two contrasting currents in Catholic theology.[2] Küng represents the return to the origins, the concern to test everything that the Church is doing against the original and primary witness; Rahner is prepared to accept that certain developments in the Church, though not covered by the original witness and apparently going beyond it, can be an authentic expression of God's will for his people. Küng has always been concerned to express himself in plain language understood of the people (and is undoubtedly the most easily readable of all theologians writing in German today), and is never afraid to call a spade a spade; Rahner's convoluted style has become so much of a byword that his own brother is said to have voiced the wish that someone would translate his books into German, while in keeping with this complex style so laden with nuances he is a master of re-interpreting past doctrinal statements in such a way as to save the appearances while allowing for the facts of change and development.

Infallibility provided an eminently suitable topic for the clash. It is first of all a doctrine that is very easily misunderstood, even by those who are ostensibly committed to believing it. A 1967 survey of what German Catholics and Protestants thought on religious questions found that 55 per cent of Catholics thought the pope could not be infallible because he was only a human being, while 11 per cent thought he was infallible every time he made a public pronouncement; only 33 per cent were able to endorse the 'orthodox' view that the pope is only infallible when he makes a solemn pronouncement on some question of faith or morals. Admittedly, in this survey Catholics included all those whose connection with the Church was limited to paying their *Kirchensteuer* and describing themselves as Catholic on official forms; but even among practising Catholics (those going to church at least once a month) 44 per cent denied papal infallibility, 14 per cent extended it à la W. G. Ward to every public utterance, and only 40 per cent got it right. By contrast, British Catholics are much readier to endorse papal infallibility: according to surveys published in 1979 and 1980, 67 per cent of Scottish Catholics and 62 per cent of English and Welsh Catholics believe that, under certain conditions, when he speaks on matters of faith and morals the pope is infallible. Nevertheless, 31 per cent of English and Welsh Catholics regard this statement as false, and the younger they are the less likely they are to accept it.[3]

Secondly, infallibility is a doctrine more than usually subject to interpretation. Not only did Vatican I not define

quite as much as some of its members would have liked –
or indeed quite as much as many Catholics, often with
official encouragement, subsequently thought it had
defined – but by the time theologians have been at the
definition there is not that much left. Before he had been
able to read and react to Küng's book Rahner had expressed
the view that for all practical purposes the exercise of
infallibility was an impossibility today: 'In the foreseeable
future there will be no further really new definitions,' he
wrote. The reason for this he found in the diversity the
Church now embraced:

> Today a pluralism exists in regional cultures, philo-
> sophies, terminologies, outlooks, theologies, and so on
> which can no longer be fully reduced to any one
> synthesis, and so vividly has the Church become
> aware of this that I can no longer imagine that any
> specific, and at the same time genuinely *new*
> proposition can be so expressed that it can be felt
> throughout to be an expression of the conscious faith
> of the whole Church, and so be capable of definition.

But this did not mean the Church's infallible teaching
office no longer had any future:

> The solemn delimitation of the ancient body of dogma
> to protect it against interpretations which would
> eliminate it is still even today an abiding task of the
> infallible teaching office of the Church.

And even when one had ruled out the kind of corrosive
interpretation that would explain things away there was
still more than enough room left to accommodate the
widest possible range of views:

> Within the last hundred years we have arrived at a
> situation in which a new definition can no longer be
> false because in any such new definition the *legitimate*
> range of interpretation is so wide that it no longer
> leaves any room for error outside it.[4]

Infallibility interpreted in this way, one is left feeling, is surely a suitable victim for Ockham's razor.

Even more striking is the defence of infallibility published after Küng's book had appeared by the American scholar Peter Chirico, for all that he describes his work as 'in no important sense a response to the content of Küng's book' but rather 'a response to a problem he has highlighted'. Chirico accuses Küng of having written primarily an attack on triumphalism, a prophetic proclamation rather than a theological study; but for his part his own work seems concerned more with the epistemology of certainty in belief than with the particular question whether the Church can make binding definitions that are *a priori* irreformable and free from error. In fact, he gives the impression of reaching precisely the same conclusions as Küng but wrapping them up in a different terminology that allows him to keep the label 'infallibility'. What in his view infallibility is concerned about is fundamental universal meanings, the understandings that gradually crystallize out from initial expressions of belief that begin by being necessarily tied to a particular culture and set of circumstances and only with time can be expressed in more general terms. Infallibility is indeed a prime example of something the Church could only become aware of at a comparatively late stage in its history. Nor is it something that can be pinned down in particular propositions:

> This relativity of expression and the consequences that flow from it lead to the basic contention that while there can be universal abstract meanings, there cannot be any universal expressions. There are no concrete expressions that always and everywhere body forth the same sort of abstract meanings. Universality belongs to the abstract, but all expressions pertain to the concrete.

Consequently, 'there are no verbal statements of the magisterium – even the verbalizations of an infallible pope or council – that, *as expressions*, have universal validity'. Infallibility in Chirico's view applies not to the formulation but to the grasp of some truth by the mind.[5]

Faced with such attempts at justifying infallibility, Brian Tierney's evocation of the Cheshire Cat, when all that remains is the infallible grin, seems entirely justified. And even if there is agreement that infallibility can after all be pinned down in particular statements there are a number of formidable hurdles to be surmounted. The Church – whether through the pope alone, through the bishops either gathered in council or scattered throughout the world, or through the consensus of all the faithful – must be trying to define something that is part of revelation (which for many Catholic theologians automatically puts birth control outside the scope of infallibility). Then, although Vatican I affirmed, against Gallican tendencies, that definitions made by the pope when exercising his gift of infallibility were irreformable 'of themselves, and not by the consent of the Church' (DS 3074), so that a papal or conciliar definition does not have to be ratified subsequently by the rest of the Church in the way that in the United States treaties are made by the President by and with the advice and consent of the Senate, nevertheless what has to be discerned by the rest of the Church (and particularly, it seems, by theologians) is whether infallibility has actually been involved in this or that actual definition. Bishop Christopher Butler has indeed suggested that the real criterion of an *ex cathedra* definition must be the Church's own acceptance, something that according to Vatican II 'will never be absent when an infallible definition has in fact been made' (*The Tablet*, 24 April 1971, p. 399).

What at this point seems to be fairly generally admitted is that there can be a difference between what a pope or council thinks he or it is doing in making a definition and what the rest of the Church concludes he or it has done, either at the time or afterwards. The language used by Pius

XI in *Casti connubii*, for example, seems pretty explicit (DS 3717):

> Since therefore some people have recently thought a different teaching should be put forward about this field of behaviour, the Catholic Church, to which God himself has entrusted the task of teaching and defending the integrity and probity of morals, placed in the midst of this moral ruin that it may preserve the purity of the marriage bond intact from this foul stain, as a sign of its divine mandate raises its voice on high through our mouth and proclaims anew: any use of matrimony in the exercise of which the act is by human ingenuity deprived of its natural power of procreating life infringes the law of God and of nature, and those who have committed such acts are defiled with the stain of a serious offence.

The pope clearly thought he was fulfilling his task of pastor and teacher of all Christians, he was pretty clearly invoking his apostolic authority (whatever that may mean), and he was certainly defining a teaching about faith or morals to be held by the universal Church. In other words, Pius XI was on the face of it fulfilling the prescriptions of Vatican I's definition (DS 3074). Up to the 1960s a number of theologians thus regarded this condemnation of birth control as infallible teaching, and no doubt some could still be found who would maintain this position. But the general theological consensus today, in the wake of *Humanae vitae* and the debate that encyclical provoked, is that this is not an infallible teaching. In other words, the Church would seem to have changed its mind about the status of one particular aspect of its teaching. At best it could be said that what at first appeared infallible turned out on closer examination not to be so. But whichever way the shift away from the teaching of *Casti connubii* is interpreted the doctrine of infallibility comes to look more and more like the Cheshire Cat.

In any case, even if it is agreed and accepted that

infallibility has come into play, what has been defined is then open to all the interpretative and hermeneutic arts that theologians have at their disposal. The doctrine is thus subject to conditions and liable to interpretations that make the more simple-minded wonder if at the end of the day it is worth all the difficulties it arouses. When it is called into play it can be a grave embarrassment to the Church: this would seem to be the case over birth control, and the time may well come when theologians will be exercising their ingenuity over Pius XII's apparently fairly explicit invocation of infallibility in his definition of the assumption (DS 3903). Richard P. McBrien seems eminently justified in comparing papal infallibility with the stockpiling of nuclear weapons as a deterrent and with the alleged intention of never actually using them: the dogma of the assumption, he suggests, might have been the equivalent of the Nevada test explosion.[6]

The complexity of the doctrine helps to explain how, after his initial outburst, Rahner fairly quickly came to recognize how very small was the practical issue in dispute between him and Küng. 'An "operative" agreement between Küng and myself seems to me to be not so impossible as it might perhaps at first sight appear to *both* of us,' he wrote in his reply to Küng's reply to his original critique (*HPR*, August/September 1971, vol. 71 no. 11, pp. 12–13):

> *If* (1) we are in agreement on the real substance of Christianity (and in Brussels [at the September 1970 *Concilium* congress on 'The future of the Church', at which the two theologians shared the platform in a session on 'What is the Christian message?'] that seemed to be clear), *if* (2) we both have a real understanding for the historicity of every dogma (and it seems to me that Küng admits this in spite of his vehement and one-sided criticism of my supposedly merely speculative and unhistorical theology, when he

says on the first page of his article that *I* taught him to understand dogma historically), *if* (3) Küng, in a truly self-critical fashion, takes the magisterial declarations of the councils and the Popes seriously and gives them a real chance over against his own thinking, *if* (4) corresponding to his own explanation he really accepts the fact that the bishops' teaching office, when it is a question 'of the existence or the non-existence of the Church of the gospel,' can utter a binding word, *if* (5) he does not practically [i.e. in practice] render his explanation ineffective by granting himself too quickly the right to decide, over against the Church of the bishops and the Pope, when the Church of the bishops and the Pope exceed the competence that even Küng recognizes in them; if these conditions were fulfilled, *then* I could think even under the presupposition of Küng's position that practically [i.e. once again 'in practice'] the meaning and the goal of the magisterium would be achieved, just as it was described in Vatican I and Vatican II and defended by me – that goal which is the foundation of the magisterium: the permanence of the complete message of the gospel.

Nevertheless, Rahner found an essential difference between their two positions in the distinction between an inadequate, one-sided dogma on the one hand and on the other a false teaching proclaimed by the Church's teaching authority with the demand that it should be accepted without reservations. He went on to defend his style of transcendental-speculative theology as against Küng's positive-historical style.

In this way the quarrel between the two theologians was able to come to a peaceful and friendly conclusion. Rahner took part in a seminar at Tübingen on infallibility and joined Küng and his colleagues for a meal afterwards. In May 1973 there was a final exchange of open letters (*The Tablet*, 23 June 1973, pp. 597–599). Making his peace with

Rahner did not mean the older theologian was expected to concur in his opinion, wrote Küng:

> But it does mean that you should allow my view to count as a Catholic. And for that reason I heartily wish also that you would stop describing me – to the joy of our common opponents – as a 'liberal Protestant', but accept me expressly as the Catholic theologian which, for all my evangelical concentration, I would like to be.

Clearly, the label still rankled. For his part Rahner expressed qualified regret for having use the expression: he had not described Küng as a 'liberal Protestant' but had merely said that on *this* one question he could only argue as if he were dealing with a liberal Protestant, and if this expression led common opponents to conclude that they were no longer agreed about anything or that what divided them was greater than what they had in common, 'then I would of course greatly regret this consequence of using the expression'. On certain conditions, including Küng making it clearer that there are in fact really binding true propositions of faith which also endure in time and can in a particular situation require an unconditional profession of faith involving life and death, Rahner would be in favour of waiting and letting their dispute rest for a couple of years:

> For I don't think that the question you raise, whether your views may be regarded as Catholic, can or must be decided in the immediate future merely by a Roman verdict and still less that it has to be answered by me. In practice, at least for the time being, a solution to the question can be sought in a different way.

His hope was that his interpretation of Vatican I could be made to coincide with Küng's opinion, 'better expressed and given a more Catholic stamp'.

Küng had earlier, in his 1971 reply to Rahner, made clear the very bruised feelings the latter's onslaught had left behind. That a theologian from whom he had learned so much and whom he revered as the founding father of modern German Catholic theology should have turned round and savaged him, without apparently so much as a hint that such a thunderbolt was on its way when the two of them were sharing the same platform and speaking on the same subject at the *Concilium* congress in Brussels in September 1970 – this stung, and Küng did not hide his feelings. Beyond this, Küng resented the way Rahner seemed to be making an easy opening for the Doctrinal Congregation in Rome and for those in Rome and elsewhere who took its part: quite clearly he feared that the label 'liberal Protestant' would be read as an open invitation to start a heresy-hunt. And not only did Rahner organize a collective volume of articles critical of Küng's book but he would not allow Küng space in it to reply to the criticisms of his work.

Understandably, Küng felt he was being ganged up against. But it was surely a little naïve of him not to foresee that his attack on what has a good claim to be *the* Catholic shibboleth would bring a whole pack of angry theologians baying at his heels. People do not take kindly to seeing their sacred cows led away to the slaughterhouse, still less to their being mocked at on the way. Küng however gave the impression of expecting the whole Catholic world to be grateful to him for having disposed so neatly and swiftly of what it could be forgiven for regarding as its badge of distinction. No doubt the small boy who pointed out the true nature of the emperor's new clothes was puzzled when the first reaction of all the grown-ups was to tell him to shut up.

The quarrel with Rahner helped to show that the central point at issue was the difference between those who stress the continuity and those who stress the change in the Church's teaching. There are those who are prepared to stretch a theory of development to the point where a doctrinal formulation in fact no longer means what it originally meant, as happened with the maxim 'No salvation outside the Church' (the history of which Küng analysed in *The Church*, pp. 313–319): a priest who in the 1950s took this 'easily misunderstood negative axiom' in the same sense in which it had originally been understood was excommunicated for doing so. There are those who, like Küng, feel that in such circumstances the only thing for the Church to do is honestly and openly to admit that it has changed its mind.

Küng's point is thus that the Church must be free to welcome new insights into what the gospel actually means and what it actually demands of us, that it must not go through history bound by the chains of its past mistakes as it fumbles its way towards the truth. On the one hand the experience of the past cannot provide a reach-me-down solution for present difficulties; on the other, the Church cannot tempt God by twisting to its own ends the indefectibility he has promised it, it cannot make use of God in this way by deciding it will make a statement that is infallibly guaranteed in advance to be true. It is not exempt from the human propensity to failure, and if it is able faithfully to proclaim and confess the truth with which it has been entrusted, that is a gift of God for which it should be humbly grateful, not an achievement of its own about which it can boast.

Besides this central issue of how the Church's indefectibility is experienced in practice, there are two other issues Küng's critics fastened on. One is his use of *Humanae vitae* and the birth control question. Many of his critics seem to have missed the point by assuming that Küng was adopting the maximalist position that would see *Casti connubii* as an exercise of infallible teaching authority and *Humanae vitae* as a reaffirmation of that infallible teaching. But in fact (for all that, as we have seen, it looks very much as if Pius XI at least thought he was making an infallible statement) what

Küng was doing was fighting on the ground chosen by the conservative theologians of the papal commission on birth control. It was their arguments that had convinced the pope, and it was their arguments he was therefore concerned to meet. They had argued that enquiring into the irreformability or infallibility of *Casti connubii* was beside the point. They had appealed not to the Church's extra-ordinary teaching office but to its ordinary teaching office. What was involved was not Vatican I but Vatican II (*Lumen gentium* § 25):

> Although the individual bishops do not enjoy the pre-rogative of infallibility, they can nevertheless proclaim Christ's doctrine infallibly. This is so, even when they are dispersed around the world, provided that while maintaining the bond of unity among them-selves and with Peter's successor, and while teaching authentically on a matter of faith and morals, they concur in a single viewpoint as the one which must be held conclusively.

And that was precisely what had been the case over birth control up until the early 1960s. The question whether an encyclical like *Casti connubii* or *Humanae vitae* could be the vehicle for an infallible pronouncement therefore did not arise.

In his use of *Humanae vitae* Küng committed a further offence. He asserted straight out that it was wrong. Many of his fellow-theologians preferred the more diplomatic approach of starting by expressing the deference due to a papal pronouncement but then robbing the encyclical of all its practical force by hedging it about with suitable qualifi-cations and interpretations. Rahner himself was responsible for a prize example of this kind of obsequious sabotage.[7]

The other issue Küng's critics jumped on was his incursion into linguistic analysis and epistemology – 'a part of his book which, like his historical sketches, even his admirers find rather embarrassing,' wrote the English

Jesuit Robert Murray (*Heythrop Journal*, 13 [1972], p. 212). In particular Küng was accused of ignoring the commonly accepted distinction between the actual judgement somebody makes and the words used to express that judgement. The Irish philosopher Patrick McGrath pointed out that Küng failed to distinguish between a propositional formula and a proposition (*Concilium*, vol. 3 no. 9, 1973, p. 66), which puts the same thing in technical language. In other words, according to Küng's critics, the Church might well on the basis of this distinction have to change its definitions and to replace a past definition with a new one; but it would do so only and specifically in order to safeguard the truth it had originally defined. The content would remain but be given a different form of expression. In Chirico's terminology a universal meaning would be given a different universal expression.

But at the very least the debate sparked off by Küng's book amply vindicated the question mark that occupied so prominent a place on the cover of the German edition. It helped to clarify that what Küng was against was not the idea of the Church being able to stand up for the gospel in the confidence that it was indeed the gospel it was standing up for, but the idea of the Church somehow having the truth in its possession and under its control instead of being possessed by the truth and at its service. It brought out precisely how dubious were the historical origins of the doctrine of papal infallibility. Brian Tierney's researches (the completion of which more or less coincided with the publication of Küng's book) showed that it was first advocated by the Franciscan Petrus Olivi in the later thirteenth century in the context of internal disputes within the Franciscan order and that it was put forward specifically to prevent a future pope from undoing the work of his predecessor – in this case Nicholas III's approval of the ideals of Franciscan poverty in his bull *Exiit* of 1279. To the alarm of the Franciscans, John XXII proceeded to do just that with the bull *Cum inter nonnullos* of 1323, and followed this up in 1324 by describing the doctrine of the irreformability of papal definitions on faith and morals (which is how papal infallibility first surfaced) as a pernicious novelty and as utterly erroneous.[8] In the Middle Ages papal sovereignty ruled out papal infallibility, since the infallible decrees of his predecessors would inevitably infringe and limit a pope's freedom of decision; it was only in the nineteenth century that papal infallibility came to be seen as an enhancement of papal sovereignty rather than as detracting from it.

Later than Tierney's work came the researches of the Swiss theologian and Church historian August Bernhard Hasler into Vatican I and the extent to which it had been manipulated and could not be regarded as enjoying the freedom essential for an ecumenical council. He published his researches in two forms: a scholarly account in two volumes which came out in 1977, and a one-volume popular version which appeared in 1979. Küng refused a request to review the two-volume study, but wrote an introduction to the popular work; and that triggered off the Doctrinal Congregation's withdrawal of his *missio canonica* in 1979.

In the immediate debate sparked off by Küng's book, what was common to all sides was recognition of the need to reconcile the promise of the Church's indefectibility with the various blunders and mistakes the Church had throughout its history committed. Küng's own view of how this reconciliation occurred is as follows (*Fehlbar?*, p. 441):

> Even a dogma that is possibly false – and how many dogmas are forgotten today or at best exert only a marginal influence on Christians' awareness of their faith – cannot do away with the existence and truth of the Church. The totality of faith consists of the totality of commitment, not the integrity of the correct propositions. And this commitment can be

complete and without reservations even if something that is false is said in the process. Errors by the Church's 'teaching authority' are a serious business, but they do not threaten the Church's existence. It is precisely this that is meant by the promise of indefectibility in the truth. And the purpose of this promise is to banish from faint-hearted Christians that fear of error that often seems greater than fear of sin. Why does the Holy Spirit not prevent such errors from the outset? That was what many people asked both before and after *Humanae vitae*. The answer is because God's Spirit does not do away with the humanity of human beings, and to err is human. But the more pressing question ought rather to be: why should the Church make such very heavy weather of correcting its mistakes when it proclaims the need for a change of mind and a change of heart? The answer is because it likes to identify itself with the Spirit of God and thus ascribes God's infallibility to itself, and from this deduces the irreformability of its decisions, the idea that they cannot be corrected. Ought not things to be the other way round, so that the Church, standing under the gospel as the *ecclesia semper reformanda*, revises and corrects its errors more easily than other bodies and thus makes its indefectibility in the truth credible?

This seems a more hopeful and more honest way than the alternative of the re-interpretation of dogma.

Helpful, too, is the image quoted by Otto Hermann Pesch. He suggests regarding the history of dogma as something like a series of signposts along a road. Each signpost points in a particular direction, but the next one may point in a slightly different direction. They are all, however, guiding the traveller to the same destination, however much the road may twist and turn in getting there (*Fehlbar?*, p. 265). This fits in admirably with the image of the Church as the pilgrim people of God. It brings out that what matters is the ultimate goal of the kingdom and the assurance that the Church will reach that goal.

Above all the debate brought out what could well be the precedent that will enable the Church to get over all the difficulties infallibility has caused it. This is the question of biblical inerrancy. Over the past century the Church has moved from being committed to the truth of everything the Bible said (suitably interpreted in accordance with the mind of the Church) to what could not unfairly be described as an acceptance of the overall truthfulness of the Bible coupled with recognition of its errors in detail. In 1893 Leo XIII argued that because the books of the Bible were divinely inspired they could not contain the least particle of error (DS 3292). In 1920 Benedict XV would not allow scholars to suggest that the Bible might contain historical and scientific errors (DS 3652). As late as 1950 (in *Humani generis*) Pius XIII had harsh words for those who resurrected 'the old argument, so often censured, which contends that the inerrancy of Scripture only extends to what it tells us about God, about morals, and about religion' (DS 3887, in the CTS translation by Ronald Knox). Vatican II's constitution on revelation thus represents quite a shift when it says: 'The books of Scripture must by acknowledged as teaching firmly, faithfully, and without error that truth which God wanted put into the sacred writings for the sake of our salvation' (*Dei verbum* § 11).

All this and more Küng points out in *Infallible?* (pp. 171–181). But his concern there is rather lest Protestants hug to themselves their slogan of *sola scriptura* without realizing that arguments that demolish an infallible teaching authority in the Church also demolish the idea of an infallible book or collection of books. Both in the Church and in the Bible, Küng argues, God is at work through men. He does not take them over, suppress their humanity, reduce them to zombies. Instead he respects their freedom and their humanity and works through these human qualities. In this way neither over biblical inerrancy nor over infallibility should there be any obstacle to agreement between Catholics, Orthodox and Protestants (*Infallible?*, p. 177):

(1) God himself acts with us and on us through the human word of Scripture in so far as he thereby moves us to faith and causes the words of man in proclamation to be the instrument of his Spirit; behind all the mythological ideas and often misleading concepts associated with it, that is the real truth in the theory of inspiration.

(2) At the same time the Scriptures are completely human documents, written by human authors with their human gifts and limitations, their human potentialities both for knowledge and for error, with the consequence that errors of the most varied kind cannot *a priori* be excluded; this should be the real limitation of the theory of inspiration in all positive statements about the workings of the Spirit.

But how are these two points to be reconciled? Just as in the Church, which is composed of men, so too in the Bible, which was composed by men, God gains his end, without doing any violence to man, though human weakness and historicity. Through all the human frailty and the historical conditioning and limitations of the authors of the books of the Bible, who are often able to speak only stammeringly and with inadequate conceptual means, it comes about that God's call, as it was finally sounded aloud in Jesus, is truthfully heard, believed and realized.

Nor is either the Church or the Bible the real basis and ground of Christian faith, Küng goes on to point out: it is God himself in Jesus Christ, who is attested in the Bible and proclaimed by the Church (*Infallible?*, p. 179).

The parallel between biblical inerrancy and infallibility may be there in the book, but it is rather tucked away in what is almost a polemical parenthesis aimed at stopping Protestants rejoicing overmuch at what might seem to them a Catholic own goal. Yet it is surely the key argument from the point of view of enabling Catholics to accept his critique of infallibility. It shows that all he is asking them to do is to follow a road they have already trodden before. At the start of his book Küng criticizes the majority on the papal commission for failing to show the pope how a change in the Church's teaching on birth control could be reconciled with the accepted Roman view of the infallibility of the Church's ordinary magisterium. But he can similarly be accused of not making it easy for Catholics to accept his thesis by playing down this precedent.

Interestingly enough, Küng's thesis on infallibility had been echoed the year before *Infallible?* came out in a study by the American theologian James T. Burtchaell of this parallel question of biblical inerrancy. Infallibility, suggested the American scholar, was as much an unprobed working assumption as biblical inerrancy, and he put forward the intriguing view that the Catholic inability to countenance error or uncertainty had its roots not just in Descartes but in the Catholic claim as against the Protestants that what their communion had to offer was authoritarian certitude – even though 'we should probably be more accurate to say that what God has promised his Church is not certitude but survival'. He proposed an understanding of infallibility in a dynamic rather than static sense that clearly reflects the root meaning of inerrancy – failing to wander, to go astray:

> The community of believers, with its clerical officers as teachers and spokesmen, will never wander or stray unrecoverably from the path of legitimate development; it will neither forget what it has been taught through revelation, nor fail to move onward to new truth; it will have power gradually to incorporate valuable insights, and progressively to slough off residual error. At any time the Church may fail to straddle firmly the center of the highway. But amid her veering and weaving, she will not get lost.

Similarly, inerrancy – when taken in a dynamic and not a static sense – 'must be the ability, not to avoid all mistakes, but to cope with them, remedy them, survive them, and eventually even profit from them'.[9]

On this kind of basis the infallibility debate could lead to a synthesis in which the Church's past doctrinal commitments would be seen as authoritative, just as the Bible is regarded as authoritative, while at the same time the possibility would be recognized of the official Church having committed itself to formulations which later on in its history it was able to recognize as not just inadequate or misleading but as just plain wrong, however right and essential they may have seemed at the time. Just as what the Bible says cannot be applied directly but has to be interpreted and understood in its context, so too the Church's dogmatic pronouncements cannot simply be applied as they stand but have to be interpreted and understood in their context. Too often the concept of infallibility suggests that this process can be short-circuited or cut out altogether. The merit of Küng's thesis is that it prevents this and restores the Church's ability to learn by its mistakes.

[1] *Stimmen der Zeit*, 186 (1970), pp. 361–377, quoted from the English translation in *Homiletic and Pastoral Review* (referred to in the text as *HPR*), May 1971, vol. 71 no. 8, pp. 10–26. This journal also published Küng's reply (June 1971, vol. 71 no. 9, pp. 9–29, and July 1971, vol. 71 no. 10, pp. 17–32 and 49–50) as well as Rahner's reply to Küng's reply and a postscript from Küng (August/September 1971, vol. 71 no. 11, pp. 11–27 and 28–31).

[2] Gregory Baum, George Lindbeck, Richard McBrien, Harry J. McSorley, *The Infallibility Debate*, edited by John J. Kirvan. Paulist Press, New York, 1971, pp. 11–13.

[3] Werner Harenberg (ed.), *Was glauben die Deutschen?: Die*

Emnid-Umfrage, Ergebnisse und Kommentare, Chr. Kaiser Verlag, Munich, Matthias-Grünewald Verlag, Mainz, 1968, pp. 41–42; Gallup Poll survey of Scottish Catholics, published 24 April 1979, table Q. 272; Michael P. Hornsby-Smith and Raymond M. Lee, *Roman Catholic Opinion: A Study of Roman Catholics in England and Wales in the 1970s, Final Report*, University of Surrey, Guildford, 1980 (dated 1979), p. 193. Neither the Scottish nor the English and Welsh survey included heterodox options in its question on infallibility: those questioned were able merely to record their agreement or disagreement with the proposition. The extent to which they misunderstood it was not probed.

[4] Karl Rahner, S. J., 'On the Concept of Infallibility in Catholic Theology', *Theological Investigations*, vol. xiv, Darton, Longman and Todd, London, 1976, pp. 66–84. The quotations are from pp. 71; 72–73; 75; and 80. The article was originally published in 1970.

[5] Peter Chirico, SS, *Infallibility: The Crossroads of Doctrine*, Sheed and Ward, London, 1977, pp. 304–305, 275, 279.

[6] *The Infallibility Debate*, p. 51.

[7] 'On the Encyclical "Humanae Vitae",' *Theological Investigations*, vol. xi, Darton, Longman and Todd, London, Seabury Press, New York, 1974, pp. 263–287. The article originally appeared in *Stimmen der Zeit* in 1968.

[8] Brian Tierney, *Origins of Papal Infallibility 1150–1350: A Study on the Concepts of Infallibility, Sovereignty and Tradition in the Middle Ages*, E. J. Brill, Leiden, 1972, pp. 115–130, 181, 186.

[9] James T. Burtchaell, *Catholic Theories of Biblical Inspiration since 1810: A Review and Critique*, Cambridge University Press, 1969, pp. 288, 300, and 303.

13

The Dispute with Rome

In publishing *Infallible?* Hans Küng was risking his future career as a Catholic theologian. Rome was already unhappy over some of the things he had said in *The Church*, and now he had probed Roman theology's most central and neuralgic point. Excommunication might be a punishment Rome no longer brandished as it used to, but a disturbing possibility was what eventually happened nine years later when he and everyone else might have been excused for thinking the matter closed – the withdrawal of his official Church recognition as a teacher of Catholic theology. This was a fate that had already befallen someone he knew, the catechetical expert Hubertus Halbfas, who in 1968 and 1969 was squeezed out of his post at the College of Education at Reutlingen (only seven and a half miles southeast of Tübingen) mainly because of his demythologizing approach to Jesus's miracles and to the virgin birth. That admittedly was something the German bishops had been responsible for on their own, but at the international level the Doctrinal Congregation was still very much a power in the Church. As we have seen, it had already in 1969 acted against Monsignor Ivan Illich and the institute he had founded in Cuernavaca (pp. 162–163 above). In the early 1970s it was pursuing other victims besides Küng, and in their cases with greater success. In particular there was the case of the Danzig-born Dominican Stephan Pfürtner, who was eased out of his post as professor of moral theology at the university of Fribourg, Switzerland, after a lecture in 1971 in which he had suggested that masturbation and sex

223

before marriage might not always be mortal sins. An especially disturbing feature of the Pfürtner case was that, although there were prolonged negotiations between the Dominican theologian and the Swiss bishops in an effort to settle the affair amicably, the Doctrinal Congregation had in fact decided from the start that Pfürtner must either retract or go; and go he eventually did in April 1974, after the Master General of the Dominicans, Father Aniceto Fernandez, had in the autumn of 1972 withdrawn his *missio canonica* or official recognition as a teacher of theology. Not only did Pfürtner complain that he had been sentenced without a hearing and without being able to put his defence, but the Swiss bishops too admitted that they had not known what was going on. Nor was Pfürtner's the only case. At Innsbruck in Austrian the Jesuit Franz Schupp was dismissed from his professorship in 1974, once again with the Doctrinal Congregation reaching a verdict but staying in the background and leaving the man's religious superiors to do the dirty work. Also in 1974 there were other cases of theologians falling foul of the Church authorities, but in these the Doctrinal Congregation does not seem to have been involved. In Belgium there were the cases of Father Jean Kamp and Father Giulio Girardi, SDB (who in 1969 had been abruptly moved from Rome to Paris by his Salesian superiors in a purge of the Salesian University in Rome), and in France that of Father Robert Argeneau.[1]

All these sanctions against theologians who in the judgement of Rome had stepped out of line must be borne in mind in considering Küng's relations with the Doctrinal Congregation. They show that what in a more civilized society might be construed as suspiciousness bordering on paranoia or even as boorishness expressed nothing more than an understandable wariness and a legitimate desire for self-preservation. Küng was throughout concerned that the Church should remain a place where questions could be asked and where the attempt could be made to provide an honest answer. He did not wish to see Charles Davis's reproaches justified, the English theologian's accusation that the Church was marked by a lack of concern for truth and a lack of concern for people.

Nor for Küng would the withdrawal of his *missio canonica* be simply a disagreeable administrative sanction that would leave his social and economic position unaffected. What he resented about this threat that was hanging over his head in the early 1970s and that was put into effect at the end of the decade was that it impugned his standing as a Catholic. It was precisely because he was so attached to the Church that he subjected it to so much criticism. The awkward and embarrassing questions he raised were in fact the measure and proof of his loyalty as a Catholic. Küng was well aware that according to the classical theological tradition a Christian should follow his or her conscience even at the cost of excommunication (*Structures*, pp. 342–343; *Infallible?*, p. 39); but were such a penalty ever to befall him it would exact a higher price than in the case of others who superficially may appear more 'loyal' but whose loyalty is not as fierce or deep-rooted. Beyond this Küng was aware throughout of acting as a spokesman for all those in the Church or pushed out to its fringes whose views tended simply to be swept aside as irrelevant or unworthy of consideration by the Monsignor Talbots of our age. For their sake, rather than his own, he should not let his voice be silenced.

The first reaction came from the German bishops' conference. After further clarifications from Hans Küng had failed to satisfy the bishops and after talks with him had failed to remove their misgivings, they issued a statement on 8 February 1971 which remarked that in *Infallible?* some of the fundamental elements of the Catholic understanding of the faith and of the Church did not seem to be preserved. They admitted that it was not the bishops' job to intervene in specialized theological disputes. But they saw it as their duty to point to certain data that could not be renounced, certain facts the denial of which meant that a theology could no longer be described as Catholic. They reaffirmed the power of ecumenical councils and of the pope to issue ultimately binding doctrinal definitions.[2]

The French and the Italian bishops' conferences also issued warnings against the book. In Italy pressure was exerted on the publishing house of Queriniana of Brescia to stop them producing a second edition after the first edition (of four thousand copies) had sold out, on the grounds that the book lacked an *imprimatur* (*The Tablet,* 19/26 December 1970, p. 1260): a second edition duly appeared from Anteo of Bologna. The fact that the book had no *imprimatur* was indeed the first point to be raised with Küng by the Doctrinal Congregation. The lack of one was deliberate (*Infallible?,* p. 24):

> No imprimatur will be sought for this book; not because it is not intended to be Catholic, but because – as we hope – it is Catholic without it. In recent years the imprimatur has become increasingly meaningless. It did not prevent my book *The Church* from becoming involved in Roman inquisitionary proceedings which have not yet closed. On the other hand, more than one bishop has asked authors to refrain from seeking an imprimatur, which might be interpreted in Rome and elsewhere as implying episcopal recommendation of the book.

Clearly in Rome they were not in the habit of taking any notice of the disclaimer appended to *imprimaturs* in Britain which stated that what was involved was simply a declaration that the book was considered free from doctrinal or moral error without any implication that those granting the *imprimatur* agreed with its contents or with the opinions or statements expressed. Küng could have illustrated his case by pointing to the absurd goings-on over the Dutch *New Catechism,* the English translation of which appeared in

September 1967 with the *imprimatur* of an American bishop in the English edition but with the Dutch Cardinal Alfrink's original *imprimatur* in the American edition. This was because the American bishop concerned had withdrawn his *imprimatur* when he learned of an agreement between Rome and the Dutch bishops not to publish any translations until agreed changes had been made, but had been too late to catch the English edition, which was already printed. Even more farcical were the goings-on over the German edition. Herder of Freiburg were unable to obtain an *imprimatur*, and after waiting a year they transferred the rights in the German translation to a Dutch firm which promptly, to the fury of the German bishops, brought out an edition.[3]

The letter from Cardinal Šeper of 12 February 1971 complaining of this lack of *imprimatur* is worth quoting from:

> Quite apart from whether the questions posed in your book ought in any case to be put by a Catholic, the following point needs to be made for a start: you have, unequivocally and not for the first time, disregarded a provision of Church law that is still valid and that despite a great deal of discussion has not in any way been done away with. You have made use of your reputation publicly to call for disobedience to the legitimate authorities [*Obrigkeit*] in the Church, for example on the question of mixed marriages. Allow me to invite you to reflect very carefully over your position in the Church and over the scope and effect of what you undertake. I hope you will then come to the conclusion that this is not the way in which one can really love and serve the Church.

The statement on mixed marriages had clearly infuriated not just the German bishops but the authorities in Rome too. But most revealing of all is the admission that from the point of view of the Doctrinal Congregation there are certain questions that Catholics just should not ask.

Five months later the Congregation sent Küng its list of the theses in his book that struck it as irreconcilable with Catholic doctrine and as creating difficulties in the way of a Catholic interpretation. It began by noting that Küng had put his views forward as subjects for discussion. But it felt that even opinions put forward in this way by a Catholic theologian should stay within the bounds of Catholic doctrine. Its difficulties centred on four points: Küng's refusal to limit the assistance of the Holy Spirit to the pope and the bishops and his rejection of the idea that the authentic proclamation and exposition of the Christian message was reserved to them alone (*Infallible?*, pp. 192–193); his indication of the extremely shaky foundations on which the doctrine of infallibility rested (pp. 70 and 103); his substitution of indefectibility for infallibility and his definition of it as a fundamental remaining in the truth which is not destroyed by errors in detail (p. 149); and his rejection of the idea of infallible propositions (p. 123).

The Congregation's letter was dated 12 July 1971 and required an answer within the statutory thirty days. But, even though it was sent express, it reached Küng in Tübingen only a few hours before he left on a lecture tour taking him right round the world, as he explained to Cardinal Šeper in a handwritten note from the Hotel Budapest in Moscow. He only got back to Tübingen on 6 December, and within a fortnight the Congregation sent him a reminder, dated 17 December 1971 and timed to reach him just before Christmas, asking for a reply to its questions within thirty days. Küng's reply was eventually dated 24 January and reached the Doctrinal Congregation on 2 February 1972. It fell into two parts. First came an expostulation against the whole manner and style of the proceedings. He objected to not having been shown the famous dossier 399/57/i with all the documents relating to his case. He objected to the Congregation appointing a *relator 'pro auctore'* and felt he should be able to choose the person to speak for him in the Congregation's investigations. He objected to the multiplicity of overlapping proceedings his book was being subjected to, with various bishops' conferences opening their own proceedings and now the Doctrinal Congregation's investigation coming on top of these without any apparent delimitation of competences and responsibilities. He wanted to know if there was any right of appeal and if so where to. Finally, he wanted to know how long it was proposed to let the proceedings drag on for. The Doctrinal Congregation gave authors thirty days in which to reply, but there was no time-limit to their activities: proceedings against *The Church* had already dragged on for four years (and in the event were to continue for another three).

In answer to the specific points the Congregation raised, Küng first pointed out that it was no good simply reaffirming the assertions that had come under his critical scrutiny. The whole point was to discover what precisely the theological basis for them was. He thus asked the Congregation to supply a defence of the possibility of infallible propositions that would not simply ignore but would take into account the difficulties he had raised with regard to certain statements by the Church's teaching authority. He indicated the extent of the debate and discussion his book had provoked, and wondered how the Congregation would judge this. From his own observations the following picture emerged:

> (a) There are hardly any serious Catholic contributions to the debate that do not regard my questions as justified.
> (b) There are hardly any serious Catholic contributions to the debate that do not subject the traditional Roman view to what is in part very strong criticism, even if they do not agree with my solution or do not fully agree with it.
> (c) My critics very often contradict each other, and

do so both with regard to the interpretation of the Roman doctrine of infallibility and with regard to the answer to my enquiry.

(d)   So far no single writer – and in my view this is decisive for the outcome of the debate – has offered a convincing argument for the possibility of infallible propositions.

All the responses to his book he would continue to subject to intensive study, he added. As part of this he invited the Congregation to send one of its own experts to the top-level seminar on the infallibility debate which he was proposing to hold in Tübingen that coming summer term and to which he was inviting his oponents to put their case (with their expenses met by the Institute for Ecumenical Research): this invitation was not taken up by the Congregation. All he was concerned with, Küng went on, was the objective clarification of a question that was so decisive for the theory and practice of the Church they belonged to.

Kung concluded with a powerful direct appeal to Cardinal Franjo Šeper, the Congregation's prefect:

> Your Eminence,[4] I do not know what your judgement is of the present situation of the Catholic Church. What I am referring to is the world-wide mistrust felt by clergy and laity towards the bodies responsible for running the Church and above all towards Rome; and the negative effects of this mistrust are quite incalculable. It is something that has arisen not from ill will but from disappointment. I have been able to substantiate this in thousands of conversations with people all over the world and through letters and statements that reach me every day from Catholic lay-people, theology students and priests from the most varied parts of our Church. Rome's loss of credibility since Vatican II has been dramatic, and the reasons for it must for the most part be found in the situation there. In our own Church today I am often reproachfully asked why on earth I write a book on

papal infallibility and go to the bother of conducting correspondence with the authorities in Rome. My answer is always that for my part I haven't written Rome off, that I am not working for the downfall of the Catholic Church. I do not share the conviction that virtually everything must collapse before we can start to build anew. In a statement that has won considerable attention and provoked a very positive response I have explained publicly why along with all my criticism of certain institutions and procedures I am staying in this Church that I belong to and how, undeterred by all the attacks on my outlook as a Catholic, I mean to go on working in it as I have done up to now. At a time when tens of thousands of priests and nuns are giving up their ministry or leaving their order or congregation I have used innumerable private letters, conversations and lectures to give students, priests, religious and lay people the hope and the courage to persevere and to renew their commitment and contribution to the Church, to its ministry and to the religious life. During my recent round-the-world trip that lasted several months I tried everywhere to combat this boundless feeling of frustration and resignation by showing on the basis of the Christian message how important and meaningful this kind of commitment was, despite all the difficulties. I have received impressive testimonials both orally and in writing from men and women who have gratefully reaffirmed their existence in the Church again with new strength and hope.

Your Eminence, Rome too could inspire Christians with new courage and new confidence by means of fundamental renewal and convincing reforms according to the gospel of Jesus Christ. I do not regard myself as infallible. I am not pig-headed and am always ready to stand corrected by those who know more than I. I do not want to demolish Rome, as from certain quarters I am accused of wanting to do, nor in any case do I fancy I am capable of doing so. This is something that only Rome is capable of doing through its lack of understanding and its

backward-looking rigidity. Although Rome is a name
other Catholics do not even want to hear any more, it
is something I am concerned with in my theology
because I am convinced of the necessity and of the
usefulness of a Petrine ministry not just for our own
Church but for the whole of Christendom. What I am
aiming at is a Church that, acting in the spirit of the
gospel of Jesus Christ, does much more than hitherto
for the men and women of today and for their
anxieties and needs. For the sake of this gospel and
people's salvation I take on much extra work and
trouble that I am not in any way obliged by my
position to undertake. It is for the same reason that I
direct my criticism at the Roman authorities, at
various traditional ecclesiastical practices and
theological concepts. If relatively speaking much of
this letter has had to be taken up with a few formal
questions, with certain demands of justice and fairness
[he uses the English word] in the Church and in the
Roman Curia, nevertheless all this is completely
secondary as far as my theological work is concerned
but in this context had to be said to you as the
representative of an official Roman body. The
administration of a Church that talks so much about
'justice in the world' must in principle first let
humanity and justice flourish within its own walls if it
is to be credible in the world.

This peroration serves as a reminder of the strength of
Küng's passionate loyalty to the Church. It would have
been very easy for him simply to have lost patience with the
institution – as a number of his contemporaries did – and
to have withdrawn into his own shell.

But Küng's plea fell on deaf ears. The Doctrinal
Congregation's response came over a year later and took the
form of the declaration *Mysterium Ecclesiae*. Published on 5
July 1973, this document, as we have seen (p. 163 above),
did not mention Küng by name but was clearly aimed at his
views. The first and last of its six sections dealt with views
objected to in *The Church*, the middle four with those in

Infallible? The Congregation's starting-point was the infallibility of the Church as a whole:

> God, who is absolutely infallible, thus deigned to bestow upon his new people, which is the Church, a certain shared infallibility, which is restricted to matters of faith and morals, which is present when the whole people of God unhesitatingly holds a point of doctrine pertaining to these matters, and finally which always depends upon the wise providence and anointing grace of the Holy Spirit, who leads the Church into all truth until the glorious coming of her Lord.

But, while ordinary Christians contributed 'in many ways' towards increasing the Church's understanding of what it believes, ultimately their only privilege was to assent to what the pope and the bishops taught:

> But by divine institution it is the exclusive task of these pastors alone, the successors of Peter and the other apostles, to teach the faithful authentically, that is with the authority of Christ shared in different ways; so that the faithful, who may not simply listen to them as experts in Catholic doctrine, must accept their teaching given in Christ's name, with an assent that is proportionate to the authority that they possess and that they mean to exercise.

We seem to be back with the over-sharp distinction between the *ecclesia docens* and the *ecclesia discens* and with the curious idea that the credibility and acceptability of what the Church teaches depends not on its intrinsic authority, whether it is true or not, but on the extrinsic authority of who is proclaiming it.

The Congregation went on to assert that Jesus Christ wished to endow the teaching authority of the pope and the bishops 'with a fitting charism of infallibility in matters regarding faith and morals' – while adding that this did not exempt them from the normal methods of finding out where the truth lay. This infallibility, the Congregation said, extended not only to the deposit of faith but also to those matters without which that deposit could not be rightly preserved and expounded. The extension of this infallibility to the deposit of faith itself was 'a truth that the Church has from the beginning held as having been certainly revealed in Christ's promises.'

On this basis the Congregation was now able formally to reject Küng's central thesis:

> From what has been said about the extent of and conditions governing the infallibility of the people of God and of the Church's magisterium, it follows that the faithful are in no way permitted to see in the Church merely a fundamental permanence in truth which, as some assert, could be reconciled with errors contained here and there in the propositions that the Church's magisterium teaches to be held irrevocably, as also in the unhesitating assent of the people of God concerning matters of faith and morals.

The declaration did admit the existence of 'as it were a hierarchy of the Church's dogmas', though it went on to rob this admission of most of its force by insisting that 'all dogmas, since they are revealed, must be believed with the same divine faith'. More importantly, it admitted that doctrinal formulations were historically conditioned and that some dogmatic truths could begin by being expressed incompletely (but not falsely) and later be amplified. It recognized that dogmatic pronouncements did not, in a very important sense, say anything new: their purpose was to confirm or clarify something somehow contained in scripture or in previous definitions, while at the same time they were usually intended to solve certain questions or to remove certain errors. It distinguished between the truths the Church intended to teach through its dogmatic formulas and the changeable conceptions of a given epoch, and while claiming that the former could be expressed without the latter it stated that such truths might sometimes be enunciated in terms that bore traces of these changeable conceptions.

The dogmatic formulations of the Church's teaching authority thus remained for ever suitable for communicating revealed truth 'to those who interpret them correctly', even though it did not follow 'that every one of these formulas has always been or will always be so to the same extent'. That was why old formulations sometimes gave way to new. But the *meaning* of doctrinal formulations always remained the same:

> The faithful therefore must shun the opinion, first, that dogmatic formulas (or some category of them) cannot signify truth in a determinate way, but can only offer changeable approximations to it, which to a certain extent distort or alter it; secondly, that these formulas signify the truth only in an indeterminate way, this truth being like a goal that is constantly being sought by means of such approximations. Those who hold such an opinion do not avoid dogmatic relativism and they corrupt the concept of the Church's infallibility relative to the truth to be taught or held in an determinate way.[5]

That would seem to rule out of court many of Küng's views about the essential ambiguity of human language.

In a public statement in response Hans Küng claimed that his enquiry had been not answered but rather side-stepped. Rome might have spoken, but the case was not closed: it was still open. He recognized the advance implied by the Congregation's acceptance that formulations of belief could be historically conditioned rather than timeless. And not only were no names named but there were no excommunications or condemnations. Rome seemed to have learned that issues such as these could not be solved by condemnations: creating martyrs did not pay off (*The Tablet*, 14 July 1973, pp. 670–671).

Privately Küng was offered a choice: accept the teaching

contained in this declaration, in which case the proceedings involving *The Church* and *Infallible?* would be brought to an end; or agree to a discussion with representatives of the Doctrinal Congregation on the points it had already raised about the two books. Originally the Congregation had intended to face Küng with an ultimatum: accept the declaration, or else . . . The fact that he was given a choice was due to last minute negotiations with the Congregation's secretary, Archbishop Jérôme Hamer, OP, by Cardinal Julius Döpfner, Archbishop of Munich and president of the German bishops' conference, Cardinal Hermann Volk, Bishop of Mainz (whose research assistant Küng had been at Münster in 1959 and 1960), and Bishop Carl Joseph Leiprecht of Rottenburg, in whose diocese Tübingen was situated (*Wahrheit*, p. 24). The three German bishops did their best to persuade Küng to take part in a discussion; but their efforts – which were presumably the condition for Rome dropping its ultimatum – proved unsuccessful.

Küng continued to insist on the conditions he had laid down in 1968: the right to see the dossier on himself; the ability to appoint his own 'counsel for the defence' in place of some unknown *relator 'pro auctore'* appointed by the Congregation; an indication of what rights of appeal were open to him; and some time-limit on the Congregation's procedures. To his mind a discussion under the Vatican rules would amount to an interrogation; and what he was concerned about was getting a fair trial. What he objected to was the Doctrinal Congregation acting at one and the same time as legislator, prosecuting counsel, judge and jury while operating on the principal enunciated by the Queen of Hearts in *Alice in Wonderland*: 'Sentence first – verdict afterwards.' What, clearly, he was afraid of was of somehow being manoeuvred into appearing to acquiesce in whatever disciplinary measures the Congregation might deem necessary. In such proceedings it always looks better if the victim apparently accepts, or even welcomes, the fate meted out to him.

The controversy thus dragged on. The Doctrinal Congregation wrote on 16 August 1973 wondering why it had not yet received a response to *Mysterium Ecclesiae* and giving Küng till 20 September to reply. Küng wrote to the pope asking whether both sides had not now said all they needed to say and whether it would not be better now to let Catholic theologians argue the question out uninhibited by any disciplinary measures and to allow the question at issue between him and the Congregation to drop, leaving any verdict to history. The same day (22 September 1973) he put the same proposal to the Congregation in his long-awaited reply to its declaration. In his long letter he repeated his objections to the Congregation's mode of procedure and also pointed out that it was of no use their resting their case for infallibility on the statements of Vatican I and Vatican II: it was precisely the theological basis of these statements that he had been questioning.

Private conversations with those responsible during a visit to Rome in October led Küng to hope that a tacit agreement to let the matter drop might indeed be possible, as he revealed the following summer in an article provoked by an interview given by the Doctrinal Congregation's secretary, Archbishop Hamer (*The Tablet*, 6 July 1974, pp. 662–663). There were also talks with Cardinals Döpfner and Volk in February 1974. But hopes of a cease-fire proved groundless. The Doctrinal Congregation replied to Küng on 30 March with a letter nearly as long as his own. Its tone was that of someone patiently trying to expose the false accusations brought against his or her good name. The Congregation accused Küng of trying to divert attention from the doctrinal issues to questions of procedure. It remained convinced that its procedure was just and fair, and although it had sent Küng a copy of its rules of procedure nearly three years earlier (see p. 158 above) it went on to give a painstaking exposition of how these worked. What was involved was not the equivalent of criminal proceedings but an investigation into whether a theological opinion could be brought into agreement with divine revelation and with the Church's magisterium. Such an investigation fell into two phases. First, the Congregation would mount an internal study to see whether the views expressed in the work under investigation were or were not in conflict with the Church's teaching: it was in this context that the *relator 'pro auctore'* was appointed to make sure that the author's positive arguments and concerns were fully taken into account (in other words, as a kind of devil's advocate). Then, if the Congregation decided that certain views could not be reconciled with the Church's teaching, the author would in the second phase be invited to explain and defend his views.

The Congregation suggested that Küng was largely responsible for proceedings having been dragged out so long. It rejected the conditions he was still insisting on: just as its investigation was not the equivalent of criminal proceedings, so too the dossier on Küng was not the equivalent of trial documents, and the essential dossier was the author's published writings; similarly the *relator 'pro auctore'* should not be equated with counsel for the defence but merely played a role in the Congregation's internal investigation, and it was the author himself who enjoyed the right of defence; and if the author believed irregularities had occurred he was guaranteed the right of appeal 'by the general norms of existing law'. In passing the Congregation revealed that sometimes an investigation into someone's work could take place and lead to the conclusion that it fell within the bounds of orthodoxy 'without the author learning of this or being unnecessarily disturbed'.

The discussion to which Küng was invited should not be understood as a free academic discussion among theologians or as an exchange of views like a congress or conference. The aim was to give him the opportunity to explain why he thought his views were open to debate without prejudice or detriment to doctrines a Catholic was bound to believe. In this way the Congregation had seen itself obliged to act in the defence of Catholic doctrine:

> The publication of the declaration *Mysterium Ecclesiae* became necessary because, despite the fact that proceedings were under way and in the face of the Congregation's express invitation in December 1967 and with disregard for the law currently in force about the need for an *imprimatur*, you continued . . . to disseminate in your writings in various languages and in lectures in various parts of the world views which have caused the profoundest confusion to the faith of the community of the Church. These were not the least of the reasons why the Church's competent authority was obliged to take steps to defend the faith and to intervene to clarify matters, something that the faithful have a right to.

And the Congregation put in a brief complaint against Küng's use of publicity in his dispute with it.

What emerges clearly from this part of the Doctrinal Congregation's letter is that it saw not the slightest difficulty over its deciding whether or not a view conflicted with the Church's teaching when the very point at issue was what precisely the Church's teaching was and whether it might turn out to be not quite what everyone had been assuming it was. Not so long ago it was thought the Church was committed to believing that the human race was descended from a single couple, and indeed Pius XII insisted strongly on this point in *Humani generis*. But now it is generally accepted that the doctrine of original sin can be combined with other views of human origins. Yet despite such examples the Congregation blithely assumed that there was no difficulty about recognizing what the Church's teaching in fact was. There could be no question of the Congregation changing the teaching of Vatican I and

Vatican II or of *Mysterium Ecclesiae* in any eventual discussion, it said in its letter. Yet precisely what was at issue was whether the Church was in fact committed to what Vatican I and Vatican II had said about infallibility. The Congregation's attitude thus threatened to leave the theologian under investigation able to do no more than murmur the remark attributed to Galileo after he had been forced to recant by the Inquisition: '*Eppur si muove* – but all the same it *does* move.'

Turning to the doctrinal issues, the Congregation made its position on the limits set to legitimate theological enquiry quite clear:

> A Catholic theologian is undoubtedly allowed to raise a question that affects a truth of faith and in that case to look for a clarification. But even if he were not at once to find a reasonable justification of this truth a Catholic theologian cannot cast into doubt or even deny the truth of faith itself. No Catholic theologian, as long as he is a Catholic, regards as permitted the denial or calling into question of a dogma of faith in the name of theology.

It took up what it saw as Küng's distinction between infallibility and infallible propositions, which it described as 'interesting', and suggested it might form a subject for discussion when the proposed discussion took place in the form of the question: 'How can infallibility, in the manner in which it was dogmatically proclaimed by the First and Second Vatican Councils, be maintained if the possibility of infallible propositions is denied?'

The Congregation answered Küng's appeal to the freedom theologians should enjoy by stressing the theologian's responsibility to the Christian community and to the authority of the Church. A believing Catholic did not enjoy the freedom to deny a revealed truth in the name of theological freedom, it said. For all these reasons it rejected Küng's proposal simply to let the proceedings drop and allow history to judge where the truth of the matter lay:

> There is in the Church a different criterion than the verdict of history: the authority of the living magisterium that has been established for the service of the revealed truth. The declaration *Mysterium Ecclesiae* has appealed to a defined dogma with regard to the infallibility of the Church and of the pope; we cannot see how a defined teaching of this kind could be left to the 'verdict' of the future.

If the silence Küng proposed meant obscuring the unambiguous clarity of doctrine, the Congregation could not accept this. But if it could be understood and interpreted as an act of respect towards the magisterium and as providing time for reflection in which he could examine his views and bring them into line with the magisterium, then this proposal might perhaps have some sense.

This turned out to be the point which enabled both sides to back down with dignity. In his eventual reply, dated 4 September 1974, Küng once again objected strongly to the Congregation's way of going about things. But he concluded by saying he certainly did not want to exclude the possibility that his views could in the course of time come into line with those of the magisterium, while he was sure the Doctrinal Congregation would for its part always be open to new developments and insights.

The Doctrinal Congregation's response was its declaration of 15 February 1975 formally bringing the proceedings against *The Church* and *Infallible?* to an end – that is, until the complaints against the latter book and against *On being a Christian* were resurrected and made the excuse for stripping him of his *missio canonica* in December 1979. The Congregation rejected the reduction of the doctrine of infallibility to some kind of indefectibility in the truth coupled with the possibility of errors in detail: this contradicted the teaching reaffirmed by Vatican I and

Vatican II. Küng was criticized for departing from the genuine teaching on the Church's teaching authority whereby the task of authentically interpreting the word of God was entrusted to the Church's living magisterium. Finally Küng's view about the possibility in an emergency of a valid eucharist being celebrated by a lay person was mentioned as incompatible with the Fourth Lateran and Second Vatican Councils. But, despite the heinousness of these views, since in his letter of 4 September 1974 Küng had not excluded the possibility that deeper study might help to bring his views into line with the doctrine proclaimed by the Church's authentic magisterium, the Congregation for the moment warned him not to go on putting these views forward. It reminded him 'that the authority of the Church has empowered him to teach theology in the spirit of the Church's doctrine, not to advocate views that turn this doctrine upside down or call it into question'.

As Cardinal Döpfner made clear in his press conference to introduce the German bishops' commentary on this declaration (a commentary which was also the first of their statements criticizing *On being a Christian*, which had meanwhile been published), there was no recourse to disciplinary measures. But, as events were to prove four and a half years later, Küng had not been acquitted or discharged. He had merely been bound over to be of good behaviour. Disciplinary measures remained in reserve if Küng should be judged to have broken the silence on the question of infallibility which, to the mind of the Doctrinal Congregation, was the price he had to pay for the proceedings being brought to an end.

The long-drawn-out battle with the Doctrinal Congregation was, to put it mildly, a wearying time for Hans Küng. At times he understandably felt himself to be the victim of a well-orchestrated campaign against him. The pressures could become intense. Writing to Cardinal

Volk in the wake of *Mysterium Ecclesiae*, he explained that in the course of a week he had received or been exposed to: the Doctrinal Congregation's declaration (and that in two copies, one via a messenger from the nunciature in Bonn, one via registered post); two Vatican press conferences; two articles in *L'Osservatore Romano*; two statements by the German bishops' conferences; a visit from a bishop; and a letter from Cardinal Volk himself. And all this was not to mention all the telephone calls, letters, conversations, enquiries from reporters, etc., inseparable from such goings on. Outside events added their pressure too: the Doctrinal Congregation's success in removing Fr Pfürtner from his post in Switzerland in April 1964 more or less coincided with its lengthy letter to him of 30 March.

But if what turned out to be merely a temporary cease-fire had been won in one battle another was just beginning to flare up. That arose over *On being a Christian*, and this time the Roman authorities left the conduct of the dispute strictly to the German bishops. But before we consider this dispute and the book that gave rise to it we need to go back and look at Küng's earlier treatment of Christology, a treatment centred on the philosopher Georg Wilhelm Friedrich Hegel.

[1] For the Halbfas case see 'Freedom for Halbfas?', *Herder Correspondence* vol. 6 no. 2, February 1969, pp. 55–59. For Monsignor Illich see 'The Cuernavaca Dossier', ibid. vol. 6 no. 4, April 1969, pp. 110–119. For the Pfürtner case see Peter Hebblethwaite, *The Runaway Church*, Collins, London, 1975, pp. 219–221, and two articles by Ludwig Kaufmann, SJ, in *Orientierung*, 30 April 1974, vol. 38 no. 8, pp. 89–92, and in *Choisir*, June 1974, no. 174, pp. 2–12: a French translation of Pfürtner's offending lecture was published in the March 1972 issue of *Choisir* (no. 149). Both the Pfürtner and the Schupp cases

were the subject of a leading article in *Orientierung* (30 November 1974, vol. 38 no. 22, pp. 238–239). For the other cases see *Le Monde*, 11 and 21 December 1974, and for the action taken against Father Girardi in 1969 see 'The Girardi Case', *Herder Correspondence*, vol. 7, no. 2, February 1970, pp. 52–55.

2 An English translation of the German bishops' statement, for some odd reason shorn of its first three sentences, can be found in *The Month*, vol. 132 no. 1249, September 1971, p. 73, along with Küng's statement of 25 June 1971.

3 *Herder Correspondence*, vol. 5, no. 12, December 1968, p. 363.

4 This is precisely the form of address Küng did *not* use in his letter. He has not addressed a cardinal as 'Your Eminence' since Vatican II. But there is no English equivalent to the form of address he did use, *Sehr verehrter Herr Kardinal*, which is formal, polite and respectful while avoiding addressing him as *Eminenz*. 'My dear Cardinal' would be insufferably patronizing.

5 Quotations are from the translation of *Mysterium Ecclesiae* published in *The Tablet*, 14 July 1973, pp. 667–670

14

Hegel as a Theologian

Infallible? brought to an end a series of works concerned with the Church and our understanding of it. They can be seen as representing the most immediate and obvious response on Küng's part to the Second Vatican Council, which by the mere fact of being summoned and taking place affected our perception of the Church. But underlying this series of works was the realization that the Church is not an end in itself, that the only justification for its existence is the message it is empowered to preach. And in the 1970s Küng concentrated more and more on what precisely this message is.

Indeed, it was a theme with which he began the decade. At the theological congress on 'The Future of the Church' organized by *Concilium* and held at Brussels in September 1970 Hans Küng gave a paper entitled 'What is the Christian message?' which already foreshadows many of the key points of *On being a Christian* to be published four years later. Expressed in a single phrase, the Christian message, he said, was Jesus as the Christ. Jesus preached the reign of God (and here we look back to *The Church* and the chapter on 'The Preaching of Jesus', pp. 43–54); but he defied all accepted classification, was neither Sadducee nor Zealot nor Essene nor Pharisee, was provocative both to right and left (and here we anticipate the chapter on 'The Social Context' in *On being a Christian*, pp. 177–213). The life Jesus led and the message he preached led to his death; but his disciples somehow came to realize (and the how, when and where is not decisive, only the that) that he who

245

had been crucified was alive, that God had raised him up. In 1970 Küng thus presented a five-and-a-half page synopsis of *On being a Christian* which shows that much of the essential foundations of the later work had already been laid. At Brussels he described the Christian message in these terms:

> In the light and in the power of Jesus we can in the world of today live, act, suffer and die in a truly human way; utterly committed to our fellow-man because utterly sustained by God.

In the book the final answer to the question: 'Why should one be a Christian?' is (*Christian*, p. 602):

> By following Jesus Christ man in the world of today can truly humanly live, act, suffer and die: in happiness and unhappiness, life and death, sustained by God and helpful to men.

The book can thus from one point of view be regarded as a filling-out of the skeletal framework presented at the Brussels congress.

But in order to present the Christian message in terms accessible to the men and women of today Küng needed to explore the immediate intellectual tradition which supplied the concepts in which this message would need to be expressed. And an outstanding shaper of this intellectual tradition was the thinker whose stature was such as to lead Barth to ask why he had not become for Protestant theology the equivalent to what Thomas Aquinas was for Catholic, why for the modern world he had not become what Thomas Aquinas had been for the late middle ages: Hegel (*Menschwerdung*, p. 335). Küng's preoccupation with Hegel went back to his student days. Originally he had thought of presenting a dissertation on Hegel's Christology for a doctorate of philosophy at the Sorbonne. Then it was to be the subject of the *Habilitation* that in the event was made unnecessary by his sudden call to Tübingen. The first draft of the book he wrote on Hegel's Christology,

Menschwerdung Gottes, was completed while he was still at Münster as a research assistant preparing for his *Habilitation*; and it was only finally published, a couple of revisions later, in 1970 – in fact, just before *Infallible?*

This preoccupation with Hegel may seem a little puzzling to English-speaking readers, especially as Küng's book has so far remained untranslated into English. Hegel is the kind of philosopher whom they are apt gladly to pass by on the other side. In pursuit of an all-embracing synthesis that would make sense of the entirety of human experience, he plunged into linguistic thickets that to the non-German-speaker can seem impenetrable. 'Hegel's philosophy is very difficult – he is, I should say, the hardest to understand of all the great philosophers,' was Bertrand Russell's comment.[1] Hegel's own ambition was to teach philosophy to speak German; and those who are unimpressed by the complex profundity of which philosophical and particularly Hegelian German is capable may feel he succeeded only too well. Not only is his syntax frequently tortuous and his language opaque, but he revelled in the deliberate ambiguity of a term like *aufheben*, which means both to cancel, to put an end to, and to preserve, to raise up: Hegel liked to use it to denote both contradictory meanings at once, and to the despair of their translators he has been followed in this linguistic vice by both Barth and Küng. Küng is indeed warm in his defence of Hegel's language and quotes both Adorno and Bloch as staunch advocates of his use of German. Hegel's fully developed language is, to Küng's mind, the expression of fully developed thought (*Menschwerdung,* pp. 245–247).

Nor is it just Hegel's language that creates obstacles for him in the English-speaking world. The English philosophical tradition is suspicious of attempts to build an all-embracing system and prefers a piecemeal approach, tentative, empirical, pragmatic. Hegel may have dominated English academic philosophy for a century or so after his death; but with the resurgence of the empirical tradition he has been largely ignored, and students have tended to jump from Kant to Moore, Russell and Wittgenstein.

A further puzzle about *Menschwerdung Gottes* for English-speaking readers is that they would expect a theologian to grapple with a contemporary philosopher rather than with one dead for nearly a century and a half, with Wittgenstein or Sartre, say, rather than Hegel. They would assume that his ideas would by now have been so thoroughly absorbed into the intellectual bloodstream that the kind of exercise undertaken by Küng in this book would no longer be necessary. But this is to reckon without a number of factors. For a start, ideas in the German-speaking world enjoy a persistence and power that hardly obtain elsewhere. They exert a fascination that most other cultures are exempt from:

> For the Germans cherish a hopeless passion for the absolute, under whatever name and in whatever guise they imagine it. The Russians have had stranger visions; the French have shown themselves more capable of embodying abstract ideas in political institutions; but the Germans are unique perhaps in the ardour with which they pursue ideas and attempt to transform them into realities. Their great achievements, their catastrophic failures, their tragic political history are all impregnated with this dangerous idealism. If most of us are the victims of circumstances, it may truly be said of the Germans as a whole that they are at the mercy of ideas.[2]

Theory thus comes to count for more than practice, as Hegel himself held. Küng quotes from a letter written during that curious period in his life after Jena when he was first an editor and then a headmaster (*Menschwerdung*, p. 306):

> Theoretical work, I am daily more convinced, accomplishes more in the world than practical; once a

revolution has taken place in the realm of ideas, reality offers no resistance.

We are a long way from Dr Johnson's celebrated refutation of Bishop Berkeley's theory of matter by striking his foot against a large stone until he rebounded from it.

Beyond this, ideas in the German-speaking world retain a novelty that elsewhere they have long since lost. Ideas that in England were thrown up in the turmoil of the Commonwealth and that in France were given legitimacy by the Revolution can still retain a dangerous novelty in Germany. In that country intellectual discussion tends automatically to reach back to the eighteenth-century Enlightenment in order to establish its foundations and credentials. The whole business of people asserting their own intellectual autonomy instead of accepting ideas ready-made for them by outside agencies still retains a freshness and daring which makes the Enlightenment somehow relevant and contemporary to twentieth-century Germany in a way that comparable movements of thought in eighteenth-century Britain or America are not to their twentieth-century legatees. This is not just because the break with the habit of deference to authority and to received wisdom marked by the Enlightenment towards the end of the eighteenth century in Germany had been heralded by comparable shifts in attitude in seventeenth-century England and earlier in the eighteenth century in France. It is also because this shift in attitudes, as happened elsewhere, took time to work its way through the system, and this process was, to say the least, hardly helped or encouraged by Germany's political development.

Hegel thus retains a certain contemporary relevance. He came to maturity in an age of political turmoil. When he was a student at Tübingen he allegedly joined with Hölderlin, Schelling and others in planting a liberty tree, while Schelling was accused of translating the Marseillaise. These dangerous revolutionary stirrings led to the personal intervention of the Duke of Württemberg himself to put an end to this student unrest and restore a proper respect for authority (*Menschwerdung*, p. 59). But it was not only the subversive ideas of liberty, equality and fraternity that affected Hegel along with his contemporaries, aided in their case at Tübingen by the presence of French students: Württemberg then included a portion of what is now French territory the other side of the Rhine around Montbéliard. Küng points to two other influences: the revolution in ways of thinking initiated by Kant's critique and continuation of the enlightenment; and the early romantic movement that represented a reaction both to this and to the French Revolution (*Menschwerdung*, p. 60). There was at this time a fourth, but it would be a long time before its influence was felt in continental Europe. This was the industrial revolution that was already transforming Britain from a predominantly rural and agricultural society into a predominantly urban and industrial one, at the cost of alienating the vast mass of the population from their work and occupation. This surely had far more effect on the pattern of people's lives than the ferment of ideas, but it was a piecemeal, pragmatic process going on largely unobserved even among those affected by it – witness the esteem in which landed wealth is held in Jane Austen's works and the way industrial wealth is ignored – and its investigation and analysis would have to await a future generation of thinkers coming to maturity half-a-century later.

It was, in any case, a world of change, often dramatic and violent change. There may have been equally dramatic and violent change in the past; but now change was coming to be accepted as the stable feature of human history, not as some anomaly to be got out of the way so as to enable mankind to revert to an ideal of static perfection. All this had its effect on how people thought of God – if, indeed, there were a God at all. The scientific outlook that had begun to predominate made it impossible to think of God as some medieval puppet-master continually intervening in the morality play of his creation. But even less satisfactory was the remote watchmaker implied by Paley's argument from design in his *Evidences,* or the unknown creator enthroned beyond the stars whom Schiller offered in his 'Ode to Joy' — for all that Schiller also describes him as a beloved father. What now inescapably demanded resolution was the tension that had been built into the Christian idea of God when the challenging, unpindownable God of the Old Testament was expressed in the categories of Greek thought. God was by definition absolute perfection, and for this absolute perfection to become involved in this human world of passion and suffering and change could seem to cast doubt on this very perfection. This was why the Christ crucified whom Paul preached was to the Greeks foolishness.

How any link, any bridge could be established between the absolute and the contingent, between the infinite and the finite, was one of the major dilemmas which Hegel grappled with throughout his career. Despite the rather unprepossessing religious background of a somewhat flabby and uninspiring Lutheran orthodoxy overlaid by the rationalism of the Enlightenment, the question not just of God but of God's involvement with and in the world remained a lifelong pre-occupation. It is this question that provides the theme of Küng's book, the scope of which is defined by his title and sub-title: 'God's Becoming Man: an introduction to Hegel's theological thought as prolegomena to a future Christology.' Küng traces not just the development of Hegel's theological thought, right from his final years at the *Gymnasium* in Stuttgart and his first years as a student at Tübingen, but also provides as much in the way of biography as most people are likely to want, even if one or two piquant details may be missing — such as Hegel's 1800 dissertation in which he set out to prove that there could be no more than seven planets just before an eighth (Ceres) was discovered on 1 January 1801.[3] Ideas retained a disconcerting habit of being refuted by facts, if not by Dr Johnson's foot.

For Hegel the incarnation, the fact that God had become man, was what distinguished revealed religion from earlier stages of religion (*Menschwerdung*, p. 262). What had previously been hinted at or dreamed of now became reality:

> The Self of existent Spirit has, as a result, the form of complete immediacy; it is posited neither as something thought or imagined, nor as something produced, as is the case with the immediate Self in natural religion, and also in the religion of Art; on the contrary, this God is sensuously and directly beheld as a Self, as an actual individual man; only so *is* this God self-consciousness.
>
> This incarnation of the divine Being, or the fact that it essentially and directly has the shape of self-consciousness, is the simple content of the absolute religion. In this religion the divine Being is known as Spirit, or this religion is the consciousness of the divine Being that is Spirit. For Spirit is the knowledge of oneself in the externalization of oneself; the being that is the movement of retaining its self-identity in its otherness. This, however, is Substance, in so far as Substance is, in its accidents, at the same time reflected into itself, not indifferent to them as to something unessential or present in them as an alien element, but in them it is within itself, i.e. in so far as it is Subject or Self. Consequently, in this religion the divine Being is *revealed*. Its being revealed obviously consists in this, that what it is, is known. But it is known precisely as its being known as Spirit, as a Being that is essentially a *self-conscious Being*.[4]

This passage offers an admirable illustration of the barrier to communication that Hegel can raise between himself and his readers. It does admittedly occur in chapters where

Küng notes a lack of conciseness and precision that reflects the haste and confusion surrounding their composition (*Menschwerdung*, p. 263). The completion of the *Phenomenology* coincided with the battle and sack of Jena, and Hegel carried the final pages of the work around with him in his overcoat pocket for a whole week – he had his home looted – before he was able to send them to his publisher in Bamberg. It was the time Hegel was so impressed by his sight of Napoleon, 'this world-soul', riding through the city on reconnaissance, the domination of the world embodied in a single individual sitting on a horse (*Menschwerdung*, pp. 243–244).

Hegel may indeed introduce a dynamic image of God, an evolutionary God, even. The incarnation may indeed play a central role in his thought. But the incarnation and above all the redemption achieved on the cross do not seem to be completely central as they need to be in any fully Christian way of looking at the world. For Hegel, contradictions are continually being resolved in a series of ever higher syntheses. Such a philosophy may provide an admirable framework for understanding a world that is in a continual process of development and evolution. But it leaves the impression that for Hegel the incarnation is not the definitive and ultimate focus that it has to be in any fundamentally Christian way of looking at the world. Indeed, it appears as if the incarnation is itself something that is to be transcended. As far as Hegel is concerned it seems to be not Christianity but early nineteenth-century philosophy (and, his critics would add, early nineteenth-century Prussia) that represent the culmination of all that human history has been striving towards:

> This is then the demand of all time and of Philosophy. A new epoch has arisen in the world. It would appear as if the World-spirit had at last succeeded in stripping off from itself all alien objective existence, and apprehending itself at last as absolute Spirit, in

developing from itself what for it is objective, and keeping it within its own power, yet remaining at rest all the while. The strife of the finite self-consciousness with the absolute self-consciousness, which last seemed to the other to be outside of itself, now comes to an end. Finite self-consciousness has ceased to be finite; and in this way absolute self-consciousness has, on the other hand, attained to the reality which it lacked before. This is the whole history of the world in general up to the present time, and the history of Philosophy in particular, the sole work of which is to depict this strife. Now, indeed, it seems to have reached its goal, when this absolute self-consciousness, which it had the work of representing, has ceased to be alien, and when spirit accordingly is realized as spirit. For it becomes such only as the result of its knowing itself to be absolute spirit, and this it knows in real scientific knowledge.[5]

On the one hand God's dealing with the world is in the biblical perspective a matter of his free grace, not as Hegel would have it of speculative necessity; and on the other hand the mystery of God and the world is something that yields not, as Hegel would have it, to absolute knowledge but to the faith that is based on trust in God (*Menschwerdung*, p. 517). Nevertheless, not only can there be no going back behind Hegel, as Küng frequently emphasizes, but Hegel's concept of God 'is in its dialectical dynamic clearly better suited to express what has to be expressed on the basis of a classical Christology that is thought through to the end' (*Menschwerdung*, p. 553).

Küng's tracing of Hegel's successive attempts to grapple with the question of God and God's relations with the world thus culminates in a section setting out the preconditions for any future Christology. This, however, is a Christology from above, one that takes as its starting-point the qualities of God and sees how these are realized in the life and work of Jesus. It is not a Christology from below such as Küng was to provide in *On being a Christian*, one that starts from the man Jesus of Nazareth and sees what his life and work have to tell us about God. In the present book Küng's starting-point is a decidedly Hegelian God, even if the Hegelian picture has been corrected by the biblical evidence (*Menschwerdung*, p. 548):

> This, then, is the living Christian God: a God who does not exclude but rather includes his opposite – not because of some essential deficiency, as Greek metaphysics was obliged to suppose, not as some preliminary stage due to find completion through self-development, but as the power of grace, as a positive 'possibility' that from the start belongs to his complete reality. To put it in more concrete terms: a life that includes death, a wisdom that includes folly, a lordship that includes servitude, an eternity that includes time, an immeasurability that includes the capacity of being measured, an infinity that includes the finite, and that includes all this as the positive 'possibility' and power of grace – this in the light of a consistent classical Christology is the good dialectic of God's qualities which even through the power of grace includes as its opposite what is ungodly and finite and in its superabundance settles the conflict. More than this: a goodness that encloses evil within itself by the redeeming endurance and suffering of grace, a holiness that encloses sin by the forgiveness of grace that takes sin on itself, a love that encloses hatred by the self-sacrifice of grace that brings about reconciliation – this is the dialectic of God's qualities that not only is good but at the same time makes good and that with grace embraces not only what is ungodly and finite but even what is against God and of nothing, embraces it as a contradiction that is not from God and transcends it, as something become a *felix culpa*, in its superabundance of grace. It is here that there occur genuine alienation, mediation and reconciliation.

In particular, the God we have to deal with is a God who suffers, whose inner life is a dialectic, who evolves

(Menschwerdung, p. 554). It is in fact the historicality of God that has to be seen as both precondition and opportunity for the Christology of the future *(Menschwerdung,* p. 557).

From Hegel, however, comes the whole development of modern critical exegesis, through David Friedrich Strauss and his application of the concept of myth to interpret the gospels, on through the quest for the historical Jesus to Karl Barth on the one hand and his dialectical theology, and on the other Rudolf Bultmann and his programme of demythologization. At the same time the classic doctrine of the two natures in Christ as established by the Council of Chalcedon in 451 bristles with difficulties. Küng's book thus concludes with a sketch of how a Christology from below might be worked out on the basis of the biblical evidence about what Jesus was proclaiming, how he behaved and what his fate was, and what the significance of all this is *(Menschwerdung,* pp. 598–610). He was approaching it from a different angle from that which he adopted at the Brussels congress, but again it was the programme for the same book – the book that was to be Küng's first really popular best-seller and was at the same time to cause him probably even more trouble with the Church authorities than his previous works.

[1] Bertrand Russell, *History of Western Philosophy*, Allen and Unwin, London, [2]1961, p. 701.
[2] E. M. Butler, *The Tyranny of Greece over Germany*, Cambridge University Press, 1935, pp. 3–4.
[3] J. Bronowski and Bruce Mazlish, *The Western Intellectual Tradition*, Hutchinson, London, 1960, p. 480.
[4] G. W. F. Hegel, *Phenomenology of Spirit*, translated by A. V. Miller, Clarendon Press, Oxford, 1977, p. 459, §§ 758–759. This translation also includes a paragraph-by-paragraph analysis by J. N. Findlay which offers as clear an interpretation as can reasonably be demanded of what Hegel actually meant – though

the reader may still be left wondering why, if that was what Hegel was trying to say, he could not be bothered to say it.

⁵ G. W. F. Hegel, *Lectures on the History of Philosophy*, translated by Elizabeth S. Haldane and Frances H. Simson, Kegan Paul, Trench, Trübner, London, 1895, vol. iii, pp. 551–552.

15

Apologetics for
the Twentieth Century

The background to *On being a Christian* may involve the
complexities of Hegelian philosophy. But the book itself is
a simple response to a simple dilemma: how can one can be
a Christian without being forced back into holding a view
of the world that is no longer tenable. Too many people
have been put off Christianity by being given the
impression that Christian belief involves accepting ideas
and assumptions that are totally incompatible with the
ideas and assumptions that govern all the rest of their lives
apart from a tiny segment labelled 'religion'. The
presentation of myth as literal historical truth instead of as
interpretation of the historical data, the emphasis on the
miraculous that when exaggerated can make Jesus of
Nazareth seem a prototype of Superman – all this erects a
virtually impassable and totally unnecessary barrier in the
way of Christian faith for those whose view of the world is
based on what can be measured, what is tangible, what is
predictable, what is quantifiable, what is subject to
experimental proof and disproof. It makes it all too easy to
see Christianity at best as something mankind has now
grown out of, a beautiful dream that can no longer be
sustained in the harsh light of reality.

Ordinary Christians, particularly if they were Catholics,
were not helped in coming to terms with this problem of
expressing their belief in language fully compatible with
the rest of their lives by the attitude to scholarship adopted

by the Church authorities. The responses of the Pontifical Biblical Commission gave the impression that a special indulgent set of criteria existed when it came to evaluating the impact of modern scholarship on our understanding of the bible: Catholic scholars were expected to take the first three chapters of Genesis as a trustworthy historical account, were warned off treating Isaiah as the work of two or three separate authors, were expected to uphold the Pauline authorship of the pastoral epistles (DS 3512–3, 3508–9, 3587). It was all a bit reminiscent of the legend of King Canute trying to stop the rising tide. Indeed, in 1927 the Holy Office duly retreated from the impossible position it had put itself in over the authenticity of the Johannine comma, a sentence that has crept into the Latin text of 1 John 5:7–8 but is not to be found in the original Greek (DS 3881–2).

When the attitudes created by this fear of scholarship percolated down to the ordinary Catholic what they encouraged was at best a pious schizophrenia, at worst a refusal to think about what one believed. Faith tended to be pushed out from the centre of people's lives towards the margin. In this way the believers were often hanging on despite reason and common-sense, the unbelievers rejecting what no Christian is bound to believe.

Much of the dispute caused by *On being a Christian* was, I suspect, due not so much to the questions of Christology the row was ostensibly all about but to the fact that Küng had breached the quasi-taboo that surrounded such issues as the distinction in the Christian message between fact and myth, between the historical datum and the Christian interpretation of it. What Küng did was to put down on paper the kind of Christian belief that many Christians had been forced more or less to work out for themselves, though few could express it so persuasively. Here was someone who asserted the incarnation while denying the historical – though not the symbolic – reality of the virgin birth. Here

was someone who accepted charismatic powers of healing
on the part of Jesus but remained sceptical about miracles.
Here was someone who stressed the absolute and literally
crucial centrality of the resurrection but cast doubt on the
historicity of the accounts of the resurrection to be found in
the New Testament. The book thus answered a felt need;
and this was shown by its becoming a best-seller.

On being a Christian in this way expresses the pastoral
concern that has throughout been fundamental to Küng's
career. The ministry which the newly ordained Hans Küng
expected to find realized in some Swiss town or village
found its realization in the seven hundred or so pages of
this volume. Of course, this fundamental pastoral concern
had underlain his previous writings, particularly those like
The Council and Reunion and *Truthfulness* aimed at an
educated lay audience rather than at his fellow-theologians.
Of course, he had directly tackled some of these obstacles to
belief in the collection of letters to young people published
as *That the World May Believe.* But here he is concerned
with the central question: why be a Christian at all? What
difference does it make? What is distinctively Christian?

The result is a book that re-establishes apologetics as a
valid category of Christian writing. In the recent past
apologetics had acquired a bad name as an unconvincing
defence of the indefensible, a rehearsal of plausible excuses
for the sins of the Church's past life, a polemical exercise
conducted on a fiercely partisan and denominational basis.
Küng by contrast offers what can certainly be described as
eirenic, and probably as ecumenical, apologetics. It is a
powerful plea first for belief in Jesus Christ, because this is
what matters, and only then for membership of the Church
as the only possible suitable context for being a Christian.

Küng's starting-point is the world of today, a world in
which Christianity can too often and too easily appear an
optional extra. But Christianity cannot be regarded as
transcended by the modern humanist outlook or by the

spirit of science and technology or by Marxism, nor can it simply be put on the same level as such world religions as Buddhism, Hinduism or Islam. Christianity remains disturbingly different and disturbingly challenging, and its distinction and its challenge centre on the person of Jesus Christ.

The core of the book is thus an exposition not so much of the message as of the person of Jesus. Jesus proclaimed a kingdom brought about not by the works of man but by the act of God: 'Unlike the sinister threats of judgment uttered by the ascetical John [the Baptist], this from the beginning is a friendly, joyous message of the goodness of the approaching God and of a kingdom of justice, joy and peace' (*Christian*, p. 182). It is an urgent appeal for that fundamental change of outlook called *metanoia* or conversion. What this means for man is in Küng's words (*Christian*, p. 225):

> That *he cannot take existing things* in this world and society *as definitive*. That for him neither the world nor he himself can be the first and last. That the world and he himself simply as such are utterly relative, uncertain and unstable. That he is therefore living in a critical situation, however much he likes to close his eyes to it. He is pressed to make a final decision, to accept the offer to commit *himself to the reality of God*, which is ahead of him. It is a decision in which everything is at stake: an either-or, for or against God . . .
>
> This conversion is possible only by relying confidently on the message, on God himself, with that confidence which will not be put off and which is called *faith*.

Not only is there a surely Barthian stress on the absolute transcendence of God's claims on us, but there is also an anticipation of the need Küng will later, in *Does God Exist?*, establish for a fundamental act of trust as the basis for a rational and rationally defensible belief in God.

In proclaiming the kingdom and calling for conversion

Jesus is presented by Küng as challenging all possible purely human efforts towards a betterment of the human condition. Jesus cut through the claims of the priestly hierarchy to interpret God's will to men. His uncompromising critique of the present order of things did not spare revolutionary movements: these too were challenged by his vastly more radical demand for a non-violent revolution in man's outlook, a turning away from selfishness towards God and neighbour. He did not proclaim an ascetic withdrawal from the world, a programme for a disciplined élite, but rather the unmerited forgiveness of precisely those seen to be the most worthless members of society. Nor did he follow the compassionate casuistry of the Pharisees: he was proclaiming something at once much simpler and much more demanding.

Küng thus presents Jesus as standing somehow askew to the world, as operating as it were in a fifth dimension that transcends and cuts across our human categories and rationalizations. He is provocative on all sides, someone who cannot be fitted into the moral typology (*Christian*, p. 212):

> He seems to have something of the most diverse types (perhaps more of the prophet and reformer than of the others), but for that very reason does not belong to any one of them. He is on a different plane: apparently closer than the priests to God, freer than the ascetics in regard to the world, more moral than the moralists, more revolutionary than the revolutionaries.

Küng thus stresses that Jesus is disturbingly different.

Not only did Jesus present such an uncomfortable challenge to the conventional and even unconventional wisdom of his (and our) day in all its varied efforts to cope with the human condition, but he could not be fitted into the expectations generated by such titles as Messiah that were to be applied to him (*Christian*, p. 290):

Apparently none of the familiar concepts, none of the usual ideas, none of the traditional offices, none of the current titles were appropriate to express his claim, to define his person and mission, to reveal the mystery of his nature. The messianic titles of majesty themselves make it clearer than the human, all-too-human roles assigned to the Messiah by the priests and theologians, the revolutionaries and ascetics, the religious or irreligious small people, that this Jesus is different.

Again there is a stress on Jesus's absolute uniqueness which can be taken as implying an orthodox Christianity. Certainly it would hardly seem to go with any Unitarian or Arian devaluation of Jesus's status and role as Küng has too frequently been accused of.

In Küng's view Jesus probably did not describe himself as Son of David, Messiah, or Son of God, and may not even have used the term Son of Man despite its occurrence in the New Testament only in sayings attributed to Jesus in a recognizably early stage of the synoptic tradition. But everything he did or allowed to happen raised a claim equivalent to that of a Messiah (*Christian*, p. 294):

> Rightly or wrongly, in practice, in word and deed, he acts as God's advocate for man in this world. Thus it becomes clear at the same time how false it would be simply to deny any messianic character to the story of Jesus and to say that this character was only subsequently imposed. Jesus' claim and influence were such that messianic expectations were roused by his proclamation and activity as a whole and were believed, as the saying recorded of the disciples on the way to Emmaus clearly expresses: 'We had hoped that it would be he who would redeem Israel' (Luke 24:21). Only in this way is it possible to understand the absolute call to follow him, the calling of the disciples and the selection of the twelve, the stirring of the whole people and certainly the violent reaction and permanent irreconcilability of his opponents.

As the public advocate of God and man, Jesus had become in person the great sign of the times. By his whole existence he confronted men with a decision: for or against his message, his activity, and indeed his person. To be scandalized or to be changed, to believe or not to believe, to continue as before or to repent. And, whether one said 'Yes' or 'No', he was marked for the coming kingdom, for God's final judgment. In his person God's future throws its shadow, its light for man, in advance.

But it is not just in an external sense that Jesus is God's advocate (*Christian*, p. 317):

. . . He is an advocate in a deeply intimate-existential sense, a personal ambassador, trustee, confidant, friend of God. In him, without any compulsion, but inescapably and immediately, man was confronted with that ultimate reality which challenges him to decide what he is ultimately seeking, where he is ultimately going.

These claims and this challenge provoked his death. One of the many merits of Küng's book is that it brings out how intolerable a challenge Jesus presented to the authorities of his time (*Christian*, p. 335):

Jesus' violent end was the *logical conclusion of his proclamation and his behaviour.* Jesus' passion was the reaction of the guardians of the law, of justice and morality, to his action. He did not simply passively endure death, but actively provoked it.

Against the background of the gospels as a whole it becomes completely clear why Jesus was killed (*Christian*, p. 336):

Or should the hierarchy have let this radical go who arbitrarily proclaimed God's will without giving any reasons or justification?
This *heretical teacher* who regarded the law and the

whole religious and social order as irrelevant and brought confusion into the minds of the people who were ignorant of religion or politics?

This *false prophet* who prophesied the fall of the temple and relativized its cult as a whole and plunged particularly the traditionally devout into the most profound uncertainty?

This *blasphemer* who, in a love that knew no bounds, accepted among his followers and friends irreligious and morally unstable people; who thus, in his underground hostility to law and temple, degraded the sublime and just God of this law and temple and reduced him to the God of these godless and hopeless people; who in his monstrous arrogance even encroached on God's most essential sovereign rights by personally assuring and guaranteeing forgiveness here and now?

This *seducer of the people* who in person presented an unparalleled challenge to the whole social system, a provocation of authority, a rebellion against the hierarchy and its theology: all of which might have resulted, not only in confusion and uncertainty, but in real disturbances, demonstrations, even a new popular revolt, the always threatening great conflict with the occupying army and the armed intervention of the Roman imperial power?

Here as elsewhere Küng is concerned that we should remember precisely how dangerous Jesus was and is, that we should not domesticate him and his message and rob the challenge he presents us with of its sting. With nearly two thousand years of Christianity behind us, we live in a world where Jesus of Nazareth has, as it were, become part of the furniture of everyday life; and one of the achievements of Küng's book is that it recaptures the vivid urgency and the crucial life-and-death character of the original gospel message.

Not only did Jesus die, his death 'the fulfilment of the

curse of the law' and the unmistakable sign that he was wrong (*Christian*, pp. 339–340): he died not merely forsaken by men but absolutely forsaken by God (*Christian*, p. 341). Yet it was only after this God-forsaken death that the movement invoking his name really began. Küng argues that to suppose that Jesus's resurrection was the projection of the disciples' psychological need or an expression of the perseverance of their faith in his decisive significance, mission and authority despite his death creates more difficulties than it solves (*Christian*, p. 373):

> If we do not indulge in historical speculation but keep strictly to the testimonies themselves, there can be no doubt about the unanimous agreement of the New Testament writings that the disciples did not conclude from Jesus' fate to his resurrection but in fact *experienced* after his death the living person himself.

But he is at pains to point out that God's raising of Jesus from the dead is an act of God within God's dimensions and therefore cannot be a historical event in the strict sense (*Christian*, pp. 349–350):

> It is not an event which can be verified by historical science with the aid of historical methods. For the raising of Jesus is not a miracle violating the laws of nature, verifiable within the present world, not a supernatural intervention which can be located and dated in space and time. There was nothing to photograph or to record. What can be historically verified are the death of Jesus and after this the Easter faith and the Easter message of the disciples. But neither the raising itself nor the person raised can be apprehended, objectified, by historical methods.

This of course does *not* mean it is something merely fictitious or imaginary. In the profoundest sense possible the resurrection is a real event, a radical transformation into the all-embracing and utterly different dimension of God. It is corporeal not in the sense of involving the physiologically identical body but in the sense of raising up the identical personal reality, the same self with its whole history.

Küng is thus arguing for the reality of the resurrection against any attempts to rob it of its force and meaning by reducing it to the categories of our present world of space and time. It is an interpretation far different both from attempts at a purely psychological explanation – those that would see the impact the historical Jesus made on the disciples as so strong that they became convinced he was still with them – and from what can only be described as science fiction interpretations of what lies beyond death. The latter include not just naïve interpretations that would think of the resurrection in terms of the resuscitation of a corpse but more sophisticated efforts such as the English theologian John Hick's bizarre hypothesis of 'a series of lives, each bounded by something analogous to birth and death, lived in other worlds in spaces other than that in which we now are'[1]. Küng's interpretation is an assertion of the central object of faith in a way that is proof against rational and scientific objections because it is seen in categories that transcend our present world rather than in categories limited to this world: in the latter case any interpretation would become liable to refutation as soon as some further area of human experience was opened up to scientific understanding.

The resurrection, as Küng points out, means a re-interpretation of Jesus's relationship to God (*Christian*, p. 383):

> Jesus' assumption into the life of God therefore does not bring the revelation of additional truths, but the revelation of Jesus himself: he now acquires final credibility. In a wholly new way Jesus thus justified becomes the sign challenging men to decide. The decision for God's rule, as he demanded it, becomes a decision for himself. Despite the break, there is a continuity in the discontinuity. Already during Jesus'

earthly activity the *decision for or against the rule of God* hung together with the *decision for or against himself.* Now they coincide.

Already the problems of Christology start to loom up: 'Jesus as exalted to God has become the *personification of the message of the kingdom of God*' (*Christian*, p. 383). A variety of contemporary titles of dignity and mythical symbols became applied to Jesus and in being applied were radically changed: Son of Man, Messiah (or Christ), Lord, Son of God, Logos (*Christian*, pp. 384–389). The man Jesus of Nazareth, as finally exalted to God, is now definitively and comprehensively, once and for all, God's representative to men, and at the same time in the same way the delegate, deputy, representative of men before God. In reaching for such terms as 'plenipotentiary', 'advocate', 'spokesman', 'representative', 'deputy', 'delegate', Küng is trying simply to convey what used to be conveyed by such words as 'king', 'shepherd', 'saviour', 'son of God', and even by the traditional teaching of Jesus's triple role as priest, prophet and king (*Christian*, pp. 390–391).

Küng thus takes the reader through the stages whereby the classic Christological titles and definitions came to be applied to this Jesus whom God had raised from the dead. Not only does such a Christology from below reach the same conclusions as provide the starting-point for a Christology from above, but it helps the reader to understand how they have been reached and what they mean (*Christian*, p. 443):

> As became clear through all the previous chapters, it was in Jesus' *whole* life, in his *whole* proclamation, behaviour and fate, that God's word and will took on a human form. In his whole speech, action and suffering, in his whole person, Jesus *proclaimed, manifested, revealed* God's word and will. Indeed, it can be said that he, in whom word and deed, teaching and life, being and action, completely coincide, *is* the

embodiment of God's word and will: *God's word and will in human form.*

Jesus's relationship to God, suggests Küng, can be positively expressed by saying: 'The *true man* Jesus of Nazareth is for faith the real *revelation* of the one *true God*' (*Christian*, p. 444), neither simply identifying the Son with the Father nor setting them up as two separate gods.

Küng concludes his exposition of the classic Christological definitions by offering 'an up-to-date positive paraphrase' of the Chalcedonian formula 'truly God and truly man' (*Christian*, pp. 449–450):

> *Truly God:* The whole point of what happened in and with Jesus depends on the fact that, for believers, *God himself* as man's friend was present, at work, speaking, acting and definitively revealing himself *in this Jesus* who came among men as God's advocate and deputy, representative and delegate, and was confirmed by God as the Crucified raised to life. All statements about divine sonship, pre-existence, creation mediatorship and incarnation – often clothed in the mythological or semi-mythological forms of the time – are meant in the last resort to do no more and no less than substantiate the *uniqueness, underivability and unsurpassability* of the *call, offer and claim* made known in and with Jesus, ultimately not of human but of divine origin and therefore absolutely reliable, requiring man's unconditional involvement.
>
> *Truly man:* Against all tendencies to deify Jesus, it must constantly be stressed even today that he was *wholly and entirely man* with all the consequences of this (capacity for suffering, fear, loneliness, insecurity, temptations, doubts, possibility of error). Not merely man, but *true man.* In describing him as such we insisted on the truth which has to be made true, the unity of theory and practice, of acknowledging and following him, of faith and action. As true man, by his proclamation, behaviour and fate, he was a *model of what it is to be human,* enabling each and everyone

who commits himself to him to discover and to realize the meaning of being man and of his freedom to exist for his fellow men. As confirmed by God, he therefore represents the permanently reliable *ultimate standard of human existence.*

But, Küng goes on to remark, the final test of being a Christian is, according to the New Testament, not assent to this or that dogma or agreement with a particular Christology, but the acceptance of faith in Christ and imitation of Christ. Orthopraxis must ultimately hold the primacy over orthodoxy.

The core of the book is thus formed by the preaching and proclamation of Jesus, the crucified and risen one. But in addition Küng grapples with a host of subsidiary questions. How, for example, should we interpret the idea of having been redeemed by the cross – an idea too often seen as a cruel and angry God bought off by the blood of his son (*Christian*, pp. 419–436)? Küng investigates the story of Jesus's virginal conception and birth, remarking that 'no one can be obliged to believe in the biological fact' of these (*Christian*, p. 457). He cuts Mariology but especially Mariolatry down to size.

In his final section he works out the practical implications of faith in Christ Jesus. First of all, faith entails membership of the Christian community. Küng is only too well aware of the many people who are able to decide for God and Jesus but who cannot decide for the Church, for any Church. He has the fullest respect for their stand and for that of committed and informed Christians who have simply opted out of the Church and left it. But in his view the alternatives to Church membership – another Church, no Church – are not convincing, and there are indeed positive reasons for staying in the Church (*Christian*, p. 524):

We should, we may remain in the Church because we are convinced of the cause of Jesus Christ and because

the community of the Church, despite and in all its
failings, has remained and will still remain in the
service of the cause of Jesus Christ.

The large number of those who call themselves
Christian did not get their Christianity from books,
not even from the Bible. They got it from this
community of faith, which has kept going reasonably
well for two thousand years, despite all weaknesses
and errors, and constantly in one way or another
awakened faith in Jesus Christ and issued a challenge
to commitment in his Spirit. This call of the Church
does not ring out unmistakably as the pure word of
God. It is a very human, often too human call. But,
even distorted by false notes and crooked actions, the
real meaning of the message can be perceived and has
in fact continually been perceived.

Or, as an English Dominican commented on one very
public departure from the Church:

It is because we believe that the hierarchical
institutions of the Roman Catholic Church, with all
their decadence, their corruption and their sheer
silliness, do in fact link us to areas of Christian truth
beyond our own particular experience and ultimately
to truths beyond any experience, that we remain, and
see our Christian lives in terms of remaining,
members of this Church.[2]

Küng's interpretation of the Church's essential
indefectibility, its remaining in the truth despite errors of
detail, thus has an apologetic edge. But it is a commitment
to the Church that is made with one's eyes open, fully
aware of that body's inseparable dark shadow, its un-nature
inextricably mingled with its true nature.

Second, Küng sketches the distinguishing features of
Christian ethics. There can be no question of a new
legalism, of a set of absolute rules to be applied more or less
blindly. Nor can there be any question of an antinomian
free-for-all: remember Corinth. Just as overall the central

point about Christianity is not a set of beliefs but a person, so too with regard to ethics (*Christian*, p. 544):

> What is specifically Christian therefore is the fact that all ethical requirements are understood in the light of the rule of the crucified Jesus Christ. It is then not a question merely of what is moral. The gift and the task coincide under the rule of Jesus Christ; the indicative already contains the imperative.

The distinctive feature of Christian ethics is thus not a set of abstract principles but the concrete person of Jesus Christ, who both for the individual and for the community is invitation, appeal, and challenge, the basic model of a new way of life and a new meaning to life (*Christian*, p. 553).

Third, just as Jesus himself provided an uncomfortable challenge to the four normal responses to the way things are – supporting the establishment, working for revolution, internal or physical emigration, and the compromise of casuistry – so too the Christian and even more the Church must present an uncomfortable challenge to the certainties of the age, must always be aware that the solutions and accommodations proposed never go far enough and cannot go far enough without the eschatological dimension that is brought into our lives by Jesus's proclamation of the kingdom. Both an integralist support of the prevailing capitalist system and the Christian socialist critique of capitalism, suggests Küng, lack 'a critical dissociation from and a genuine respect for the modern secular autonomy of politics, state and society' and 'fail to see the true political relevance of the Christian message, from which it is impossible directly to deduce a particular policy and particularly detailed solutions for questions of law and constitution, for economic, social, cultural and foreign policy' (*Christian*, p. 557). Küng draws a sharp distinction between the Christian's and the Church's duty of political involvement (*Christian*, p. 568):

The individual Christian must take a stand on all
outstanding questions. The Church as community of
faith and its representatives must not, cannot and may
not take a stand on all outstanding questions.

The Church and its representatives may, should
and must take a stand publicly even on controversial
social questions *where,* but *only where,* it is empowered
to do so by its special mandate: *wherever* and *as far as*
the Gospel of Jesus Christ itself (and not just any sort
of theory) unambiguously (and not only obscurely)
demands this.

There seems to be a much more rigorous construction of
what is demanded by the gospel when this passage is
compared with one of the specific tasks Küng had six years
earlier suggested should be undertaken by a Church
undergoing reform (*Truthfulness,* p. 232):

Deliberately unpretentious and realistic undertakings,
to enable christians to contribute to the solution of
important problems of the time wherever and in so far
as the gospel of Jesus Christ itself is unambiguously
involved (the racial question, over-population,
reconciliation of nations, social distress, and so on).

The qualifications are spelled out much more clearly, but
the kind of witness that is demanded by the gospel is no
longer suggested by specific examples. This is a pity, given
the ability of a number of Christians to convince
themselves that the Soviet treatment of believers, apartheid
in South Africa, and Latin American régimes based on
torture and terror are all somehow defensible on the basis of
the gospel or at least far less black than they are usually
painted: the best-known example of this kind of attitude is
the 1978 Reith Lecturer.[3] Such views may be eccentric, but
they can exert a fatal fascination on the Church as
institution, as shown by both the Catholic and the
Protestant reaction to Hitler's rise to power.

However, the Christian must in Küng's view be very

careful about how he gives his allegiance and pledges his loyalty (*Christian*, p. 569):

> The appeal of which Jesus Christ in person is the living embodiment, the distinctively Christian reality, must be the criterion everywhere. Christians may never identify themselves *totally* with any party, institution or even Church. Only totalitarian systems demand total identification. Christians may never join uncritically in every cry of the age. Only *partial* identification can be justified: *insofar as* this party, institution or Church corresponds to the Christian criterion or at least does not clearly contradict it.

This insistence that, because his or her primary commitment is to Jesus Christ, the Christian can pledge only a conditional and critical loyalty to any human institution or organization helps to balance Küng's fierce insistence on the limits to the involvement of the Church as Church in social and political questions.

In all this lengthy book there is one major – and admitted – lacuna. There is no treatment of what for many people today, perhaps especially for many Christians, is the most baffling and problematical aspect of being a Christian – prayer. When we pray, aren't we just talking to ourselves, indulging at best in some kind of autosuggestive mental therapy? What do we mean when we talk about God 'answering' our prayers? If we have been praying for some specific need or intention, doesn't this often mean that we are thinking in terms of a God who has favourites, who will grant our request and by doing so turn down someone else's? Can we really in some sense 'listen' to God in prayer or do we merely hear the echo of our own voice? Prayer has thus become a problem in a world that can no longer accommodate the idea of an interventionist God 'up there'; and it is a problem Küng originally meant to deal with in his book. In a note which may well escape the attention of many readers because, like all the notes (including even the scriptural references), it has irritatingly been relegated to the end of the book at the author's request, Küng explains what happened (*Christian*, pp. 686–687, n. 80):

At this point especially it becomes clear how closely faith and prayer are linked and how far prayer is an essential part of being a Christian. As a logical continuation of the reflections on prayer in Part C [the central section of the book expounding Jesus's life and message], I had planned to devote a special section here to prayer, meditation and Christian worship (in particular, the Sunday act of worship). The tiresome disputes forced on me afresh by Rome cost me at least two months of working time and working energies in the final, decisive phase of producing this book, which could not be made up in view of the tight schedule. The section planned therefore had to be dropped: a victim of the policy of the Roman Inquisition.

Nor were Küng's readers any luckier when it came to *Does God Exist?*. A section on prayer – thirty or so pages, with another three pages of notes – got as far as being set up in type, but was omitted at the final stage. This time it was not the Roman inquisition but space that was responsible.

[1] John Hick, *Death and Eternal Life*, Harper and Row, New York, 1977, p. 456.
[2] Herbert McCabe, OP, commenting in *New Blackfriars*, February 1967, on Charles Davis's decision to leave the Church; quoted from Simon Clements and Monica Lawlor, *The McCabe Affair*, Sheed and Ward, London and Melbourne, 1967, p. 13.
[3] Edward Norman, *Christianity and the World Order* (*The BBC Reith Lectures, 1978*), Oxford University Press, 1979. For religious freedom in the Soviet Union see pp. 33–42; for South Africa pp. 60–71; and for comments on Latin American régimes pp. 20–22 (Chile) and pp. 43–50.

16

The Battle with the Bishops

Why *On being a Christian* should have sparked off a dispute that outdid in fierceness and bitterness that sparked off by *Infallible?* may seem a little odd. In the earlier book Küng had after all called into question what for many was the lynch-pin of the Catholic system of belief. This was something that few would expect to be allowed to go unchallenged – least of all by Rome itself on seeing the axe laid to the root of its power and authority. But in the present case Küng was not challenging or criticizing anything. He was simply using all his resources of scholarship and his not inconsiderable skill in rhetoric to persuade a generation often disillusioned with Christianity in its institutional form why being a Christian was ultimately the only valid way of being human. For the Church authorities to find fault with *that* may seem a little perverse.

The trouble was that Küng lay under suspicion not of explaining what the Church believes but of explaining it away. The dispute in many ways lay between those who need the security of fixed dogmatic formulae and those who are more interested in what these formulae mean. Beyond this, another element was the frustration of those who had hoped to see the earlier dispute end with Küng condemned for heresy. The new book provided a fresh opportunity to nail this dangerous thinker. There was in addition a specifically German component reflecting the German inability to tolerate nonconformity. During the four-hour-long discussion with representatives of the German bishops' conference and its doctrinal commission held in Stuttgart on 22 January 1977 Küng remarked that it was only in Germany that *On being a Christian* had aroused such controversy – not in Italy, not in the United States, not in Ireland, not in England (*Wahrheit*, pp. 235–236). He had a point, even though his mention of the last two countries was hardly fair. He had only just come back from visiting them to launch the book's publication there five days earlier.

Certainly the book was accorded a calm and unhysterical reception in the English-speaking world. It came in for criticism, often searching criticism, but tempered by solid appreciation of Küng's many achievements. Thus the English theologian Nicholas Lash began his review by pointing to the book's strengths: the attractive and enviable clarity with which it was written; the fact that it is an outstanding work of 'apologetics', a persuasive, articulate, provocative apologia for Christian belief which does not seek to bludgeon the reader by 'proof' but seeks to persuade him towards taking the risk of seeing, and so sharing, the Christian programme; Küng's insistence on the interdependence of Christian speech and action, life and reflection; and the way in which the book is resolutely Christocentric, concerned with the following of Christ. But Lash found Küng paradoxically guilty of abstraction, not in the sense of ignoring the particular, the urgent, the personal, not in the sense of attending to one thing at a time, but in the sense of 'making unimpeachable general assertions while insufficiently attending to the problem of their instantiation':

> What Küng is doing is taking a short cut past those practical and theoretical historical mediations of meaning which create that 'distance' between Jesus and ourselves which hermeneutics seeks to overcome. I am not saying that this 'distance' *cannot* be overcome, but that it can only be overcome in

particular times and places, by particular forms of speech and action. If we attempt, this side of the reign of God, to overcome the distance in completely *general* patterns of action and speech we evade, by illegitimate abstraction, the particularity (and agony) of concrete choice and affirmation. Thus, for example, Küng says that 'it is possible to follow [Jesus] without an explicitly political or socio-critical commitment' (p. 187). Yes, but is it possible so to follow him in *all* situations, in *every* time and place? Or again: 'We must therefore again insist . . . that a *Christian can be a socialist* (against the "right"), but a *Christian is not bound to be a socialist* (against the "left")' (p. 567). But are there not particular situations in which obedience to the 'supreme norm' may indeed, in the concrete, take the form of an *obligation* to be, or not to be, a 'socialist'?

Earlier in his review Lash remarked: 'When I reflect on the fact that both Ian Smith and Robert Mugabe are committed Christians, I find intolerably abstract recommendations to "speak of Jesus" in the style of "present-day speech" that seem to be untroubled by the complex urgency of the question: *whose* present-day speech?' But despite all his criticism Lash concluded by admitting that he partly shared the considerable enthusiasm with which in many quarters the book had been received.[1]

Similarly the American biblical scholar Raymond E. Brown and the American theologian Avery Dulles offered praise tempered with criticism. Brown saw Küng's strength in his developing his theology out of the Bible, and found this refreshing when contrasted with the amount of bad Catholic theology (whether liberal or conservative) stemming from ignorance or neglect of New Testament scholarship. But in his view Küng did not always realize the limits of the exegetical work he depended on (even if Küng's exegesis, though defective in part, was overall 'much better than that of some of the Roman theologians who have been called in to criticize him'). Nor did Küng always make it clear that he was preserving essential points even when challenging past doctrinal formulations. And finally in Brown's view he made little allowance for theological developments that came after the New Testament but went in a different direction from biblical thought. Dulles for his part described the book as 'successful as apologetics, but somewhat less than successful as dogmatics'. Its obvious strength lay in its fundamental theology: 'Küng gives a highly effective apologia for basic Christianity.' Its high point was the central section on the life and teaching of Jesus:

> Küng splendidly illuminates the significance of Jesus' miracles, the originality of Jesus' doctrine of God and the reasons why he came into conflict with the religious leadership of contemporary Judaism. His description of Jesus' final abandonment on the cross is rhetorically powerful, and his account of the rise of the Easter faith is, in my judgement, both persuasive and inspiring. Küng makes it quite clear why the Christian cannot be content with psychological and mythical explanations of the Resurrection, but will insist on the reality of Jesus' new life with God.

But Dulles found the book's treatment of dogmatic questions its most controversial and least satisfactory sections: 'Küng's methodology almost guarantees that he will come into conflict with the dogmatic tradition both of Roman Catholicism and of other Christian Churches.' On what at the time of this review was already the central Christological issue Dulles remarked that Küng in effect affirmed Christ's divinity in functional terms but was unwilling to translate this affirmation into ontological or essential terms and therefore stopped short of saying that Jesus is truly God. Nevertheless, 'in his effort to present a meaningful, credible and challenging statement of why one might wish to be a Christian in our time, Küng performs brilliantly'. Dulles concluded by noting that his difficulties

over some of Küng's doctrinal positions were shared by
other Catholic theologians, but remarked that perhaps in
the course of time these positions would win an
acknowledged right of existence within the Catholic
community.[2] That in effect was the issue thrown into
prominence nearly three years later when the Roman
authorities suddenly withdrew Küng's right to teach as a
Catholic theologian.

Küng may have aroused the most ire from the Church's
Philistines, but he was hardly alone either in his approach
or in his conclusions. The same year that saw the original
German edition of *On being a Christian* also saw the
publication of two other studies in Christology: the book
Jesus the Christ by Küng's Tübingen colleague Walter
Kasper, and the complex and richly subtle work by the
Dutch Dominican Edward Schillebeeckx, *Jesus: an experiment in Christology*, a book that was to embroil its author
with the Doctrinal Congregation.[3] Kasper, for example, is
fully aware of the pressures towards wholesale
demythologization (*Jesus the Christ*, p. 43):

> Can we honestly and sincerely continue to hold and
> pass on the message that God came down from
> heaven, assumed human form, was born of a virgin,
> walked about working miracles, descended to the dead
> after his death, rose again on the third day, was
> exalted to the right hand of God, and now is present
> and effective from heaven through the Spirit in the
> proclamation and sacraments of the Church?

Demythologization becomes 'not only permissible but
necessary' in the face of the difficulty felt by the average
Christian in accepting that Jesus was truly man (ibid.
p. 46):

> It is undeniable that, in generally current ideas of
> Christianity, Jesus Christ is often thought of more or
> less as a god descending to earth whose humanity is
> basically only a kind of clothing behind which God
> himself speaks and acts.

Docetism – the view that regarded Christ's humanity and suffering as apparent rather than real – was thus not merely a theological temptation but a danger to the Church's life and faith (ibid. p. 199):

> In the history of Christian piety the figure of Jesus had often been so idealized and divinized that the average churchgoer tended to see him as a God walking on the earth, hidden behind the façade and costume of a human figure but with his divinity continually 'blazing out', while features which are part of the 'banality' of the human were suppressed. In principle we can scarcely say that the doctrine of the true humanity of Jesus and its meaning for salvation have been clearly marked in the consciousness of the average Christian. What is found there often amounts to a largely mythological and Docetist view of Jesus Christ.

Schillebeeckx similarly points to the danger that the process of Christologizing Jesus of Nazareth may leave us with only a celestial cult mystery (*Jesus*, p. 671):

> the great Ikon Christ, shunted so far off in a Godward direction (God himself having already been edged out of this world of men) that he too, Jesus Christ, ceases to have any critical impact on the life of the world. To contend for the divinity of Jesus in a world of which God had long since taken his leave may well be a battle lost before it has begun . . . To put it starkly: whereas God is bent on showing himself in human form, we on our side slip past this human aspect as quickly as we can in order to admire a 'divine Ikon' from which every trait of the critical prophet has been smoothed away.

And Schillebeeckx places the Christological debates on a new level of complexity by throughout his work bringing out the diversity of Christologies to be found in the New Testament itself.

Nevertheless in Germany not only was Küng's book

subjected to strong criticism, but he got the impression that the criticism was being orchestrated by the bishops' conference. That body indeed concluded its statement expounding the Doctrinal Congregation's declaration of 15 February 1975 bringing to an end the proceedings against *The Church* and *Infallible?* with a preliminary listing of aspects of Küng's latest book that it found questionable. The bishops felt that conflicts with the Church's teaching authority could not be avoided if Küng did not take as the basis for his theological work the principles they had laid down in their statement on the normative significance of tradition in the Church, on the relationship between theology and the magisterium, and on the actual binding nature of doctrinal statements (*Wahrheit*, p. 151):

> For this reason 'elucidations' on particular points by Professor Küng, however necessary they may be, are insufficient. Thus in his latest book *On being a Christian*, while we recognize the theological work that has gone into it and its pastoral aims and intentions, there are a number of statements which do not allow one to see how they are to be brought into agreement with the basic principles mentioned above (cf. especially Christology, the doctrine of the Trinity, the theology of the Church and the sacraments, and the role of Mary in the history of salvation).
>
> Closely linked with this basic attitude is the demand for arbitrary changes in Church order put forward once again in the form of 'proposals for reform' that contradict responsible statements by the competent organs of the Church's administration (cf. for example once again *On being a Christian*, pp. 490 ff., 525–527: mutual recognition of ministries, intercommunion, etc.).
>
> The German bishops' conference thus urgently appeals to Professor Küng to re-examine in the light of the principles expounded above the methodology of his theological work and the actual statements of his to which objection has been taken.

This provided as it were the charge sheet on which proceedings were based.

The next move came not from the bishops themselves but from a group of theologians associated with them through being members of the bishops' doctrinal commission or close collaborators with it. Eleven of them published a volume of essays critical of Küng's book.[4] Küng was given the impression that the German bishops had indicated to the Doctrinal Congregation in Rome that this volume was one of the steps they were taking to cope with the threat presented by *On being a Christian* – specific action against which seems to have been left to the German bishops to undertake following Rome's failure to emerge as the undisputed victor from the proceedings against his two earlier works.

Several things upset Küng about this volume, perhaps above all the unpleasantness of seeing old friends and colleagues apparently ganging up against him – particularly when they included not only Karl Rahner, the doyen of German theologians, his former Tübingen colleague Joseph Ratzinger, now translated to a chair at Regensburg on his way to becoming cardinal archbishop of Munich, and his present Tübingen colleague Walter Kasper, but above all his old mentor and fellow-countryman Hans Urs von Balthasar, the man who had come all the way to Paris to give him moral support at the oral examination for his doctorate. There was the one-sidedness of it all: he was not given the chance to answer his critics and put his case within the same set of covers. There was above all the suggestion that he was not quite orthodox. From his point of view what he had been trying to do was to express the doctrine the Church had committed itself to in a way that actually made sense to people today. Too often such doctrines were kept in their traditional and by now often misunderstood formulations to fence the Church round with some kind of protective barrier against the barbarian hordes outside. Clearly for some of his critics Christianity was an arcane mystery admission to which depended on its officially empowered interpreters condescending to interpret its central secrets. In keeping with this kind of attitude Ratzinger evaluated Küng's book as a precatechesis for the pagans of the modern post-Christian world, a necessary preliminary stage before their initiation into the fullness of the Christian mysteries, but not as a compendium of the entire Christian message (op. cit. pp. 17–18); and in making this judgement Ratzinger was clearly doing his best to find something nice to say and to end his critique on a positive note.

Küng's irritation with this volume of criticism found expression in a robustly written article in the *Frankfurter Allgemeine Zeitung* of 22 May 1976 (*Wahrheit*, pp. 191–207). He enjoyed himself pointing out the inadequacies of the various different ways which the members of this football team that had come out against him adopted in order to cope with the problem of reconciling continuity and change in the Church. He gleefully underlined the contradictions between their various different views. The volume was in fact made up of two kinds of critique: those that are basically sympathetic, but naturally with some reservations and questions; and those that think Küng has got some basic point essentially and dangerously wrong. In a letter to Cardinal Döpfner a month later Küng indeed remarked that quite a different reaction would have been possible on his part if the contributions by Balthasar, Grillmeier, Rahner, and Ratzinger had shown the same constructive readiness to engage in dialogue as those by Deissler, Kasper, Kremer, Lehmann and Schneider (*Wahrheit*, p. 211). In his newspaper article Küng summed the volume up as 'professorial theology for professors of theology'. His critics, too, were for the most part a self-selected group of German dogmatic theologians. Absent for the most part were the biblical scholars, the Church historians, the fundamental theologians, the moral theologians, the pastoral theologians, and the catechetical experts – quite apart from theologians outside the German-speaking world (*Wahrheit*, p. 206–207). In fact the contributors to the volume did include one Old Testament scholar (Deissler), one New Testament scholar (Kremer), and one moral theologian (Stoeckle), and Küng was able to use their contributions as sticks with which to beat their colleagues. At the Stuttgart discussion Küng was to remark that it was the dogmatic theologians who were upset by what he had written, whereas the biblical scholars tended to be on his side; while Stoeckle's isolation as apparently the sole moral theologian to come out against him made one wonder quite how representative he was in view of his recent appointment to the bishops' doctrinal commission (*Wahrheit*, pp. 234–235).

But the criticism in this volume was comparatively restrained compared with the vicious attack on Küng's book and on his orthodoxy made by another member of the bishops' doctrinal commission, Leo Scheffczyk, in an article that Küng's opponents distributed as widely as possible in offprint form. Among those circulating what Küng regarded as a piece of scurrilous defamation were apparently members of the bishops' conference itself, and nearer home on Küng's doorstep the parish priest of St John's, Tübingen, Dr Fridolin Laupheimer, a man according to Küng known throughout the diocese as among the most reactionary of the clergy (*Wahrheit*, p. 272). Scheffczyk accused Küng of taking pluralism to the point of equivocation. Küng's view that the laws of nature were not violated in the resurrection meant to Scheffczyk that it was no longer a case of the *resurrectio carnis* taught by the Church. He suggested that what Küng had received from the Church had on his (Küng's) view been transmitted in so distorted, corrupt and degenerate a form that there was no intellectual and moral justification for staying in the Church. He objected to Küng's assertion that there was neither any rational disproof of atheism nor any rational proof of belief in God. He thought it was probably not going too far to suggest that Küng's exposition of the Christian belief in the Trinity approached the rigid monotheism of Judaism or Islam, and he suggested that the book's Christology did not go beyond the Moslem pattern of the one God and his prophet. He accused Küng of denying the mystery of the Trinity and the pre-existence of Christ. He accused him of sacrificing the truth of the blotting out of our sins by the sacrifice of the cross and of peddling the old Pelagian doctrine of Jesus's merely exemplary life and death. He accused him of completely misunderstanding the Church's sacramental structure: he (Scheffczyk) was very worried at the prospect of people in a state of sin being admitted to the eucharist without having received the sacrament of penance – a sacrament which the book did not even mention. In Scheffczyk's eyes Küng had sacrificed what was specifically Christian: his book would merely strengthen the conviction of genuine atheists and the real radical humanists that Christianity was moving a stage nearer self-dissolution.[5]

The importance of Scheffczyk's article is that it brings out the hostility Küng was able to arouse among adherents of a rigid, legalistic Catholicism that bordered on superstition and magic. It was a reaction that was theologically and rationally indefensible, and so the accusations that Scheffczyk hurled against him did not formally surface during the dispute between Küng and the bishops. But they undoubtedly provided much of the unconscious impetus behind the harassment to which Küng was subjected, and their existence beneath the surface helps to explain the intensity with which the whole quarrel was pursued. Küng was indeed himself aware, as he explained in a letter to Cardinal Döpfner, that in certain circumstances his book, or often tendentious reports or reviews of it, could make traditionally minded Catholics feel insecure, especially if their religious education was deficient (*Wahrheit*, p. 188).

What the German bishops wanted was for Küng to re-examine his methods and conclusions, as they had asked at the end of their statement commenting on the Roman declaration concluding proceedings against *The Church* and *Infallible?* Cardinal Döpfner urgently appealed to Küng to undertake this re-examination and regretted that the latter's article in the *Frankfurter Allgemeine Zeitung* gave the impression that such a re-examination was out of the question (*Wahrheit*, pp. 208–209). Küng replied somewhat indignantly that since the book had appeared he had striven to clarify, re-examine and study more deeply those disputed dogmatic questions that in *On being a Christian* he had noted as being in need of further theological investigation. To show that this was not just a purely verbal promise he listed the study-sessions and seminars he had undertaken: one lasting three days with his doctoral students comparing his book with Walter Kasper's; another of the same length devoted to the volume of critical essays produced by Balthasar and his team; several lengthy discussions with prominent biblical scholars on the Balthasar volume that concluded with a disputation between Kasper and himself; and discussions or correspondence with most of the contributors to that volume. He defended his newspaper article as a factual reply to his critics and rejected Cardinal Döpfner's suggestion that he had faced the bishops with a new situation. What he thought was needed on all sides was further constructive work (*Wahrheit*, pp. 210–212).

The course of the dispute was now dramatically affected by Cardinal Döpfner's sudden and unexpected death on 24 July 1976. Döpfner clearly found Küng a sore trial in some respects, but was nevertheless sympathetic to much the theologian was doing. Thanks to the fact that they had both studied at the Germanicum they were able to address each other with the familiar *Du*, which at once gave the correspondence between them a friendlier tone and helped to banish the impression of an inquisitorial proceeding. By contrast, relations with Cardinal Döpfner's successor as president of the German bishops' conference, Cardinal Joseph Höffner, Archbishop of Cologne, were throughout more formal, more strained, less friendly. Cardinal Höffner too may have been at the Germanicum, but he does not seem to have addressed the theologian as *Du*. Nor was he exactly sympathetic to Küng's approach. A letter he wrote to Küng on 23 December 1974 explaining why he could not reconcile the theologian's views on the infallibility of popes and councils with the faith of the Church as he understood it brings out the difference of attitude:

> Do new developments in theology and society possess the authority to change the faith of the Church? And again theology today does not present one single teaching. One person acknowledges, as does the faith of the Church, that the pope is infallible when in the supreme exercise of his teaching authority (*ex cathedra*) he makes a final decision on a matter of faith; another says that neither the pope nor councils nor the apostles would be able to proclaim doctrinal statements that would be infallible.
>
> The one acknowledges that God has created not only the visible world but also the angels; the other says that there aren't any angels and that when sacred scripture talks about angels it means merely God's loving concern for us.
>
> The one acknowledges the real existence of evil spirits, in other words beings whom God created naturally good but who through their own fault have revolted from God; the other says goodbye to the devil and holds that belief in the devil is a dubious legacy of biblical ideas that were conditioned by their age.
>
> The one acknowledges that the virgin Mary bore 'the Father's Son on earth', and did so 'without

having knowledge of a man, overshadowed by the Holy Ghost'; the other says that Mary conceived her son through sexual intercourse with a man.

The one acknowledges that Jesus Christ rose from the dead and appeared to his own; the other says that after his death the memory of Jesus was so strong among his disciples that they ventured to say in vivid metaphorical language that he was no longer dead but had been raised up.

The one acknowledges that the eucharistic sacrifice can *only* be validly celebrated by an ordained priest; the other says that all Christians are empowered to perform the eucharist.

The one acknowledges that sacramentally contracted and consummated marriage is by God's will indissoluble; the other says that the indissolubility of sacramental marriage is only an ideal commandment, so that remarriage during the lifetime of the other partner is permitted if the first marriage has irrevocably broken down, in other words is 'dead'.

The one acknowledges that Jesus laid down the missionary task of making all men his disciples and baptizing them in his name; the other says the missions should only be concerned that the Hindu becomes a better Hindu.

Clearly there is no one single teaching proclaimed by professors of theology. There are not a few who are not merely saying things differently but are saying something different. Who decides who is right? The better arguments? That is something both groups claim.

The essential question I have to put to you is: according to what authority do you put your views forward?

Oddly enough Walter Jens does not include this revealing letter in his collection of documentation; but it indicates pretty clearly what Cardinal Höffner thought he was up against. It may also have been significant that the cardinal admitted he had not yet had time to read *On being a*

Christian, a copy of which Küng had sent him two months earlier. At the beginning of December Cardinal Döpfner had already been able to form some kind of preliminary judgement on the basis of reading a few selected passages (*Wahrheit*, p. 137).

Cardinal Höffner did however implement a proposal Cardinal Döpfner had made just before his death. This was that a discussion should take place between Küng and representatives of the bishops' conference and of its doctrinal commission in order to clarify some of the central theological issues involved in Küng's book. This discussion eventually took place at Stuttgart on 22 January 1977. Present were Cardinal Höffner; Küng's former professor at Münster, Cardinal Hermann Volk, Bishop of Mainz; Bishop Georg Moser of Rottenburg, the diocese that includes Tübingen; Dr Josef Homeyer, secretary of the bishops' conference; Professor Karl Lehmann of Freiburg-im-Breisgau; Professor Otto Semmelroth of Frankfurt; Küng himself; and as his one supporter his Tübingen colleague Professor Johannes Neumann. Küng had successfully objected to the presence of his former Tübingen colleague Joseph Ratzinger on the grounds that his participation could introduce into the discussion an emotional streak that would serve no useful purpose – an indication of the deterioration of relations between two men who only ten or so years earlier had been close colleagues.

The three hours planned for the discussion stretched to four, with Cardinal Höffner becoming increasingly agitated: it was a four-hour journey to Cologne, and he had to get back to meet a crowd of between forty and sixty bishops waiting to celebrate his seventieth birthday. Presumably, too, having to wait an extra hour for lunch – the discussion went on from 10 a.m. to 2 p.m. – did not improve at least some participants' patience or concentration.

One point the discussion brought out was the intense

pressure Küng had been under during the past nine years of dispute with Rome over his two previous books coupled with a full teaching schedule at Tübingen, various engagements abroad, and the labour of writing a book of the length and complexity of *On being a Christian*. That book had brought him to the limit of his physical resources, said Küng (*Wahrheit*, p. 291): a remarkable admission from someone of his energy and stamina. He could not manage on less than five hours' sleep a night, he pointed out (*Wahrheit*, p. 307) when explaining why it would be physically impossible for him to produce the kind of clarificatory appendix that was suggested as one way of resolving the conflict – and that threatened, if the subject-matter included all the questions his critics had raised over *On being a Christian*, to turn into a summa longer even than the original. Not only did he have to complete *Does God Exist?* ready for publication, but he had an important lecture to prepare for Tübingen university's five hundredth anniversary that October, quite apart from all his normal university work and three trips to the United States inside six months. For the immediate future all he could promise was to clear up some of the difficulties in the final section of *Does God Exist?* Moreover, he did not see why the whole burden of clarifying the issues that had been raised should fall on him alone. He favoured a co-operative approach. What he wanted to see were study sessions by theologians on particular points at issue and the commissioning by the bishops' doctrinal commission of studies on these points that would involve not just the dogmatic theologians but also the biblical scholars, experts in the history of dogma, Church historians and others (*Wahrheit*, p. 303).

The transcript of the four-hour discussion suggests a difference that was never resolved. Küng was looking forward to an intensification of theological study at the professional level to help resolve what were admitted to be not just his own personal difficulties but problems encountered by any serious attempt to grapple with the Church's Christological tradition within the context of the twentieth century. The bishops for their part wanted from Küng some clear and explicit acknowledgement of simple dogmatic formulae. Cardinal Höffner in particular was alarmed at being unable to find in the book any suitably clear statement of the doctrine that Christ was 'begotten, not made': he felt that if one restricted oneself to functional rather than ontological terms there was no reason why one could not say of Mohammed that he was Allah's deputy, plenipotentiary, spokesman, ambassador, confidant and friend, or why one could not say that God's love had been revealed in Francis of Assisi (*Wahrheit*, pp. 254–255).

This difference was in fact where the attempted settlement between Küng and the German bishops broke down. Following the Stuttgart discussion a press communiqué was issued stating that the main subject of the talks, which had been under consideration for some time to deal with the disputed theological questions raised by *On being a Christian*, was Küng's statements in this book on the person of Jesus Christ and his work of salvation. The communiqué went on (*Wahrheit*, p. 313):

> Agreement was reached on the need to supplement some Christological statements.
> The German bishops' conference regards these supplementary clarifications as urgently necessary to avoid misunderstandings. Professor Küng said he was ready to make an appropriate contribution to clarifying the questions discussed.

The ambiguity lay in the different interpretations each side put on this process of clarification.

The points needing clarification were listed a week later by Bishop Moser in a letter urging Küng to write to Cardinal Höffner as president of the bishops' conference taking up the points raised during the Stuttgart discussion, as Küng had promised the bishop he would do. The points were: the binding nature of the classical Christological definitions made by the early Councils; the doctrine of the two natures in Christ; a more exact treatment of functional Christology; more detailed consideration of Johannine Christology; the relation between a Christology 'from above' and one 'from below'; the fundamental underivability and unsurpassability of the person of Jesus Christ; and a more detailed and precise description of the form of the unity between Jesus and the Father (*Wahrheit*, pp. 314–315).

Küng's letter to Cardinal Höffner followed on 21 February, a week before the bishops' conference was due to meet. It was written and despatched just before he flew to Washington for the second of his three trips to the United States. He stressed the book's pastoral intentions and the practical help it had provided for the pastoral clergy and for teachers of religion in putting over the Christian message. He explained that it was written as it were from the perspective of Jesus's first disciples, a perspective that also happened to be that of questioning men and women today. He did not dispute that the Church had to abide if not by every letter then by the major intentions and contents of the general councils of the past, particularly Nicaea and Chalcedon with their fundamental importance for classical Christology, even though throughout his work it had become more and more clearly necessary to measure the tradition of the Church and its councils against the Christian message to which scripture bore the original witness and against Jesus Christ himself as the primary criterion of any and every theology. He rejected comparisons with the French rebel archbishop Marcel Lefebvre: unlike the latter he had not called Rome's orthodoxy into question, he had not condemned Vatican II as neo-protestant and heretical, he had not formed his own 'progressive' organisation, and he had not tried to give exclusive scope to his particular views in the education of priests. He claimed that critics of his efforts to preserve the New Testament insights that the major Christological dogmas were drawn up to defend had not read *On being a Christian* carefully enough. He pointed out that the difficulties of interpretation in the Christological field were something brought home not just to every Catholic theologian but to everyone trying to proclaim the Christian message: his expositions were not in any way meant to curtail or conceal the truth or to make people insecure and anxious but to help those who were worried, clarify ideas for the perplexed, overcome polarization and strengthen Christian faith. He rehearsed yet again what he had done in the way of theological discussion with his colleagues of the questions at issue. He repeated his defence of his *Frankfurter Allgemeine Zeitung* article. He hoped to find time in the foreseeable future to tackle once again the questions of exegesis, history of dogma, systematic theology and hermeneutics thrown up by the Balthasar volume of criticism and by other writings: some of the disputed issues, including the underlying questions of the relation between faith and reason and the whole business of our understanding of God, as well as Jesus's relationship to God the Father, would be tackled in *Does God Exist?*, which was intended to supplement *On being a Christian* and was due to appear the following year. He stated that even in the most difficult phases of the dispute over infallibility he had always asserted the use and value of a pastoral ministry of teaching or proclamation exercised by the pope and the bishops. He recapitulated the proposals he had put forward at the Stuttgart discussion for study projects and study sessions on individual issues. He repeated his call for the German bishops' doctrinal commission to be more representative of the present state of theology in the Catholic Church and to take a more positive approach to its job. Finally he suggested that the point had now been reached when the conflict could be allowed to die out. 'I would be grateful to you and to the German bishops if I could be left in peace and quiet to get on with my theological work,' he wrote (*Wahrheit*, pp. 316–327).

The German bishops, however, were impressed neither by this apologia nor by whatever common ground might have been discerned at the Stuttgart discussion. Their second public statement on Küng's book once again called on him to clarify what he had said (*Wahrheit*, p. 330):

> Despite moves towards agreement, the German bishops' conference regards Professor Küng's unsatisfactory and misleading statements as so open to suspicion that it must again demand a more precise clarification that would put matters right.
>
> In particular the German bishops once again affirm what they said in their statement of 24 September 1975 on the Nicene creed: Jesus Christ is not simply an exemplary human being, not simply God's spokesman and representative; he is rather the eternal Son of God, 'God from God, light from light, true God from true God, begotten, not made, of one being with the Father', as the Church teaches in its profession of faith. It is only when, in keeping with this affirmation, Jesus Christ is presented and borne witness to without possibility of misunderstanding as true God and true man that the Christian message of redemption and salvation remains undiminished and unfalsified.
>
> Because the book *On being a Christian* does not do justice to this central truth of the faith, the German bishops' conference, in order to avoid readers being given a wrong orientation or becoming confused, insists on corrections or clarifications being made soon to statements of this kind by Professor Küng, such corrections or clarifications to have regard to the Church's binding teaching. As long ago as 17 February 1975 the German bishops' conference mentioned the book's treatment of Christology, but it

also pointed to the doctrine of the Trinity, the theology of the Church and the sacraments, and the role of Mary in the history of salvation.

In his covering note Cardinal Höffner told Küng he 'very much regretted' that the bishops' conference was unable to be satisfied either with the Stuttgart talks or with his letter.

Küng replied with a brief press statement (*Wahrheit*, p. 332):

> The mere repetition of traditional creeds does not help the men and women of today in the difficulties they experience with regard to belief. I have never denied the creeds but have rather attempted to make them understandable to the men and women of today. It is precisely this that people expect from the bishops. The clarification of theological difficulties – which are not something encountered just by me alone – is not a burden that can be left to a single theologian. Unfortunately the bishops have not said a word about the constructive proposals I put forward: study projects on important questions in dispute; study conferences bringing together the best-equipped experts in the field; and reconstituting the German doctrinal commission on an impartial basis.
>
> I am of course ready to make further clarifications of my theological position. Important fundamental questions will soon be clarified in my forthcoming book on the question of God. But for this reason, as I said in my recent long letter of explanation to the bishops' conference, I would be grateful to the German bishops if I could be left in peace and quiet to get on with my theological work.

Neither statement seemed to leave much hope of a compromise.

The next move came from Cardinal Höffner. In a letter apparently drafted by a dogmatic theologian on the German doctrinal commission (*Wahrheit*, p. 333) he set out three questions to which he would like an answer from Küng within three months. Küng was asked neither to refer back to previous writings nor to promise clarification in future publications: a brief and concise answer should be quite easy, since two of the three question involved merely credal formulations. First Cardinal Höffner took up Küng's statement in his letter of 21 February that it had never been his intention to call into question Jesus's divine sonship or the Trinity. In that letter he had remarked in parenthesis: 'Jesus *is* really God's son,' but to Cardinal Höffner's mind this seemed almost to contradict what he said in his book. So the first question was: 'Is Jesus Christ the uncreated, eternal Son of God, consubstantial with the Father?' Second came the Chalcedonian formula that Jesus is true God and true man: 'If in Jesus it was not God himself who sacrificed himself for mankind,' remarked the cardinal, 'then the heart is torn out of the Christian revelation.' The second question thus ran: 'Do you ultimately agree without reservations, always presupposing the explanations or profounder explorations that may be possible or necessary, with the Church's avowal that Jesus Christ *is* true man and true God?' Third was the central methodological question of Küng's approach which led to a question in two parts: 'Does not a return to the "perspective of the first disciples" – at least in the theological sense – require mediation through the Church's living awareness of faith? Is the Church's confession of faith (e.g. in Jesus being the Son of God) the datum that theology has to expound with the help of all the methodological possibilities at its disposal – or is it in your eyes a hypothetical historical reconstruction that on its own and in itself provides sufficient access to the theological understanding of Jesus Christ?' As to Küng's proposals about study projects, the bishops' conference had nothing against these, but the cardinal stressed that theological scholarship should not be the sole criterion for deciding what was and what was not the Church's teaching. Küng's suggestion that members of the bishops' doctrinal

commission were chosen not for their professional
competence but for their stance in Church affairs was
firmly and rather fiercely rejected (*Wahrheit*, pp. 335–340).
Cardinal Höffner had wanted an answer in writing by 15
June 1977. On 13 June Küng wrote to explain that he had
just returned from a fairly lengthy visit to the United States
to take up all the work awaiting him as a university teacher
in the middle of the summer term. This third of his three
trips across the Atlantic had been to take part in a
theological conference at Notre Dame, Indiana, organized
by *Concilium* and the Catholic Theological Society of
America: Küng had been one of the team of five responsible
for planning and preparing the 'colloquium', as it was
called, and gave a paper himself on the present state of
affairs in the ecumenical field and what needed to be done
in the immediate future.[6] In his letter Küng reminded
Cardinal Höffner that at Stuttgart he had explained in
detail why it was physically impossible for him to devote
any more time to the present dispute for the moment: the
questions of form and content that were raised demanded
more than a brief answer. He went on:

> With the Stuttgart discussion and particularly with
> my long letter of 21 February I have, in the opinion of
> many who are competent to judge, done more than
> could fairly be expected of me. And I was in fact
> surprised that, in contrast to the impression you gave
> me at least after the Stuttgart talks, you are still not
> satisfied with the answers I have given both orally and
> in writing.

He concluded by asking the cardinal to understand that he
would not be able to furnish a suitable answer to his letter
until he had completed his book on the God question and
had given his lecture at the Tübingen quincentenary in
October (*Wahrheit*, pp. 341–342).
It was now Cardinal Höffner's turn to be surprised. The
whole matter had to be seen against the background of

official misgivings about what Küng had been saying in his
books that went back for the best part of ten years, while
the German bishops had been waiting for clarification of a
number of urgent and fundamental questions raised by *On
being a Christian* for no less than two and a half years.
Meanwhile the book was being sold unamended both at
home and abroad. The bishops' conference now wanted an
answer in time for their autumn meeting, which began on
19 September. This meant a new deadline of 10 September
at the latest, and Küng could have no more urgent
priorities (*Wahrheit*, pp. 342–343).

Küng's answer came two days after the new deadline.
Once again he stressed the pressure of work he was under
and pointed out that he had to give absolute precedence to
completing his book about God and preparing his lecture
for the Tübingen celebrations. Nevertheless he had done
his best to examine more closely the extremely complex
Christological questions which the cardinal had raised and
which in his view could not be answered in the question-
and-answer form of the catechism. He had now subjected
the entire complex of problems to fundamental
reconsideration in connection with the question of God and
the root question of faith and knowledge and expressed the
results of his labours in a book of nearly nine hundred
pages. He felt that placing the questions the cardinal had
raised in a broader theological context better served their
clarification. He would send the cardinal a copy of the book
as soon as it was available, and hoped the German bishops'
conference would appreciate not only its pastoral intentions
but also the weight of its theological argumentation
(*Wahrheit*, pp. 344–345).

This was too much for Cardinal Höffner. He replied
(*Wahrheit*, pp. 345–346):

Dear Professor Küng,
    Thank you for your letter of 12 September 1977. In
it you once again refuse to answer questions relating

to the book *On being a Christian*. You were asked
about fundamental truths of the Catholic faith. The
confession of this faith – which is something surely
that cannot be relinquished – was all that was needed
to answer these question. I am very sorry that you
have failed to do this. Your failure has shown that an
unequivocal assent to fundamental statements of the
Catholic faith is not possible on the basis of the
theology represented in your book.

That in effect seemed to write Küng off as a Catholic,
though the full effects were not to be felt for another two
years.

It was now Küng's turn to be amazed. In a letter dated 7
November he decisively rejected Cardinal Höffner's
charges. He had not refused to answer questions arising
from *On being a Christian*: what else had he been doing at
the Stuttgart talks, in his letter of 21 February, and in *Does
God Exist?*, due to appear in three months' time? Taking up
the cardinal's suggestion that all that was needed by way of
an answer was an acknowledgement of the irrelinquishable
core of the Catholic faith, Küng felt it was unreasonable to
demand of a professor of Catholic theology a confession of
faith as if this was something he had denied. He strongly
rejected, too, the imputation in the second of the bishops'
collective statements that he regarded Jesus Christ as
merely God's spokesman and representative and that he
denied parts of the Nicene creed: he felt a public
rectification would be in order of these imputations that
defamed his orthodoxy. He had never thought to deny the
irrelinquishable credal statements of their faith, nor did he
see any fundamental contradiction between the statements
of the early ecumenical councils and what he had said in *On
being a Christian*, though of course he regarded the former
as standing in need of interpretation for the men and
women of today. He hoped that in the future they could
start from the assumption that they shared the common

ground of the Catholic faith. The imputation that an unequivocal assent to fundamental statements of the Catholic faith was not possible on the basis of the theology represented in his book he rejected as untenable. Involved were extremely subtle and complex problems that not just in his judgement but in that of other Catholic theologians too could not be dealt with by means of catechism answers. In conclusion Küng once again stressed the extreme pressure of work he had been under: so far that year he had not been able to take a single day off (*Wahrheit*, 346–348).

All this was to no avail. Ten days later, on 17 November 1977, came the German bishops' third collective statement criticizing *On being a Christian*: the decision to issue it was presumably taken at the bishops' meeting two months earlier. It quoted the first of their collective statements against the book. It said that despite repeated warnings Küng had not answered the questions put to him by Cardinal Höffner. It took up a remark Küng might well have been tempted to regret having made in his preface – that his book had in effect turned into something like a small-scale 'summa' of the Christian faith (*Christian*, p. 20) – and, noting that the book was still being distributed unamended both in German and in other languages, went on (*Wahrheit*, pp. 350–351):

> Since this book is put forward as a 'small "summa" ' of the Christian faith and is taken and used by many people as a kind of manual of Catholic belief, the German bishops' conference sees itself obliged to comment on it once again. They would not do so if they did not regard it as their duty for the sake of the faith of the faithful. Küng's *On being a Christian* has, as has often been shown to us, made a considerable contribution to the distressing erosion of security and stability in belief.
>
> The aim of this statement is not to pass judgement on what Professor Küng personally believes or does not believe. Nor is it concerned with what he has

written in earlier books or will write in future ones. What is at issue here is the book *On being a Christian*, even if this book presupposes the style of theological content and method propounded in earlier works. On this the German bishops have commented in the statement mentioned above [that of 17 February 1975, p. 282 above]. Although *On being a Christian* sees itself as a 'small "summa" ' it does not deal with everything that forms an irrelinquishable part of the Catholic faith, e.g. the seven sacraments and their significance for the Christian life. The question must nevertheless be asked whether what is dealt with is dealt with in conformity with the faith. It is not a question here of listing everything the presentation of which is inadequate, e.g. the doctrine of the Trinity, the doctrine of the Church, of the sacraments and of Mary. The theological method followed by Professor Küng, which as already mentioned in the statement of 17 February 1975 involves an unsatisfactorily narrow approach, has as its consequence – if it is applied consistently – a breach in important questions with the Catholic tradition of faith and doctrine. The freeing of theological methodology from the tradition of belief put forward by the Church and the arbitrary selection from scripture lead to a curtailment of the content of faith. This is not to call Professor Küng's positive intentions into question. But he does not present the reader with the whole Christ nor with his saving action in its entire fullness. It is not enough for him to protest in general terms his loyalty to the irrelenquishable confessions of faith: these must rather be stated unequivocally and their contents expounded.

The two and a half years of argument and discussion seem if anything to have hardened the bishops' position.

The bishops then tackled three specific doctrines on which they found Küng's position unsatisfactory. First came the Chalcedonian doctrine that Jesus Christ is true God and true man (*Wahrheit*, pp. 351–352):

In this book Jesus Christ's divine nature is neglected. Jesus of Nazareth is however true man and true God. These two statements cannot be reduced any further, nor can they be resolved into the other: both are necessary. For Jesus Christ cannot do what he does if he is not what he is: the eternal uncreated Son of God, equal in divinity with the Father and of one being with the Father, is in the incarnation united with the man Jesus to become a personal unity. This may be a great mystery. But it must be held firm and also expressed, otherwise the doctrine of salvation as the fruit of Jesus of Nazareth's act of redemption is seriously called into question; otherwise the gospel, the good news of our salvation in Jesus Christ, in which God has intimately united himself with mankind, can no longer be expressed and indeed proclaimed in its essential basic meaning. Simply to say in passing that Jesus was the son of God does not suffice as a description of Christ, because for example the grace of redemption also bestows the status of a child, of a son: 'For in Christ Jesus you are all sons of God, through faith' (Gal. 3:26). In this way we too, in keeping with what our Lord has said, can and may call God our father.

Although Küng's book pointed to the row of titles that were uniquely applied to Jesus, the Christ, describing him as uniquely God's representative did not in the bishops' mind suffice to provide an adequate description of the reality of Jesus Christ. The language used of him in the New Testament would be completely incomprehensible if in distinction to all other representatives of God Jesus were not himself God: 'Jesus Christ is not the Son inasmuch as and because he is God's representative, but he is God's representative because he is the Son of God' (*Wahrheit*, p. 353).

Next was the question of God's sacrifice of himself for us in Jesus Christ. Innumerable people had through their life and death borne witness to their faith in God. But however many there were of them they could not redeem us. Jesus Christ in contrast had redeemed us by his life, suffering and death, because he was not only true man but also God's divine Son, sent by his heavenly Father for our redemption. In this God's love for us found its fullest expression. Abraham, who had been ready to sacrifice Isaac, his only son, could only faintly prefigure the action of our heavenly Father. And this self-sacrifice was fully accepted and brought to fruition by Jesus. In an apparent reference to Küng's stress on Jesus's God-forsaken death on the Cross (*Christian*, pp. 341–342) the bishops emphasized the triumphal nature of the cross. When Jesus said: 'It is finished' (John 19:30) this did not only mean that his sufferings were at an end but that he had completed and fulfilled his task. All this the bishops found insufficiently represented in *On being a Christian*. They felt it was not made clear that the Father revealed himself as love in sending his divine Son. Nor did they find in the book's final section (*Christian*, pp. 513–602) an adequate treatment of the supreme commandment of love (*Wahrheit*, pp. 353–357).

Finally by diminishing God's act of salvation in Jesus Christ Küng was accused of presenting a diminished account of the mystery and reality of our redemption. The bishops took exception to Küng's question: 'But does a reasonable man today want to become God?' (*Christian*, p. 442) – as if anyone thought or taught that in being redeemed man ceased to be man: 'In the incarnation the divine Son does not cease to be God, and in redemption man does not cease to be man,' said the bishops. Man did not become God but shared in God's life and blessedness. In this way the description of the reality of salvation was in the bishops' mind distorted and diminished in Küng's book. Their concluding warning was that on these points *On being a Christian* could not be regarded as an adequate representation of the Catholic faith (*Wahrheit*, pp. 357–359).

In his covering letter Cardinal Höffner picked up Küng's indignant assertions that he had never thought to deny essential elements of the faith and that the theologian and the bishops shared the same Catholic faith. This personal avowal he accepted unreservedly and gratefully, but the bishops' reservations were due to Küng's inability to express this common faith satisfactorily in his book. The bishops were aware of the complexity of the theological issues involved, but the effort to attain a deeper understanding of the Christian faith in the world of today should not lead to essential elements of the faith being presented in a misleading form or discussed in such a way as to give the impression that they were disputed: 'Even today the faithful have a right to a complete and unambiguous presentation of the inalienable truths of the faith,' said the cardinal (*Wahrheit*, pp. 371–372).

Together with their statement the bishops published some of the correspondence that had passed between them and Küng, along with the other documents in the case. Küng was annoyed not only that they should have done this without seeking his permission but that they should have published what he saw as a tendentious selection and that they should also have released confidential information, such as the letter he wrote to Cardinal Döpfner on 27 April 1976 telling him about his five hours' private conversation first with Cardinal Šeper and then with Archbishop Hamer, prefect and secretary of the Doctrinal Congregation, when he was in Rome for the publication of the Italian translation of *On being a Christian* (*Wahrheit*, pp. 184–189) – a meeting which among other things confirms that throughout Küng had not the slightest objection to talking things over with officials of the Doctrinal Congregation: it was merely that he objected to being forced into proceedings analogous to a trial with the rules biased against him. His friend and fellow-professor at Tübingen Walter Jens was thus prompted to bring out a much fuller selection of documents, in fact virtually the entire documentation of the dispute right from 1973 and *Mysterium Ecclesiae*. It bore the provocative title 'Nothing but the Truth', and carried a pungent introduction by Jens treating the dispute as a Kafkaesque gladiatorial contest between Küng and the Church authorities.

The volume concluded with a final apologia from Küng himself in which he subjected the bishops' statement to a scathing analysis. He did not propose to bore the reader by pointing out all the half-truths, twisted statements, misunderstandings and downright lies it contained. It was indeed of a lower standard than many documents that had emanated from Rome and he wondered whether the person who had drawn it up had actually read his book and tried to come to terms with the issues it raised. The statement picked up his heavily qualified remark about the book having become a kind of small 'summa', but ignored his disclaimer half a page higher that it was *not* meant to be 'a miniature dogmatic theology with the answer to all old or new disputed questions' (*Christian*, pp. 19–20). It hunted for evidence of his having diminished or curtailed essential elements of the faith, as if this kind of process did not occur in episcopal statements and in officially approved catechisms and prayer books. The statement confused the theological question whether the man Jesus of Nazareth was the son of God (which Küng affirmed) with the methodological question whether in the field of Christology one was obliged to start 'from above', with God (which Küng denied). It showed little regard for serious biblical scholarship. Where the New Testament spoke of the cross, it spoke of the sacrifice of the Father and indeed by its comparison with Abraham seemed to make him responsible for the murder of his son. It used the term 'mystery' as an excuse for dodging the issue, and was stuffed with theological commonplaces, abstruse statements, and paradoxes. In fact it relied on the dogmatic approach of neoscholasticism which in practice made tradition the guiding norm of scripture and the magisterium the guiding norm of tradition, as if there had never been a Second Vatican Council. The Catholic tradition of faith and teaching to which it appealed needed handling with care: perhaps the German bishops would care to recall their predecessors' condemnation of the Darwinian theory of evolution in 1860 as incompatible with the Catholic faith.

With this background Küng was forced to renew his protest against the blanket condemnations to be found without any justification in the first of the bishops' statements; against the imputation in the second statement that as far as he was concerned Jesus Christ was 'just an exemplary human being' and 'only God's spokesman and representative' and that he denied the Christological statements of the Nicene creed; against the unfounded and unspecified charges brought against him once again in the third statement with regard to ecclesiology, the Trinity, the sacraments and Mariology; and against the accusation of separating himself from the tradition of faith and of making an arbitrary selection from scripture, as well as against the reduction of his acknowledgement that Jesus is the son of God to a remark made in passing. Indeed, after repeating his objections to being expected to behave like a prize pupil and give prompt answers to questions put by the magisterium, he reaffirmed his acceptance of Jesus's divine sonship and of the Chalcedonian formula 'truly God and truly man' – while pointing out that for him the central issue was that this should be understood correctly. He outlined both the problems involved in handling the classic Christological definitions today and the theological consensus within which these problems could be tackled. In this way he could join in saying: 'I believe in the only-begotten Son of God.' Simply parroting past doctrinal formulae was not enough: 'What the men and women of today, with all their doubts and hopes, expect both from the theologians and from the bishops is not the simple repetition of the creeds but their interpretation for today in a manner that can be justified by the original Christian witness of the New Testament,' said Küng.

While conflict was unavoidable even in the Church and was in fact a sign of life, it should be not just endured but put to fruitful use. Both bishops and theologians had their role and function in the Church, which would be helped not by one side's victory at the expense of the other but by their mutual co-operation with all the tension involved. Küng thus concluded with an appeal for an end to disputes about orthodoxy, to secret proceedings, to endless correspondence, to inquisitorial interrogations, authoritarian hearings, public sentencings (*Wahrheit*, p. 389):

> Let us do away with mistrust, overcome polarization, and decide the issues between us fairly. Let us work together again at the real front where we both stand, to meet the demands of the time and to be a real help to people in their problems both as individuals and socially: in order to make progress towards the unity of the still divided Churches and once again give people in our country 'an account of the hope that is in us' (1 Peter 3:15).

They should jointly get down to the tasks awaiting them in both Church and world, tasks the men and women of today expected them to tackle. 'Let us end the quarrel,' said Küng. 'We have more important things to do' (*Wahrheit*, pp. 374–389).

Once again, it looked as if the dispute had ended in a draw. But a warning sign of what was to come was contained in the fact that the German bishops' statement was apparently presented as final merely for the time being (*Wahrheit*, p. 375).

1 Nicholas Lash, 'Reflections "On Being a Christian",' *The Month*, March 1977, vol. 238, no. 1314, pp. 88–92.

2 Both reviews were originally published in *America*, 20 November 1976; quoted from their reprint in *The Tablet*, 15 January 1977, pp. 54–56.

3 Walter Kasper, *Jesus the Christ*, Burns and Oates, London, Paulist Press, New York, 1976; Edward Schillebeeckx, *Jesus: an experiment in Christology*, Collins, London, 1979. The originals of both works appeared in 1974.

4 Hans Urs von Balthasar, Alfons Deissler, Alois Grillmeier, Walter Kasper, Jacob Kremer, Karl Lehmann, Karl Rahner, Joseph Ratzinger, Helmut Riedlinger, Theodor Schneider and Bernhard Stoeckle, *Diskussion über Hans Küngs 'Christ sein'*, Matthias-Grünewald-Verlag, Mainz, 1976.

5 Leo Scheffczyk, '*Christentum an der Schwelle der Selbstauflösung?: Zu H. Küngs Buch "Christ sein"*,' in *Die Entscheidung* (Vienna) 61 (1975), pp. 4–12. He has since expounded his misgivings about this and other of Küng's works (including *Does God Exist?*) and his conviction that Küng has departed from the orthodox mainstream of Catholic tradition in a 96-page booklet, *Kursänderung des Glaubens?: Theologische Bilanz zum Fall Küng*, Christiana-Verlag, Stein am Rhein, 1980.

6 'Vatican III: Problems and Opportunities for the Future', in David Tracy, Hans Küng and Johann B. Metz (ed.), *Toward Vatican III: The Work That Needs to be Done*, Gill and Macmillan, Dublin, 1978.

17

The Question of God

In their criticisms of what they took to be a comprehensive manual of dogmatic theology for the layman the German bishops made great play with the omissions they found in *On being a Christian*. But the danger Küng was constantly having to guard against in writing it was of the book outgrowing any reasonable compass. Originally he had promised his English publisher a volume of only two hundred pages. In the German edition it ran to 676 pages, and that – regrettably – is without an index; in the English (with an index) it comes to 720 pages, and at 2 lb 10 oz is nearly double the weight of the German. Küng was up against the difficulty of finding no middle way between a comprehensive treatment of the subject matter and a brief sketch that is forced merely to allude to far more than it can actually say. Once the book had been written he was able to present its basic message in aphoristic form and extract its skeleton as twenty theses that fill a mere forty pages or so. Beyond that he was able to produce an abridgement of the work at only half the length which came out in 1979 under the title *The Christian Challenge*.

But in whichever version – full length, abridged, or summarized in theses with brief explanations – Küng was conscious of having had to treat summarily one major topic that cried out for fuller investigation. This was the whole question of God and whether belief in God still makes any kind of sense today when God is no longer felt to be an essential hypothesis to explain how the world works. Christianity itself may seem problematic enough in the modern world, but at least it has in its favour the sociological necessity of belonging, the existence of the institutional Church, and the disturbing impression left behind by the man Jesus of Nazareth. But God seems to have become dispensable. The shift from a world in which God seemed an essential ultimate explanation to a world where mention of God appears merely a gesture to ancestral piety has left many believers floundering. Can twentieth-century men and women still honestly believe in God? Or is belief in God merely a cover for psychological or sociological inadequacies? A response was already sketched out in one of the early chapters of *On being a Christian* (A II: 'The Other Dimensions', pp. 57–88). But the question needed to be explored in far fuller detail than was possible in a few pages of a work with a different theme. It involved, in fact, the entire Western intellectual tradition from Descartes to the present day. The scope of the exploration demanded helps to explain why the German original of *Does God Exist?* runs to nearly eight hundred pages of text alone.

Once again, however, there is something like a skeleton key. Among the many pressures on Küng during the final year of his dispute with the German bishops over *On being a Christian* was the vitally important lecture he was to give as the high point of Tübingen university's celebration of its five hundredth anniversary. His theme was science and the question of God, and the central question his lecture was trying to answer was: 'Can a modern person who thinks rationally and has a scientific training still believe in God?' (*Reden*, p. 103). He was thus covering much the same ground that he had already covered at length in *Does God Exist?* when he shut himself up in his cottage by the lake at Sursee for a month to work out the text of his lecture. It was delivered on 8 October 1977 before an audience of the learned and eminent, including the President of the German Federal Republic, Walter Scheel (who also gave a speech), the Austrian Chancellor, Bruno Kreisky, the Prime Minister of Baden-Württemberg, the Mayor of Tübingen, and both the Protestant and the Catholic bishop, at a ceremony held in the town's collegial church, a building only a few years older than the university, of which it served as the *aula* or great hall during the institution's early years.

When the university was founded five hundred years ago, Küng reminded his audience, there was not felt to be any contradiction between piety and reason, faith and knowledge, belief in God and science. Now the question was whether God should be mentioned at all within the confines of the University – apart of course from the twin faculties of theology. What had happened to bring God into such discredit?

First, God had been used as a weapon to try and curb the development of science. Nor was this just a specifically Catholic vice. Giordano Bruno, the former Dominican friar burnt at the stake in Rome in 1600, had twenty-one years earlier been refused permission to teach at that stronghold of Protestant orthodoxy, Tübingen. A generation or so later in 1620, four years after Rome condemned Copernicus, Tübingen rejected Johannes Kepler for a professorship because of the freedom of conscience the astronomer claimed. As late as the eighteenth century Tübingen made the philosopher Israel Gottlieb Canz recant when he started questioning the idea that the world had been created in six days.

The aim of such rearguard action was to defend the biblical faith in God. But the effect, Küng pointed out, was artificially to preserve the Greek and medieval picture of the world. No wonder the Catholic Church in particular was rega ded as the enemy of science. But paradoxically the major scientists – Descartes, Pascal, Copernicus, Kepler, Galileo, Leibniz, Newton, Boyle – did not merely believe in God but were committed Christians. Even Voltaire and his kindred spirits of the French Enlightenment were deists for whom God, however remote and distant he may have become, was needed to set the machine of the world in motion and keep it running.

A second reason for God becoming discredited was that he was similarly used as a weapon to beat back the rising tide of democracy. The Catholic Church in particular, though not alone, failed to face the social and political problems the modern world brought in its train. The gospel's relevance for issues of social ethics was neglected. The unholy alliance of an individualistic form of belief with princely absolutism and unscrupulous power politics wreaked untold damage on the credibility of the Christian faith. During the French Revolution the cry went up: *'Les prêtres'* – and not just *les aristos* – *'à la lanterne!'*

To the extent that theology depended on a God of the gaps it was forced into a continual retreat as science filled gap after gap. And, noted Küng, science was quite right to leave God out of account. But no one science had as its object of study all aspects of the world and of human life and behaviour. Scientists were concerned, and rightly, primarily with the analysis of data, facts, phenomena, operations, processes, energies, structures, developments; theologians, equally rightly, with questions of ultimate and primary significance, goals, values, ideals, norms, decisions and attitudes. What was needed was critical rationality, not ideological rationalism.

But, Küng went on, it was precisely in the light of this critical rationality that the question arose whether twentieth-century rational scientific man could go on believing in God. There was no way of *proving* the existence of God. To the extent that proofs of God's existence were trying actually to prove this they had nothing to say; but to the extent that they made it possible to talk about God they had a great deal to say. To critics like Feuerbach, Marx, Nietzsche and Freud it had to be conceded that it was possible to reject God, that atheism was not capable of rational refutation. But at the same time acceptance of God was possible. If atheism could not be refuted by reason, neither could it be established by reason. Feuerbach was right to point out the element of projection in religion, but he was unable to show that religion was merely the projection of man's hopes: it could also be a relationship with a totally other and deeper reality. Marx was right in pointing out that religion could be the opium of the people; but it did not have to be, and it could also be a means of enlightenment and liberation. Freud was right to point out that religion could be an illusion, the expression of psychological immaturity or even of neurosis; but again it did not have to be, it could be the expression of personal identity and psychological maturity. Nor was it possible to see religion as something that was fading away: Nietzsche's forecast of the death of God was, to say the least, a little premature.

How, then, did one today reach belief in God? An appeal to the bible would for the most part convince only those who were already believers. The idea that God exists, said Küng, could be accepted not on the basis of some proof or demonstration but in the context of a rational act of trust. In other words, it was a rational thing for someone to do to commit and entrust himself to the idea that the reality of immediate experience is not the ultimate reality but that the reality of the world and of man is founded on, borne up by and encompassed by some ultimate foundation, some ultimate support, some ultimate goal. Belief in God meant that man could escape from his one-dimensionality, offered an answer to the riddle why anything should exist at all, gave meaning to man's innate longings, showed that suffering, pain, old age, and death were not the final and ultimate reality, promised the fulfilment of man's longing for perfect justice, total meaning and eternal truth.

But, asked Küng, if God existed, how was thinking about

him to be fitted into the context and framework of
contemporary science? There could of course be no
question of God 'up there' as some kind of divine puppet-
master, nor of some constitutional monarch bound by the
laws of nature. On the other hand, although God was not
the world and the world was not God, God was in the world
and the world was in God: what was presupposed was not
some dualistic but a unitary understanding of reality. Even
for the scientist God could provide the answer to the
unavoidable questions: who are we? where do we come
from? where are we going? These questions were surely not
just a private matter that should not be admitted to public
discussion in a university: 'No, the question of God is too
important and too explosive for one to be able to leave it to
the theologians alone,' remarked Küng (*Reden*, p. 110).
What he looked for was an interdisciplinary approach
which would enable the different branches of learning to
cross-fertilize each other, with astrophysics contributing
ideas about the origin of the universe, quantum mechanics
or molecular biology insights about chance and necessity,
the law questions of legality and morality, the social
sciences questions of motivation and goals, medicine
questions of life and death. But there should be no question
at all of seeing God as a reach-me-down answer to
contemporary problems, or religion as a patent solution to
the difficulties of today. Rather, the question of God was
posed afresh within the context of modern science, looking
forward and not back.

One of Küng's major concerns in this lecture was thus to
argue forcefully that God was a proper object of university
study and not something to be confined merely to faculties
of theology – which in any case can too often be regarded
by academics of other disciplines as some kind of nature
reserve for the preservation of an endangered and no longer
viable species. But to establish this argument he needed to
develop one of the main strands that went to make up *Does*

God Exist?. Instead of merely alluding to a handful of the
intellectual giants who have shaped the way we see the
world we live in and the way we understand our place in it,
Küng needed to tackle all the major figures who have
affected our views and attitudes. In *Does God Exist?* he
gives detailed consideration to some thirty-eight or so
philosophers and theologians, including besides such
obvious names as Descartes, Pascal, Hegel, Feurbach,
Marx, Nietzsche, Darwin, Freud and Einstein such more
recondite thinkers as Carnap, Wittgenstein, Whitehead,
Teilhard de Chardin, Auguste Comte and Lenin. The
index of names contains some 1600 entries in all. And when
he discusses a major figure Küng does not assume that his
readers already have a reasonable idea of why this person
was important, what his contribution was and the context
within which he made it. Instead he carefully fills in the
basic biographical background as well as setting out the
man's views, how they developed, why he held them, and
how they have fared at the hands of contemporary and
subsequent critics – and all this without either patronizing
the ignorant or irritating the knowledgeable.

His starting point was Descartes and the latter's attempt
to import mathematical certainty into our understanding of
the world. From Descartes he went on to Pascal, for whom
certainty was to be found not in the God of the philosophers
or the scholars but in the God of Abraham, Isaac and Jacob,
the God of our Lord and Saviour Jesus Christ. Whereas
Descartes had found his Archimedean fulcrum – the Greek
mathematician had asked: 'Give me somewhere to stand,
and I will move the world' – in his first principle *Cogito,
ergo sum* ('I think, therefore I am') for Pascal (who was
nicknamed the Archimedes of Paris), Küng suggested, the
formula should run *Credo ergo sum* ('I believe, therefore I
am') (*God*, pp. 13, 44, 58). But Küng does not just start
from scratch in the early seventeenth century. Cartesian
dualism with its divorce between faith and reason, with

faith seen as an act not of the intellect but of the will, is traced to its Thomist roots, with Thomas Aquinas's reassertion of the autonomy of reason giving rise to one of Küng's least favourite intellectual structures, the two-tier theory marked by an antithesis between nature and grace, faith and reason, philosophy and theology, the temporal and spiritual power. Pascal's intellectual roots are similarly traced back to Augustine, while Pascal himself can be seen as founding a tradition leading on to Kierkegaard (though apparently Kierkgaard had not read him) and Karl Barth. And while Descartes was a founding father of modern mathematics, as was Pascal, he contributed powerfully to the development of neoscholasticism and its domination of the Church's intellectual life over the last century or so.

With both Descartes and Pascal God was in a sense taken for granted. Descartes' attempts to establish the existence of God may in fact have made that existence appear more problematical by suggesting that what was involved was the same kind of question as that involved in a geometric theorem. Pascal's reliance on the emotions ('The heart has its reasons that reason is unaware of') must surely have encouraged people to regard belief in God as somehow irrational. Both were convinced believers, even though among their eighteenth-century successors first deism and then atheism became established as intellectually respectable and fashionable. Hegel, too, placed God firmly at the head of things. As we have seen from looking at Küng's study of him, he introduced a dynamic understanding of God better fitted to a world of movement and change than the static picture usually inherited from the Middle Ages and the Graeco-Roman world. Even so, the old static image of God has had remarkable staying-power. Küng remarks that it should be not just in theology but in preaching and in religious instruction that it needs to be made clear that contemporary man no longer needs to imagine or conceive of God in the same way as did his predecessors of the ancient world or of the Middle Ages (*God*, p. 182).

It was with Hegel's heirs and assigns that God really started being pushed completely and decisively out of the intellectual picture. Feuerbach argued that God was merely the projection of human qualities (*God*, pp. 201–202). Marx saw religion as a means of persuading men to put up with what they ought not to put up with: he may have recognized that it could be seen as a protest – 'the sigh of the oppressed, the heart of a heartless world' – but the fact that attention was diverted from this world to the next robbed such protest of its force (*God*, p. 229). Freud concluded that religious ideas were illusions that fulfilled the oldest, strongest, most urgent wishes of mankind (*God*, p. 283). Nietzsche led the way to thorough-going nihilism and decried both the Christian God ('one of the most corrupt concepts of God attained on this earth') and Christianity ('Basically there was only ever one Christian, and he died on the cross') as expressing an attempt by life's failures to redress the balance that was rightly and decisively tilted against them (*God*, pp. 385 and 407).

These are views that cannot simply be brushed aside, much as many Christians would like to do so. The uncomfortable criticisms they express are not the product of wilful perversity but have to be taken seriously. Time and again Küng insists that there can be no going back behind Feuerbach, Marx and Freud, no pretending they never existed.

Feuerbach, for example, cannot be treated as a secret believer in what to non-Christians must be the extremely irritating way some Christians have of claiming those outside and against the Church as really on their side. He was instead the first proponent of a consistent and conscious atheism (*God*, p. 211). The questions he puts to religion and theology have to be taken seriously. Do not the Church and theology often defend God at the expense of man? Was he not right in seeing his philosophy as the final phase of a Protestant theology which long before had been reduced to an anthropology, having not God but man as its subject-matter? And was he not right in exposing major weaknesses in the Christian way of talking about God, an all-too-anthropomorphic style of language to which the answer cannot be a Hegelian dialectical movement of the spirit transcending and overcoming the contradiction between the world and God? The right contrast for theology to put forward against Feuerbach's accusation of theology being reduced to anthropology, Küng argues, is not the opposite extreme of theology swallowing anthropology up but for theology to have priority. The aim is not a deficient but a more abundant humanity (*God*, pp. 212–216).

Nor can there be any going back behind Marx. His justified reproaches against Christianity are a standing reminder of the need to take seriously the social implications of the gospel and never to allow religion to become a justification for the prevailing pattern of injustice. In the wake of Marx theology must be aware that 'the truth of belief in God must be demonstrated, confirmed and verified in practical behaviour' (*God*, pp. 252–261). There is thus a recapitulation of Küng's stress on the primacy of orthopraxis over orthodoxy in *On being a Christian*, as well as of the earlier book's insistence that a Christian may but does not have to be a socialist.

Nor can there be any going back behind Freud. Christians should accept the justified criticism he directed against infantile forms of religion, against the abuse of power in the Church, against the neurosis of the ecclesiastical institution, against the image of God as an angry or indulgent father-figure. The aim of Freudian psychoanalysis was emancipation, complete liberation, enabling man to become more fully human. Man needed to come to terms with his instinctive drives, with the burden of his past, with his consciousness of guilt. Here psychoanalysis and Christian faith could be partners, though both the psycholanalyst and the theologian needed to recognize the limits of their specific competences (*God*, pp. 307–312).

But accepting the justified criticisms of these determined atheists did not in any way mean accepting their atheism. In all cases that remained an assumption that lacked proof, even though Christians should always respect the atheist convictions of others and not treat them patronizingly as some kind of latent or covert believer. The answer to the abuse of religion was not no religion but better religion.

As for Nietzsche's critique of Christianity, if it really were what he thought it was then one would have good reasons for being obliged to reject it and to join him in subscribing to Voltaire's slogan *Ecrasez l'infâme*: one could no longer be a Christian but would have to be an anti-Christian. But the answer to Nietzsche was that this was how Christianity must not appear, nor should if based on a proper understanding of Christ Jesus. Being a Christian must not take place without being human, at the expense of being human, in some parallel, superior or subordinate relationship to being human. Instead, being Christian must be seen as the radical and genuinely human way of being human (*God*, pp. 409–410) – the message, in fact, of *On being a Christian*.

But, if neither the existence of God nor atheism can be proved, is it merely a matter of tossing up between them? Is there any rational basis for belief in God and ultimately for Christian belief? Nietzsche had shown how there was no limit to the corrosive power of doubt: there was no compelling reason to find either the Cartesian *cogito, ergo sum* or the Pascalian *credo, ergo sum* a stable foundation. One was faced with the choice between on the one hand accepting reality together with all the questions, doubts and misgivings it gives rise to, and on the other opting for the nihilist solution, involving ultimately a rejection of reality. Just like atheism, nihilism was possible, irrefutable, but unprovable. The antithesis however was not between belief in God and nihilism – otherwise, as Küng points out, all atheists would be nihilists, which they are not. Nihilism involves a more fundamental level of acceptance or rejection of reality. Before the question of God can arise there arises the question of one's fundamental attitude to this reality that, through the consistent use of the analytical tool of doubt, can be and has been called into question. Man has to adopt a fundamental attitude to reality as a whole, to make a fundamental decision which can be positive or negative and which will determine this fundamental attitude to himself, to other people, to society, to the world. This in its turn involves a fundamental act either of trust or of rejection (*God*, pp. 437–441).

What is involved here is in fact taking a risk that is thoroughly reasonable (*God*, p. 450). But on this basis atheism is still possible, and the option of atheism must be respected (*God*, pp. 472–473). Nevertheless, like the basic act of trust, belief in God is something that makes sense. It involves not just the human reason but the entire actual living human being; it transcends reason, but is not irrational; it is not a blind act of faith but rather a well-founded decision with its roots in reality and everyday life; it involves relationships with other people; and it is not a once-and-for-all decision but continually has to be realized anew (*God*, pp. 574–575). Küng thus steers a middle way between Karl Barth and Vatican I, between dialectical theology on the one hand and its insistence that it is only through God's revelation of himself that man can know God, and on the other Vatican I's anathematization of those who would deny that God can be known with certainty by the natural light of human reason – a decree which, as Küng points out (*God*, p. 514), was sharpened up in the anti-Modernist oath imposed by Pius X, where it became a question of believing that God could not merely be known but be proved to exist. As against dialectical theology Küng insists that belief in God must be not merely asserted but verified; as against natural theology, that it must be verified but not proved (*God*, p. 536). There can be no question of using the Bible as some *deus ex machina* to provide the answer when faced with the question of whether reality ultimately makes any sense and the question of whether the idea of God makes any sense. Faith in this way can give a rational account of itself when challenged by nihilism and atheism. But on the other hand there is no question of indulging in natural theology in the sense of building up a purely rational foundation from which the supernatural can then take off. The basic options of accepting reality and of accepting God entail not simply pure reason but an attitude of believing trust or trusting faith. There is no continuous rational progression from man to God but rather a venture, an acceptance of risk in freedom and trust (*God*, pp. 577–578).

God may in this way promise the ultimate meaning of human existence, the guarantee that the world does after all make sense. But he can seem rather remote compared with the God with a human face revealed in the Bible. Küng again takes the middle way between dialectical and natural theology. Simply to dissociate the God of the philosophers and the God of the Bible is to short-circuit the whole problem; simply to harmonize the two would be superficial. Rather the two must be seen in a genuinely dialectical relationship. In the God of the Bible the God of the philosophers is, says Küng, using that untranslatable Hegelian term, *aufgehoben* – 'affirmed, negated, and transcended at one and the same time' (*God*, p. 666).

For the Christian this God has ultimately and definitively revealed himself in the man Jesus; and here Küng provides a concise recapitulation of the disputed Christological section of *On being a Christian*. The conviction that Jesus

was the eternally begotten Son of the Father, the idea of his
eternal pre-existence, reflected the conviction that in Jesus
the eternal God and none other was definitively revealing
himself. Other Catholic scholars had warned against understanding pre-existence in a purely temporal sense and
against allowing the concept so to distort one's understanding of Jesus's life, suffering and death as to shift the
emphasis from the resurrection to the incarnation in the
sense of a miraculous birth. The incarnation in turn meant
that God's word and will had taken on a human form in
Jesus's whole life (*Gott*, p. 748; cf. *God*, p. 685):

> In everything he said and did, in his suffering and
> dying, Jesus proclaimed, manifested, revealed God's
> word and will in his whole person: this man in whom
> word and deed, teaching and living, being and doing
> completely coincide, *is* God's word, will, son in
> bodily, in human form.

At the same time Küng suggests that to avoid all possible
misunderstanding we would be well-advised to call Jesus the
Son of God rather than simply God. In this way the Nicene
formula that describes Jesus as 'God from God, light from
light, true God from true God, begotten, not made, of one
being with the Father' must not only meet with our consent
but also must be guarded against misunderstandings either
in the direction of believing in two Gods or in the direction
of simply identifying the Son with the Father. It is God
himself whom we encounter in the acts and person of Jesus.

At the time of the early councils Christians had
practically no option but to use such concepts as hypostasis,
person, nature, being, *homo-ousios* and *homoi-ousios*,
remarks Küng; but today the same things can be expressed
in different terms. What is binding is not the terminology
but what the New Testament bears witness to: Jesus
himself. Nicaea's definition that Jesus is of one being with
the Father was directed against the danger of Arius

reintroducing polytheism into Christianity and turning
Jesus into a second God or demigod (*Gott*, p. 750; cf. *God*,
p. 687):

> One will share the conviction of the fathers of Nicaea
> that our entire redemption depends on the fact that
> what is involved in Jesus is the one God who is truly,
> really and uniquely God: made manifest in Jesus as
> his son.

Alongside this equality of being with the Father Chalcedon
in 451 emphasized Jesus's equality of being with us men
and women (*Gott*, p. 751; cf. *God*, p. 687):

> In the event Jesus of Nazareth has nothing ultimately
> decisive to say to me if he is not proclaimed as the
> Christ of God. But at the same time even a divine
> Christ has little to say to me if he is not identical with
> the man Jesus of Nazareth.

There is on the basis of the New Testament no possibility
of vindicating an interpretation of the history of Jesus
Christ in which he is only a human being, only a preacher,
prophet or teacher of wisdom, only a symbol or figure for
some basic human experience. But neither is it possible to
vindicate on the basis of the same New Testament any
interpretation in which Jesus Christ in only or simply God,
raised up above human deficiencies and weaknesses.

But once again Küng stresses that what matters is being a
Christian, and that is something he is enabled to try to do
only by Jesus Christ: Christology may be important, but
belief in Christ and following Christ are more important.
And on this basis he can make bold to say without
hesitation: *Credo in Jesum Christum, filium Dei unigenitum*
(*God*, p. 688).

Originally, as we have mentioned (pp. 274–275
above), *Does God Exist?* was to have concluded with the
section on prayer that his dispute with Rome had prevented
Küng from writing for *On being a Christian*. This time it
was a desire to stop an already lengthy book from becoming

even longer that led to its omission. Nevertheless the work ends on a note of prayer that brings to a quietly triumphant conclusion this exhaustive but not exhausting, sometimes perilous but always rewarding voyage through the ocean of ideas that circumscribe our intellectual world (*God*, p. 702):

> After the difficult passage through the history of the modern age from the time of Descartes and Pascal, Kant and Hegel,
> considering in detail the objections raised in the critique of religion by Feuerbach, Marx and Freud,
> seriously confronting Nietzsche's nihilism,
> seeking the reason for our fundamental trust and the answer in trust in God,
> in comparing finally the alternatives of the Eastern religions,
> entering also into the question 'Who is God?' and of the God of Israel and of Jesus Christ:
> after all this, it will be understood why the question 'Does God Exist?' can now be answered by a clear, convinced Yes, justified at the bar of critical reason.
>
> Does God exist? Despite all upheavals and doubts, even for man today, the only appropriate answer must be that with which believers of all generations from ancient times have again and again professed their faith. It begins with praise: *Te, Deum, laudamus,* 'we praise you, O God,' and ends in trust: *In te, Domine, speravi, non confundar in aeternum,* 'in you, Lord, have I put my trust, let me never be confounded.'

Belief is thus not just possible but, like being a Christian, supremely worth while.

18

The Blow Falls

When he celebrated his fiftieth birthday on 19 March 1978 Hans Küng could seem enviably secure. He had survived a brush with the former Holy Office and a wrangle with the German bishops. Both disputes had apparently ended in a draw: the Church authorities may not have liked what he was saying, but they had not tried to stop him from saying it, and any such move was fairly widely regarded as tactically impossible. His latest book, *Does God Exist?*, was busily climbing up the German best-seller charts, as *On being a Christian* had done three and a half years earlier. To celebrate his fiftieth birthday three of his staff at the Institute for Ecumenical Research had collaborated to produce not a *Festschrift* – the collection of essays by academic colleagues traditionally presented to professors on retirement or to mark their sixtieth, seventieth or eightieth birthday – but a volume assembling some of the critiques and reviews his major works had elicited over the years, together with a long interview with Hermann Häring and Karl-Josef Kuschel covering his career and development so far, and an invaluable bibliography of his writings to date. He was a deservedly popular university teacher. His lectures were clear, concise and comprehensive. Many a foreign student must have gained from him a misleading impression of the comprehensibility of German as spoken by academic theologians: at the other end of the spectrum Rahner is apt to leave professional interpreters floundering when answering questions at conferences. In seminars and discussions Küng showed a concentrated alertness and an ability to pounce on the key points at issue without over-awing or discouraging the more nervous among his students. All in all, things seemed to be going well. It looked as if he was indeed being allowed to get on with his work as a theologian in peace and quiet.

But 1978 was also the last year of Paul VI's pontificate. Increasingly there had been a reluctance to take major decisions in Rome: for some time no new initiatives were to be looked for from the Vatican, and there was a sense that Paul VI was quietly playing out time. It had not yet seemed possible for a pope to resign and make way for a younger man, as under Paul VI had become the custom for bishops to do (with a handful of notorious exceptions). This atmosphere reinforced what seems fairly clearly to have been Paul VI's deliberate policy of refraining from pushing the dispute between Küng and the Doctrinal Congregation to the point of disciplinary sanctions. This was in line with Paul VI's overriding concern not to preside over any kind of split or schism in the Church such as might have been expected to follow the radical upheaval brought about by Vatican II, and it was something for which Küng was duly grateful (*Fall*, p. 56).

At the two conclaves which followed Paul VI's death, surprise succeeded surprise. In Albino Luciani the cardinals elected the only Italian who seemed capable of measuring up to the demands and expectations that had become centred on the papacy: someone whom few if any observers had tipped as *papabile* but someone who, with his quiff of hair peeping out from a skull-cap slightly askew and with his endearing smile, rapidly gained people's affection.[1] When after merely thirty-three days in office this Pope John Paul I suddenly died, the cardinals surprised everyone again, this time not just by electing the first non-Italian pope since the Dutchman Hadrian VI had emerged from the conclave of 1522 but by going behind the Iron Curtain to choose the Pole Karol Wojtyła. Clearly it meant a new age for the Church; but it was not equally clear what kind of a new age it would be. John Paul II had a warmth and a directness that brought an equally warm and direct response, especially from young people, as at Galway in September 1979 and in Paris in June 1980. But at the same time he could be hard and intransigent where he felt hardness and intransigence were demanded by the Church's mission. The clearest example was the abrupt halt he imposed on the process of laicization whereby priests had been able to leave the ministry, normally with permission to marry. Now all that was stopped, and priests who a couple of years earlier would have had no difficulty in leaving the ministry and getting married found themselves faced with a choice between a civil wedding that in the Church's eyes would be invalid and no marriage at all or a continuation of the celibacy they had painfully come to realize was not for them. He could also show himself obstinately insensitive to local attitudes, as when during his American trip he refused to give people communion in the hand and waited for them to open their mouths so that he could give them communion on the tongue, despite the fact that communion in the hand has been officially approved in the United States since 1977. In many ways it is tempting to apply to John Paul II the title of one of his books and to call him a sign of contradiction. He cannot simply be classified as traditionalist or reactionary. He is far too complex and subtle-minded a person for that. It is rather that he has been moulded by coming from a Church where authority and discipline had proved the key to survival.

Indeed, in the policy he has adopted towards dissent and opposition in the Church Pope John Paul II would seem to be going out of his way to disappoint the hopes that could legitimately have been read out of the work of the philosopher Karol Wojtyła. In his study *The Acting Person* he had shown himself not just prepared to tolerate opposition but ready to welcome it as an essential and constitutive element of human community. Opposition he there interpreted as essentially an attitude of solidarity, and he pointed out that those who stood up in opposition were not trying to cut themselves off from the community but rather were seeking their own place in it and the kind of constructive role that would afford them a fuller and more effective share in its life. In this way he saw this kind of constructive opposition as a condition of the proper structure of communities and the proper functioning of their internal organization. Moreover, opposition had to be able not just to express itself but to be practically effective. All this meant that the principle of dialogue had to be adopted regardless of the obstacles and difficulties it might entail.[2]

This in fact reads like a programme for a Church in which Küng's role as His Holiness's loyal opposition would be not merely tolerated but positively welcomed. But the new pope gave increasing evidence of a certain doctrinal firmness and rigidity coupled with an authoritarian streak. This was reflected in a fresh campaign launched by the Doctrinal Congregation against what it saw as dissident theologians. Material for this campaign may have been prepared some time before, while Paul VI was still alive; but the measures that were taken needed papal approval, and despite the fact that some theologians were eased out of their teaching posts in the early 1970s – notably the Dominican Stephan Pfürtner (pp. 223–224 above) – it is doubtful whether Paul VI would have sanctioned the steps John Paul II was to endorse. In September 1979 the French Dominican Jacques Pohier was banned from public teaching and from presiding at worship following the condemnation by the Doctrinal Commission in April of his book *Quand je dis Dieu* on account of its alleged denial, among other things, of Christ's bodily resurrection (*The Tablet*, 29 September 1979). A little later came the news that another and more famous Dominican, Edward

Schillebeeckx, Belgian-born but long settled in the
Netherlands, had been summoned to Rome to explain
views put forward in his book *Jesus: An Experiment in
Christology*. As we have seen, Schillebeeckx had had an
earlier brush with the Doctrinal Congregation in 1968,
when it was thought Rome was using this as a way of
getting at the Dutch Church in general (p. 155 above).
Other theologians whose work was being regarded with a
baleful eye by the Roman authorities included the
American moral theologian Charles Curran.[3]

All this gave ample scope for apprehension when Hans
Küng offered an 'interim appraisal' of John Paul II's first
year as pope in an article which appeared on 13 October
1979, three days before the actual anniversary, in the
Frankfurter Allgemeine Zeitung and subsequently in *Le
Monde*, the *New York Times* and other newspapers and
periodicals in Switzerland, Spain, Brazil, the United States
and Ireland. No doubt if *The Times* had not involved itself
in an industrial dispute which kept it off the streets for a
year it would have appeared in England too, but there was
still a month to go before the paper reappeared on 13
November: a copy of the article sent to *The Guardian* was
mysteriously lost in the post. As a result English readers
had to wait until after Rome had acted, when *The Observer*
(23 December 1979) published it as the best way of explaining what the row was all about.

Küng's article was far from one-sidedly critical. He found
much to praise in the new pope, who was clearly someone
to whom he like others could not fail to respond. As his
framework he took the profile he and other theologians
connected with *Concilium* had drawn up just after Paul VI's
death to sketch out the kind of pope that was needed: a man
open to the world; a spiritual leader; an authentic pastor; a
true fellow bishop; an ecumenical mediator; and a genuine
Christian (*The Tablet*, 19 August 1978, p. 811). Under each
of these six heads Küng had something positive and

generous to say about John Paul II. Apart from this, and to begin with, there was the tremendous impact he had made right from the start of his pontificate, an impact underlined and reinforced by the remarkable series of journeys he undertook:

> There is no significant issue on which he has not already taken a definite stand. After just one year, the contours of this pontificate stand out in bold and unmistakable relief. The intense activity of the Pope in Rome and, above all, his triumphal trips to Mexico, Poland, Ireland and the United States have presented him to world public opinion as an impressive champion of peace, of human rights, of social justice; and also of a strong Church, as a man who knows how to satisfy the desire of the masses for a morally trustworthy leader – a rarity in today's world – in a manner both impressive and highly skilful from the public relations standpoint.

But could one visualize Jesus of Nazareth as the darling of the masses and the media superstar the Pope seemed amazingly quickly to have become, a sort of living cult figure for some Catholics, very nearly something like a new Messiah for our time? And did the Pope really have Jesus's message behind him in everything he so vehemently advocated in dogma and morals?

Typically, Küng's criticisms took the form of rhetorical questions. Had the pope not re-emphasized the disciplinary and dogmatic obstacles Catholicism presented to Christian unity (including infallibility) instead of removing them? Did he not indeed give his approval to inquisitorial proceedings against representatives of directions in theology other than the traditional Roman school – and this despite his calls for human rights outside the Church? (Küng specifically mentioned Pohier, Schillebeeckx, Hasler, and two moral theologians in the United States whom he was not free to name.) Above all, was the Church under his leadership prepared to be as prophetic and critical with

itself as it was with regard to the world outside? Küng
asked bluntly:

> Is the commitment in the Church to human rights in
> the world honest, when in the Church itself, at the
> same time, human rights are not fully guaranteed —
> for example, the right of priests to marry, as is
> guaranteed in the Gospel itself and in the old Catholic
> tradition; the right to leave the priesthood with an
> official dispensation after a thorough examination of
> conscience (rather than the inhumane practice reintro-
> duced by this Pope of forbidding bureaucratically this
> dispensation); the right of theologians to freedom in
> their research and expression of opinion; the right of
> nuns to choose their own clothing; the ordination of
> women, as can certainly be justified by the Gospel for
> our contemporary situation; the personal responsi-
> bility of married couples for the conception and the
> number of their children?

Was this pope capable of changing, of learning? Küng
sincerely hoped so.

This article can hardly have improved Küng's standing
in Rome, especially as he also criticized the new pope's
insufficient familiarity with recent developments in
theology and his failure to listen, to encourage genuine
discussion, and to act in a truly collegial manner. It can
only have reinforced whatever impression had been given
by a letter Küng sent to the new pope at the end of March
1979 pleading with him to make celibacy no longer
obligatory for priests. Not only did he suggest that this
question should be examined by a commission of experts
representative of the entire Catholic Church, but he also
went on to suggest a similar way of dealing with the still
disputed question of infallibility. The letter was prompted
by advance reports of the letter to bishops and priests that
the pope issued in just under a fortnight, on Maundy
Thursday, powerfully reasserting the absolute nature of the

commitment to celibacy made by priests (and bishops) of the Latin Church (*Fall*, pp. 60–66).

By the end of the first year of John Paul II's pontificate Rome had also had plenty of time to consider what from its point of view no doubt appeared a much more impertinent and dangerous challenge to its authority. This was the publication by Küng much earlier in the year of two essays on the taboo subject of infallibility. One was another slim volume in the series 'Theological Meditations', with the title *Kirche – gehalten in der Wahrheit?* ('The Church – maintained in the truth?'). It consisted for the most part of the final section of the concluding summing-up Küng had contributed six years earlier to *Fehlbar? Eine Bilanz*, with remarkably few changes: once Küng has worked out what he wants to say he is content to leave what he has written unchanged when he comes to use it in later works. Basically the purpose of this essay was to show how by giving up infallibility the Church was not in any way giving up its essential certainty about what it was preaching and where it was going. It was in essentials simply the republication in a handier format of what Küng had said six years before without then causing any additional trouble. It seems safe to assume that its appearance did not play any major part in provoking the events that followed later in the year, even if Küng did send the Pope a copy at the same time as he sent him his letter pleading for an end to compulsory celibacy.

What does seem to have done the damage was the other essay. This was the introduction he wrote to a book by a fellow-countryman, August Bernhard Hasler, on Pius IX, Vatican I and infallibility. Hasler had previously published a two-volume study of these issues which, as Küng explained in a letter to Bishop Georg Moser of Rottenburg warning him that these writings were on the way, he had refused to review for the *Frankfurter Allgemeine Zeitung* (despite having provisionally agreed to do so) in order not to exacerbate the dispute over *On being a Christian* that was then drawing to a close and causing it to flare up again. But Küng found it impossible to refuse Hasler's request to contribute a foreword to his one-volume, 'popular' presentation of the same material. This book of Hasler's could be regarded as guaranteed to prove offensive to the pious ears that abound in the Roman Curia. It was written in a punchy style with short sentences, easy to read and never afraid to call a spade a spade. It presented Pius IX as dangerously unbalanced. It suggested that Vatican I had been subjected to so much unscrupulous manipulation by the advocates of papal infallibility as to cast doubt on the validity of its decrees: in particular, was the definition of infallibility freely arrived at and freely accepted? It analysed the Church's subsequent history in the light of the imposition of the ideology expressed by Vatican I. It even brought up not just the suggestion that Pius IX was no longer of sound mind at the time of Vatican I but that the row with Cardinal Guidi that apparently led to his outburst: *La tradizione, son' io* ('Tradition? *I* am tradition') was a row between father and son: 'not proven, but not totally improbable,' commented Hasler on the story that the future pope had fathered a child who grew up to become one of his leading opponents at Vatican I (Hasler, pp. 61–62). It was thus hardly a book to win friends and influence people (except negatively) in Vatican circles. It even proved too much for its original publisher, the Swiss firm of Benziger Verlag: it was in the event published by Piper of Munich, publishers of *On being a Christian* and *Does God Exist?*.

No doubt the mere fact of giving such a book his seal of approval by supplying it with an introduction would have been offence enough in the eyes of Rome. But Küng compounded his offence by what he said. When the Doctrinal Congregation brought the case against *Infallible?* to what proved merely a temporary close in 1975 it clearly saw the inevitable outcome of any reconsideration of the issue by

Küng to be his coming round to see the error of his ways. Instead here was Küng unrepentantly pointing out that subsequent developments had shown not just that he had been justified in raising the question in the first place but that an emerging consensus could be discerned among Catholic theologians. First, it was now being admitted with an openness that formerly would have been unusual that the magisterium could err and had often erred. Secondly, even conservative theologians were wary of the term 'infallible' with all the opportunities for misunderstanding it gave rise to, while nobody any longer wanted to have infallible definitions served up to them as W. G. Ward would allegedly have liked for breakfast each morning. Thirdly, even for those who defended the possibility of infallible statements the indefectibility of the Church in the truth represented a more fundamental level. Küng went on to claim that in the debate that had followed his book no single theologian and no single Church authority had been able to furnish any proof of the possibility of statements being not just true (something which was not in dispute) but infallibly true because they were made by certain functionaries or authorities in the Church who in certain circumstances were by the special assistance of the Holy Spirit automatically protected from falling into error: it was simply begging the question to quote the definitions of Vatican I and Vatican II, because it was precisely these that were in question. Moreover, the dispute had brought out unexpected confirmation of his position – notably with the historical researches of Brian Tierney, who had shown that papal infallibility was the invention of dissident Franciscans towards the end of the thirteenth century and that it had been condemned as the work of the devil by John XXII in 1324. (Küng forbore to suggest that this was no doubt an *ex cathedra* statement and therefore infallible: a pity, because the infallible condemnation of the doctrine of papal infallibility offers a paradox at least as mind-boggling as some of those developed by science-fiction authors writing about time travel.)

Küng went on to give Hasler's thesis his backing. It provided a historical account of how the infallibility decree came to be passed and thereby brought out more sharply the question of how firmly based it was. In particular, how free was Vatican I? Küng remarked that in many ways that Council was more like the well organized and manipulated congress of a totalitarian party than a free assembly of free Christians. Was it genuinely ecumenical? Was it really representative of the entire Catholic Church? Was its definition of infallibility really freely accepted by the entire Catholic Church afterwards? And was the cost it demanded in intellectual suppression, human suffering and the loss of credibility really worth while? The questions that emerged from Hasler's work as a historian might be uncomfortable and awkward questions, but they had to be asked for the sake of the truth and for the sake of the Church's credibility, Küng remarked. (It is noteworthy that the position he adopts here represents a hardening compared with his rejection in *Infallible?* [p. 107] of the assertion that Vatican I was not free.)

The question remained whether a Catholic theologian who adopted a critical position of this kind could remain Catholic. Excommunication, suspension, withdrawal of one's licence to teach were penalties that not only remained possible but were still applied where they were effective, Küng noted, adding: 'Even for Catholic theologians whose position is economically and legally secure they would be a sentence that would not be easy to cope with.' But events were to prove him sadly optimistic when he went on to say (Hasler, p. xxxiii):

> Excommunication, suspension, withdrawal of someone's licence to teach have however not so far occurred in the recent debate about infallibility and are not likely in the future: not only because

individual theologians who have adopted a critical position apparently enjoy so much popularity, influence, and power that they cannot be punished; but because it has been observed throughout the entire Catholic Church and in Rome too that the question at issue and the circumstances surrounding it are complex and difficult. There are too many of those who doubt: surveys of opinion have apparently shown that in many countries it is only a minority in the Catholic Church that believes in papal infallibility. It has thus so far turned out to be impossible to label critics of infallibility as un-Catholic in the eyes of the world.

The path of discriminating criticism, opposing the Roman system but defending the Catholic Church, was a narrow and dangerous one. Those who trod it would be accused from one side of being heretics and the enemies of the Church, from the other of inconsistently bolstering up the Church instead of taking their ideas to their logical conclusion and rejecting it. But it was in fact a consistent path between conformism on the one hand and escapism on the other, between uncritical adaptation and hypercritical sectarianism. In words that could well be applied to himself, Küng expressed the hope that Hasler would be able consistently to follow this path of critical loyalty without being misled, if not unaffected by well-intentioned judgements by Church authorities and by less well-intentioned journalistic mischief-making.

Küng concluded by taking up Congar's suggestion of a 're-reception' of the decrees of Vatican I and proposing a fresh examination of the question of infallibility from the exegetical, historical and theological points of view, with the setting up of an ecumenical commission composed of internationally recognized experts in the various fields of study concerned. He stressed that it was only by finding a solution to the problem of infallibility that a solution could be found to the problem of birth control, where as far as

Rome was concerned progress was for the moment blocked
– just as in the past it had been over the pope's temporal
sovereignty and the papal states. Was it too much to hope
that John Paul II, who had just returned from Latin
America where he had spoken out clearly against poverty,
underdevelopment, and the wretched conditions so many
children had to endure, would take a decisive step towards
an honest solution of this question?

Presumably that is precisely what John Paul II thought
he was doing when he approved the withdrawal of Hans
Küng's licence to teach. It happened without any
immediate warning. Küng had already slipped away from
Tübingen for a skiing holiday over Christmas at Lech, a
hundred miles to the south-east in Austria. When the
Doctrinal Congregation's letter reached his home in
Tübingen at 10 a.m. on Tuesday 18 December – delivered
by hand by a Jesuit acting as a messenger for the nunciature
in Bonn – it was impossible to get hold of Küng: he was
out skiing until lunch-time. Modern ski-slopes, however,
have such things as public address systems, and on hearing
himself paged over the loudspeakers Küng rang Tübingen
to have the gist of the letter read out to him over the
'phone. He returned to Tübingen after lunch, but it took
him until the evening to get back.

But the omens had not been exactly encouraging.
Indicative was the reaction of Bishop Moser, probably the
friendliest towards him of the German bishops, to his two
fresh contributions to the infallibility debate. Writing on 5
April to thank Küng for his earlier letter and for copies of
the two writings that had meanwhile arrived, the bishop
said he could not conceal from him that he had been
profoundly upset by reading them. All he could find in
them was the positions objected to by the Doctrinal
Congregation and regarded by the German bishops'
conference as in need of reconsideration and correction:

Hence I find it utterly incomprehensible that you are of the opinion that your latest utterances ought not to provoke any fresh dispute over infallibility. What you have done can in my view not be understood other than as a provocation. I assume therefore that unpleasant consequences are unavoidable and that great difficulties will ensue.

Bishop Moser mentioned in passing what would be one of the key factors in the eventual disciplinary measures against Küng: his position as a teacher of theology involved in training future priests of the diocese. But the bishop concluded by stressing his continued readiness to talk and to act as a mediator.

Another ominous development was the anticipation by Cardinal Joseph Ratzinger of the Roman verdict as yet hidden in the future. Addressing young people of his archdiocese of Munich the cardinal said that Hans Küng was quite simply no longer putting forward the faith of the Catholic Church: that was not what he was offering, and so he was not speaking on the Church's behalf. 'It must quite plainly be said that Küng vigorously disputes essential teachings of the Catholic Church and so does not speak in its name,' said Küng's former Tübingen colleague – who claimed always to have been on very good terms personally with the man he was attacking (*Frankfurter Allgemeine Zeitung*, 13 November 1979). A press statement from Küng and a polite exchange of letters between the two men followed, with each assuring the other of their concern to prevent theological disputes degenerating into personal rows and Cardinal Ratzinger stressing that he had resisted efforts to persuade him to intervene and to stop Küng speaking at Rosenheim, the centre for adult Catholic education thirty miles south-east of Munich, while he claimed not to have intervened on either side in the business of Bishop Rudolf Graber of Regensburg banning Küng from addressing the Regensburg university parish.

This ban – which reflected the indignation Küng's article on the first year of the new pontificate had aroused in some quarters – was got round by the theology students inviting him to give his planned lecture. On this Cardinal Ratzinger had pointed out that anyone addressing a university parish did so ultimately on the invitation of the bishop of the diocese, even if this were not a personal invitation from the bishop himself. To this Küng retorted in his press-statement that it was alarming when a bishop whose lack of contact with his own clergy had given rise to a great deal of complaint did not shrink from disparaging the loyalty to the Church of committed Catholic priests and lay people because they had ventured to invite to address their parish a Catholic professor of theology whose views apparently did not find favour.

Presumably Cardinal Ratzinger was well aware of the kind of conclusions being reached in Rome by the Doctrinal Congregation, which must already have consulted at least the leading members of the German hierarchy in preparing the measures it was to announce in little over a month's time. With the other German Cardinals he had just returned from taking part in the special consistory held in Rome at the beginning of November. Given the time needed to draft and approve the statements that were then issued both in Rome and in Bonn and for the German bishops' secretariat to prepare the two and a half pounds of documentation they issued to the press to buttress their case, the decision to withdraw Küng's licence to teach must either already have been taken or have been on the point of being taken: in the latter case Cardinal Ratzinger's outburst could have been a trial balloon to see how strong the reactions to such a step were likely to be. But to the outsider unaware of what was being prepared in Rome and Bonn it no doubt appeared yet further evidence of the quirky hostility increasingly being shown by the

Cardinal Archbishop of Munich towards his former colleagues. Earlier in the year he had intervened to prevent the appointment of Johann Baptist Metz to succeed Heinrich Fries as professor of fundamental theology at Munich university, and did so not by objecting to Metz's standing as a Catholic theologian (as under the concordat he was entitled to do but which would have obliged him to adduce 'weighty reasons') but by persuading the Bavarian Minister of Education, Professor Hans Maier, to choose not the first but the second of the three names chosen by the appointments committee: it was a piece of deviousness that just at this very time aroused a strong and outspoken protest from Karl Rahner (*'Ich protestiere'*, *Publik-Forum* no. 23, 16 November 1979, pp. 15–19).

Meanwhile Küng was keeping up with his usual hectic round of engagements in Germany and abroad while also maintaining his normal quota of lectures, seminars and other teaching work at the university. 1979 saw not only the publication of the central argument of *Does God Exist?* in thesis form (*24 Thesen zur Gottesfrage*) but also the appearance of the Italian and Spanish translations of the book, in each case involving press conferences in each country to launch it. Besides a visit to Israel, the year was also notable for a trip to China under the auspices of the Kennedy Institute of Washington, DC, to take part in a discussion with the Chinese academy of social sciences in Peking on religion and science: Küng presented them with nine theses – nine apparently being the perfect number as far as the Chinese are concerned, much as seven is with us – and distinguished carefully between religion and superstition before going on to recapitulate some of the argument of *Does God Exist?* All this activity was complicated by Küng having to move out for a whole year, from July 1978 to July 1979, while urgent repairs were done to his house: Germany too suffered its share of jerry-building during the 1930s.

From 18 December onwards all this was overtaken by a more urgent task: that of defending his good name as a Catholic and as a theologian. As already mentioned, the blow fell without Küng being given any warning in advance. Galileo had been frightened into recanting by the threat of torture. Unlike the Inquisition, the Doctrinal Congregation did not have such means of persuasion at its diposal. But it did not even give Küng the chance to change his mind. No doubt it rightly discerned that there was little prospect of such a change. Nevertheless Küng was not even presented with the immediate threat of having his official approval as a Catholic teacher of theology withdrawn. Instead, it was simply withdrawn, and he was left with no opportunity of keeping or regaining this official approval beyond that of virtually complete surrender and submission to the authorities. Nor was there ever anything approaching a fair trial in open court.

The timing, too, was extraordinary, as Küng was not slow to point out: just before Christmas. Bishop Moser, who was clearly embarrassed by the way things had turned out and uncomfortable in the role he was now being called upon to play, had done his best to persuade the authorities both to choose some more suitable time and to allow Küng to be heard in his own defence before imposing disciplinary sanctions; but without success (*Fall*, p. 127).

In its declaration dated 15 December and published three days later the Doctrinal Congregation made it quite clear that the reason for the disciplinary measures now being taken was that, far from bringing his views on infallibility into line with the teaching of the magisterium, Hans Küng had been even more explicit in putting them forward: it cited *Kirche – gehalten in der Wahrheit?* and the introduction to Hasler's book. The consequences of these views, and particularly of his contempt for the Church's magisterium, could be found in other works of his, to the detriment of several essential points of the Catholic faith, such as those connected with Christ being of one substance with the Father and those connected with the Blessed Virgin Mary, inasmuch as the meaning attributed to these doctrines was different from that understood by the Church. These views of his had been disturbing the minds of the faithful, and in 1975 the Congregation had refrained from further action on the presumption that he would abandon them:

> But since this presumption can no longer be entertained, this Sacred Congregation is now in the fulfilment of its task forced to declare that in his writings Professor Hans Küng departs from the integral truth of the Catholic faith and that therefore he cannot be regarded as a Catholic theologian nor perform the task of teaching as one.

This bleak statement was accompanied by a much longer one from Cardinal Höffner, as president of the German bishops' conference, dotting the i's and crossing the t's. The faithful had a right to a full and unequivocal presentation of the inalienable truths of faith, and to provide this was the concern of the Church's teaching and pastoral office, said the cardinal, emphasizing this point once again in slightly different language towards the end of his statement. As the Doctrinal Congregation had done, he rehearsed the history of the long dispute, presenting it as a demonstration of remarkable patience on the part of the Church authorities faced with rebellious intransigence:

> The temporary suspension of doctrinal proceedings and the publication of the 1975 exhortation – steps for which there was no previous provision in law or procedure – represented the utmost willingness to meet him half-way and a new attempt to bring the conflict to an end. Professor Küng did not make use of these opportunities. With an unparalleled inflexibility and a rare deafness to advice and instruction – and this is true despite his assertions of being ready to talk things over – he did not let himself be

influenced towards amplifying, modifying or correcting his doctrinal opinions either by the comprehensive theological discussion or by the initiatives taken
by the magisterium. To the same context belong his
sometimes extravagant attacks on the Church's
discipline and order.

Hence the Congregation's decision had become unavoidable. Another factor mentioned by the cardinal was that of
recent years Church leaders had frequently been
reproached with tolerating this kind of doctrinal deviation
within the bosom of the Church while taking severe
measures against Archbishop Lefebvre and his followers.
But, the cardinal concluded by emphasizing, Küng was not
excluded from the Church. He remained a priest. All that
he was deprived of was the commission to teach Catholic
theology in the name of the Church and as a teacher
recognized by the Church.

Although Cardinal Höffner's statement agreed with the
Doctrinal Congregation's in stressing that the latter body
saw the main reason for its decision in Küng's views on
infallibility, he gave more scope to the Christological
questions that had been at issue between Küng and the
German bishops in the row over *On being a Christian*:

> The dangerous narrowing down resulting from the
> theological method used by Professor Küng has often
> been commented on. In important questions it leads
> to a break with the Catholic tradition of faith and
> doctrine. This is especially clear in Professor Küng's
> statements with regard to the person of Jesus Christ.
> In the central Christological question whether Jesus
> Christ *really is* the son of God, that is whether he
> shares in God's rank and level of being without
> diminution, he has, despite all attempts at clarifica-
> tion, evaded a decisive confession cast in a binding
> form of words.

Quoting the Nicene creed, Cardinal Höffner went on:

> This has consequences for our salvation: if *God
> himself* has not sacrificed himself for mankind in
> Jesus Christ, then the core of Christian revelation
> collapses. All statements, including those about
> Jesus's human nature and humanity, are only really
> meaningful for Christian faith when they are
> intimately coupled with Jesus Christ's being truly
> God.

Complaining that, despite his assertions that he wished to
maintain the content of the Christological dogmas, Küng
obscured and diminished the unequivocal statements of
these doctrines, Cardinal Höffner said that fundamental
lack of clarity about the mystery of the person of Jesus
Christ threatened the core not just of Catholic but of
Christian faith in general. It was thus no accident that
Küng's presentation of the trinity, the Church, the sacraments, and Mary were in his eyes unsatisfactory.

The Christological element seems to have loomed even
larger in the minds of some of the German hierarchy.
According to a report of an interview he gave to
Südwestfunk, Cardinal Volk (Küng's former professor at
Münster who had taken part in the Stuttgart discussion on
On being a Christian) said the decisive factor in the
withdrawal of Küng's licence to teach was his Christology
(*Petrusblatt*, 11 January 1980). In this way the condemnation had a kind of domino effect: because Küng's views on
infallibility were suspect in the eyes of the authorities,
because they saw these as affecting his views on
Christology and Mariology and thus helping to bring these
too into suspicion, the result was to cast doubt on the
orthodoxy of his views in general.

Shock, indignation, alarm at what all this meant for the
future of the Church: these were common reactions. The
day after the blow fell a thousand students staged a
torchlight demonstration in the square outside the

fifteenth-century collegial church in the centre of Tübingen where Küng had given his lecture on God and science just over two years earlier. Earlier that day Küng's scheduled lecture on the apostolic creed was packed out by an overflow audience of two thousand who passed a resolution stating that they saw the arguments put forward by the Doctrinal Congregation as merely an excuse to silence a committed theologian. Ironically, Küng would not normally have given this lecture at all but would have left it to Dr Karl-Josef Kuschel, one of his staff at the Institute for Ecumenical Research: as we have seen, Küng himself was on the ski-slopes in Austria when the Roman authorities and the German bishops issued their condemnation. Küng's colleagues in the Catholic faculty of theology expressed their profound dismay at what the Doctrinal Congregation had done and their alarm over its as yet incalculable consequences: they saw serious dangers to the Church's credibility in contemporary society and to theology's freedom of research and teaching. The Catholic theological students described the Congregation's action as repressive and authoritarian. A number of prominent Catholics and Protestants set up a committee for the defence of the rights of Christians in the Church. Some of Küng's colleagues among Catholic professors of theology elsewhere in Germany declared their readiness to resign their own official approval as teachers of theology – a step which, if taken on any large scale, would severely embarrass the *Land* governments concerned by obliging them to appoint (and pay) the same number of supplementary professors.

Most disturbing of all, perhaps, were the ecumenical implications. 'If they are going to go on behaving as they did in my case yesterday,' said Küng during his packed-out lecture (which needless to say was not on the apostolic creed but presented his side of the case), 'then there is little sense in going on talking about the ecumenical dialogue.'

The professors of the Protestant faculty said they shared their Catholic colleagues' dismay and saw in the Church authorities' decision a painful obstacle on the road of ecumenical understanding between their two Churches: they appealed to the *Land* Education Minister to do what he could in co-operation with Bishop Georg Moser of Rottenburg to ensure that Hans Küng remained a teacher within the Catholic faculty of theology. The World Council of Churches issued a statement pointing out that because what was involved was the fundamental question of authority in the Church, a question which was the most sensitive point at issue in ecumenical discussions, the action taken against Küng could not simply be regarded as an internal affair of the Roman Catholic Church but had immediate ecumenical repercussions. Particularly upset were Anglicans, whose dialogue with Rome had recorded substantial agreement on the hitherto divisive issues of the eucharist, ministry and ordination, and to some extent authority itself. The *Church Times*, the English Anglican weekly, wondered in its issue of 11 January 1980 whether John Paul II would turn out to be the Ayatollah of the West, and commented: 'Anglicans know that Professor Küng has not been a typical Roman Catholic, but they also know that he certainly is typical of what Anglicans would look like if subject to Rome. And they do not want to be treated as he has been.' The Archbishop of York, Dr Stuart Blanch, said that the examination of Schillebeeckx in Rome followed the next week by the condemnation of Küng could not but be a cause of sadness: 'For these two great theologians have put the whole Christian world in their debt by their courageous – if sometimes provocative – attempts to express the gospel in intellectual categories more appropriate to our time than the categories in which they were expressed either by the theologians of the early Church or the theologians of the Reformation.' What worried Anglicans (and with them Nonconformists) was the threat of the reappearance of even a wraith of the Inquisition: this, commented *The Times* (24 December 1979), 'evokes ancestral memories whose tendency can only be to chill the carefully kindled warmth of Anglican-Roman relations'.

Many of Küng's colleagues outside Germany rallied to his defence. The editorial board of *Concilium* (which included Congar, Metz, Rahner and Schillebeeckx) said it did not see any decisive reason to stop regarding Küng as a Catholic theologian and called for proceedings on doctrinal matters to respect the generally accepted rights of man. Fifty Spanish theologians in an open letter expressed their solidarity with Küng while not necessarily agreeing with everything he said: the Vatican, they felt, should have given Küng a last chance to reconsider his position. Seventy theologians from the United States and Canada put their names to a brief statement rejecting the Doctrinal Congregation's verdict: 'We, as concerned and committed Roman Catholic theologians, cognizant that no one of us necessarily agrees with the opinions on particular issues of any other Roman Catholic scholar, including Hans Küng, publicly affirm our recognition that Hans Küng is indeed a Roman Catholic theologian,' they said. Schillebeeckx told the Rome daily *Il Messagero* (7 January 1980) that he regarded Küng's views as being in line with those of the Church. Congar concluded a long analysis of the dispute in *Le Monde* (2 January 1980) by stressing Küng's passionate devotion to the Church and by asking his mother the Church what it proposed making of this difficult child.

There were, of course, those who thought Küng was merely being treated as he deserved. The editor of *Homiletic and Pastoral Review*, Fr Kenneth Baker, SJ, thought the Doctrinal Congregation had 'bent over backwards' to get Küng to change his views (NC News Service, 19 December 1979). Hans Urs von Balthasar wrote a long article for the *Frankfurter Allgemeine Zeitung* presenting the

Church authorities as a model of patience and suggesting that one could not blame Küng for holding good Protestant views. But the consensus among theologians seemed to be that, even if justice had been done by Küng being stripped of his right to teach theology on the Church's behalf, justice had very definitely not been seen to be done.

For Küng himself the decision had come as a totally unexpected shock, however much the withdrawal of his *missio canonica* was a possibility he had had to live with ever since that Christmas twelve years earlier when the Doctrinal Congregation peremptorily wanted him to withdraw *The Church* from publication. He expressed his shame at belonging to a Church that in the twentieth century was still indulging in secret inquisitorial proceedings and pointed to the scandal created by a Church that based itself on Jesus Christ and had recently shown itself keen to defend human rights slandering and discrediting its own theologians by such means. He stressed that he intended to go on expressing, as a Catholic theologian in the Catholic Church, the Catholic concerns of numerous Catholics. He would thus fight to have the disciplinary measures reversed.

In this fight he had a strong case. He could hardly be said to have been given a fair trial. Nor was it easy to see why the Church could no longer tolerate views it had in fact been tolerating since 1970. Long discussions with Bishop Moser led to the latter going to Rome just before Christmas with a statement from Küng pointing out that he had always regarded himself as a Catholic theologian and would go on doing so; that he had not intended to provoke any fresh dispute over infallibility with his two latest publications on the subject; that along with his existing objections to the Doctrinal Congregation's procedure he had not been given any opportunity to make his position clear and justify himself before the latest measures were taken; that in addition the Congregation was making judgements on

questions of Christology and Mariology that had never
been the subject of proceedings at Rome; that he acknowledged true Church statements that could not be abrogated;
that he acknowledged the Church's duty to proclaim the
Christian message witnessed in scripture and to express it
in an unequivocal and binding form; that on questions of
Christology he based himself on the early Councils and was
concerned to make them comprehensible to people today;
that it had never been his intention to deny Vatican I's
definitions of faith or to question the Petrine ministry, still
less to make his own opinions the criterion of Catholic faith
or to make ordinary Catholics insecure in their faith; and
that the question he had raised – infallibility – was a real
and genuine one which very many unassailably orthodox
Catholic theologians had admitted the necessity and
legitimacy of raising.

With this Bishop Moser went to Rome, but he was not
able to see the Pope himself, and the best he could achieve
was for a delegation from the German bishops' conference
to go out after Christmas to see the Pope. Even then Küng
could not enjoy the remains of his Christmas holiday in
peace but had to spend Christmas day drafting yet a further
defence of his position which was worked out over the
telephone with Dr Hermann Häring back in Tübingen and
delivered to Bishop Moser for him to take back to Rome
(*Fall*, pp. 135–138). The delegation consisted of Cardinals
Höffner, Volk and Ratzinger and Archbishop Oskar Saier
of Freiburg-im-Breisgau as well as Bishop Moser himself.
Their meeting with the Pope, together with Cardinal
Franjo Šeper, prefect of the Doctrinal Congregation, and
Cardinal Agostino Casaroli, Secretary of State, produced
merely a confirmation of the earlier verdict and the pious
hope that Küng would, 'after more profound reflection,
adopt a position which will make it possible to restore his
faculty to teach with a mandate from the Church' (*The
Tablet*, 5 January 1980, p. 19). As Küng's colleague

Herbert Haag, the veteran Old Testament scholar, put it in his account of the case, 'the realists could imagine what was to be expected from mediation conducted under the leadership of Höffner and Ratzinger – and they would be proved right' (*Die Zeit*, 18 January 1980). What was to be expected from Cardinal Höffner had been made clear by a lengthy interview which he gave to the German Catholic news agency KNA before going to Rome (*Fall*, pp. 138–144) and in which among other things he repeated the misgivings he had expressed in his letter to Küng of 23 December 1974 (pp. 288–289 above).

Naturally, Küng still wanted the verdict reversed, but his more immediate concern was with its implications for his conditions of work at Tübingen. Withdrawal of his *missio canonica* meant he was not recognized as competent to teach or examine not just candidates for the priesthood (who in the 1979 winter term made up only 123 of the 807 students in the Catholic faculty of theology) but also all those who would later need Church approval in the form of their own *missio canonica* for their work — particularly would-be teachers (of whom there were 331) and pastoral assistants (of whom there were 298).

The precise legal position was a little obscure, since the concordat that Pius XI concluded with indecent haste with the newly established Nazi government in 1933 merely said that the relationship between Catholic faculties of theology and the Church authorities was to be governed by the relevant concordats that had previously been concluded with the German states. The common assumption was that it was now up to the *Land* government in agreement with the local bishop to make suitable alternative arrangements. But did these alternative arrangements mean leaving Küng where he was in the Catholic faculty and appointing someone else as a supernumerary professor to do the work he was no longer entitled to do, or did they mean moving Küng to a new professorship outside the Catholic faculty –

as a professor he could not simply be sacked – and appointing someone else to his now vacant chair of dogmatic and ecumenical theology? (Either way it would mean the *Land* paying an extra professorial salary.) Fortunately what did not seem to apply was the 1857 agreement concluded between Pius IX and the King of Württemberg. This gave the bishop the power to grant professors the authority and mission to teach 'and to revoke it when he should think fit' – as well as to demand of professors a profession of faith.[4]

Given that, as a German professor, Küng was unsackable, this dispute over how he was to continue as a professor may seem the merest quibble. But there is much more to it than that. The study of theology is conducted in Germany along fairly rigidly confessional lines. Theologians of both confessions have of course long since left behind the custom of refusing to read the other side's work, but it is true to say that the approach is inter-denominational rather than nondenominational. There does not seem to be anything like the situation in Britain where the denominational allegiance of holders of teaching posts is often immaterial and where it has proved possible for a Catholic to succeed a Presbyterian in a chair originally connected with the training of candidates for the Presbyterian ministry, as happened (to the accompaniment of some slight controversy) when James Mackey succeeded Thomas Torrance in the Thomas Chalmers chair at Edinburgh in 1979. In this way banishment from the Catholic faculty of theology to some other faculty not directly connected with theology – philosophy, say, or social sciences – would have threatened to isolate Küng both from the academic and from the Catholic community and to reduce his study of theology to the level of some private hobby. But also under threat was the Institute for Ecumenical Research, of which Küng had been director since its formation in 1963 and which came under the aegis

of the Catholic faculty. Removal of Küng from a professorship in the Catholic faculty implied removal from the
directorship of the Institute; and that would affect not just
him but the loyal and devoted staff who worked with him
there.

The complicated negotiations between the *Land* government, the university, the local bishop and Küng himself
were not helped when seven of the ten professors of the
Catholic faculty retreated from the support that body had
previously been giving their condemned colleague. The
seven, who included Alfons Auer and Walter Kasper,
expressed their fear of the affair blowing up into a total con-
frontation between 'progressives' and 'conservatives'. They
criticized Küng (without actually naming him, but it was
quite clear who was meant) for threatening to fight the issue
right the way through the courts and for a propagandist use
of language that applied such labels to his opponents as
'wire-pullers', 'hierarchs', 'inquisition', and (with its
connotations of Nazi terror) '*Nacht-und-Nebel* campaign';
on the other side they objected to procedures that corresponded neither to modern ideas of justice nor to the spirit
of Christianity, and criticized efforts to rule contemporary
theology out of court. Again, while they insisted that the
attempt should not be made to use administrative or
disciplinary means to solve disputed questions of scholarship, they argued that this did not rule out all use of such
means. What they seemed above all afraid of was an
'unholy alliance' of integralist Churchmen on the one hand
and ideological liberals on the other, both bent on doing
away with the confessional faculties of theology – the
former because they felt theology should be confined to
seminaries and similar institutions totally under Church
control, the latter because they felt it had no place at a
university. In this context they said that anyone tolerating
or wanting a theologian without a *missio canonica* to belong
on a permanent basis to a theological faculty was under-

mining the position of such faculties in the world of scholarship as well as the rights guaranteed to them under the constitution and the various concordats (*Schwäbisches Tagblatt*, 5 February 1980).

The compromise which was eventually reached on 10 April gave Küng much of what he had been asking for but without exacting the probably unacceptable cost in embittered personal relations that would have been involved in fighting the issue through the courts, as he had originally threatened to do. Küng's chair was detached from the Catholic faculty and placed directly under the authority of the university senate. So too was the Institute for Ecumenical Research. In this way, Küng's position as a Catholic theologian whose position as such was denied by the authorities of his Church was given institutional recognition. He retained his chair, he retained the directorship of the Institute, but his formal links with the Catholic faculty were broken.

Meanwhile the German bishops had issued a joint pastoral letter and a declaration on 7 January putting their side of the case and presenting the withdrawal of his *missio canonica* as an unpleasant necessity forced on them by Küng's intransigence. 'It is not a question of a wholesale rejection of his theology,' they wrote. 'But the self-contradiction within the Church was gradually becoming intolerable when an influential theologian who was teaching in the Church's name and educating future priests and future lay theologians was for years acting against the mandate he had undertaken. What is involved is the handing on of the Catholic deposit of faith intact to future generations, not a Roman bid for power or the self-preservation of a particular system.'

Küng for his part published yet another of those explanations of why he is and has remained impenitently Catholic that have had to punctuate his career. Why did he remain a Catholic when efforts were being made to expel him from his faculty of Catholic theology and to push him out to the fringe of the Catholic Church he belonged to – and this just two months after he had celebrated the silver jubilee of his priesthood? These latest developments, he claimed, had already driven some to formal apostasy and very many more to retreat silently within themselves; and, he warned, this silent drifting away from the Church would continue. He remained a Catholic not just because of his Catholic origins but also because of the experience of the great opportunity he found working as a theologian in the ecumenical atmosphere of Tübingen, where it had been possible for a Catholic theology to emerge which was truly ecumenical and sought to combine loyalty to the Catholic heritage with openness to Christendom. Being a Catholic theologian meant being bound to the Church in its entirety, both in time (refusing to reject certain periods as un-Christian or unevangelical) and in space (aware that, though rooted in a particular local Church, his theology cannot be tied to any particular nation, culture, race, class, form of society or ideology). But this did not mean accepting everything that had been officially taught, ordered and observed over the past twenty centuries: Küng's list of official blunders included the excommunication of the Patriarch of Constantinople, the ban on worship in the vernacular, the condemnation of Galileo, the refusal to allow adaptation to Chinese and Indian civilizations, the maintenance of the Pope's temporal power, the condemnation of freedom of conscience and of religion, the condemnation of historical and critical biblical scholarship, and the measures taken against such theologians as Teilhard de Chardin, de Lubac, Chenu and Congar. Catholicity needed a criterion, which could be none other than the gospel and ultimately Jesus Christ himself – 'who,' Küng remarked, 'is for the Church and, despite all assertions to the contrary, for me too God's son and word.' The theologian who was Catholic in the genuine sense of the word must thus have an evangelical (which of course in German also means Protestant) cast of mind, and vice versa. 'Admittedly,' commented Küng, 'this makes the theological demarcations objectively and conceptually more complicated than they might seem to be in the light of official documents, which are often terribly simple and display little Catholic depth and breadth.' Why then did he remain a Catholic? Because he was able precisely in this way to assent to an evangelical Catholicity that in this way was centred and ordered on the basis of the gospel, an evangelical Catholicity that was nothing other than genuine ecumenicity. Catholicity included tensions between what it gave and what it demanded, between where it came from and where it was going to, between indicative and imperative. Within these tensions Küng would like to go on doing theology and thus as decisively as he had been doing up till now to make the message of Jesus Christ comprehensible to the men and women of today. He concluded (*Die Zeit*, 18 January 1980; omitted from the version in *The Times*, 28 January 1980):

> I know I am not alone in this dispute about true Catholicity. Together with all those many people who have been supporting me up till now I will fight against any kind of becoming resigned to what is happening. It is a matter of going on working together for a truly Catholic Church that is bound to the gospel. For that it is worth remaining a Catholic.

---

[1] Cardinal Luciani did indeed write to Hans Küng in 1976 thanking him for a copy of the Italian edition of *On being a Christian* and saying that, despite his imperfect knowledge of the language, he had already read some of the German original, a copy of which had been given him by Bishop Joseph Gargitter of Bolzano and Bressanone in the German-speaking South Tirol. Some passages he found excellent; on some points he remained

doubtful; while on others he disagreed. In return he sent Küng a copy of his own *Illustrissimi*, a work he described as being without pretensions.

² Karol Wojtyła, *The Acting Person (Analecta Husserliana X)*, D. Reidel, Dordrecht/Boston, 1979, pp. 286–287. (The Polish original was published in 1969.) I have not been able to quote verbatim from this work: the publishers have refused me permission to do so because they are working on a revised edition with alterations approved by the author.

³ For an account of the way Schillebeeckx was treated and of the issues involved, together with an account of the Küng case, see Peter Hebblethwaite, *The New Inquisition?: Schillebeeckx and Küng*, Collins (Fount), London, 1980.

⁴ Vincentius Nussi (ed.), *Conventiones de rebus ecclesiasticis inter S. Sedem et Civilem Potestatem variis formis initae ex collectione Romana exceptae*, Franz Kirchheim, Mainz, 1870.

19

What is at Stake

Both inside and outside the Catholic Church many people succumb to the temptation to play down or ignore the significance of the official disavowal of Hans Küng as a theologian. He is presented as being on the fringe of the Church and not really representative of its central tradition – in his own terminology an outsider rather than a vanguard (*Theologian*, p. 49). Beyond this echoes can be heard of a whispering campaign seeking to denigrate him as bumptious, arrogant, impervious to criticism, and financially too well off. True, he has preserved a certain boyish enthusiasm intact for longer than most of his contemporaries, along with his remarkable energy and stamina; but that may merely reflect the way in which his career unfolded smoothly without any major hitches or frustrations to quell his spirit. Nor can he be regarded as arrogantly convinced of the rightness or indeed infallibility of his own position. He is rather constantly on the look-out for some more convincing presentation of what the gospel means for us and demands of us today. He may have come from a comfortably off middle-class Swiss background; but it is hardly fair to criticize him for not having been born to, say, unemployed working-class parents in the Falls Road district of Belfast. *On being a Christian* may have landed him with the problem of affluence; but in coping with it he is well aware of Jesus's warnings about giving alms in order to be seen before men, and by the standards of West Germany he leads a modest existence. The innuendos that circulate about him do not survive meeting him and are

358

evidence simply of the human capacity for envy and backbiting.

Indulging in them, however, is one way of suggesting that somehow Küng has brought all this on himself, that he has got his just deserts – in its most extreme form that he has at last achieved the martyrdom he has been aiming at throughout his professional career. Yet ultimately this is to assume that the Catholic Church is irredeemably corrupt, that Vatican II represented merely a momentary aberration in its long history, that it cannot escape from the intransigent, authoritarian mould of triumphalism, clericalism and juridicism in which for so long it had been set. For what is at stake is whether the Church is really at home in the world of late twentieth-century Western Europe, or whether Christianity cannot be translated into the ways of thinking and feeling normal in this society but demands adherence to patterns of behaviour and ways of looking at and understanding the world at variance with what is taken for granted. Of course there is an extent to which Christianity is inevitably at odds with any civilization, any secular understanding of the world, and Küng is well aware of this. But all he is suggesting is the same degree of adaptation to the surrounding culture that in earlier centuries the Church found essential if it was to get its mission across. Küng may indeed be open to criticism for playing down the prophetic, hair-shirt aspect of Christianity; but that aspect, the heroic and romantic aspect, if you like, needs to be kept in balance by the routine Christianity of everyday life that Küng presents so clearly; and in any case even the prophetic aspect of Christianity has to be expressed in a language understanded of the people. A nostalgic effort to re-create a heroic golden age that never existed is neither Christian nor realistic.

What Küng has done is thus to try to express Christianity in such a way that one no longer has to make excuses for being a Christian. For him – and, as is shown by the response he has gained, for very many others – Christianity is fundamentally reasonable, even if it necessarily transcends reason. In this endeavour he sees no cause to be bound by the dead pieties of the past, by ways of thought and practices that in their time may have been valid enough but now present a positive hindrance to the gospel. No doubt if he had shown due deference to well-established abuses, if he had developed what the English Protestant tradition would call a Jesuitical skill in paying lip service to questionable traditions while in fact subverting them, he would have survived without condemnation and could well have made himself a flourishing ecclesiastical career. But that would hardly have been honest; and it was not his way. Rather, he preferred to meet difficulties head on, to admit the contradictions instead of seeking to harmonize them at all costs.

Nor can the issues he has raised be evaded. They are the kind of issues that arise as soon as Christians start taking their faith seriously and realize that it does bear thinking about after all. It may be that his answer to the problem of infallibility is not the right one; but that there is a problem no one can deny, nor that the qualifications with which even defenders of Vatican I's definition hedge it about make Brian Tierney's evocation of the Cheshire Cat remarkably apt, nor that the essential task is to reconcile the claims the Church rightly makes on our loyalty and trust with our awareness of its blunders and misdeeds. It may be that he has not been able to hit on the right way of expressing the Christological doctrines proclaimed by the early councils in terms that speak directly to the people of today; but that we cannot simply repeat parrot-like formulations deriving from a different cultural and conceptual context again cannot be denied, nor that we need to give full weight to both poles of the Chalcedonian assertion that Jesus Christ is truly God and truly man instead of letting the manhood be swallowed up by the divinity.

Again, other people might have been more deferential and diplomatic in raising the same issues. But is committed active membership of the Church to be confined only to those who are diplomatic and deferential and willing to tug their forelocks? Is it only for those who are willing to burn a pinch of incense on the altars of outmoded ways of thought?

If the Church has no room for someone like Hans Küng among its accredited theologians, someone who is fired by a passion for truth and a love for the Church such that he finds it difficult to accord its defects the tolerant welcome others do, then there will be many humbler people, people to whom his books and writings and lectures have given new heart and new hope in the daily struggle of trying to be a Christian, who will conclude that there is no room for them either. The Church would then court the danger of allowing itself to be narrowed down to a sect, the congregation of those with a particular antiquarian and romantic appreciation of the gospel, rather than as the universal assembly of believers that finds room for all genuine expressions of the human spirit within its fellowship.

In all this Küng's position has been rather like that of the small boy in Hans Christian Andersen's story. As readers will recall, the ostensible virtue of the emperor's new clothes was that they were invisible to anyone who was either unfit for his job or unforgivably stupid. It took the small boy to blurt out the truth that everyone privately was uncomfortably aware of; and the first reaction of his elders and betters was to tell him to shut up.

Index

Index